The Art of
Facilitating Participation

The Art of Facilitating Participation

Releasing the Power of Grassroots Communication

Edited by

Shirley A. White

Sage Publications
New Delhi/Thousand Oaks/London

First published in 1999 by

Sage Publications India Pvt Ltd
M–32 Market, Greater Kailash–I
New Delhi – 110 048

Sage Publications Inc.
2455 Teller Road
Thousand Oaks, California 91320

Sage Publications Ltd
6 Bonhill Street
London EC2A 4PU

Published by Tejeshwar Singh for Sage Publications India Pvt Ltd, photo-typeset by Line Arts Photosetters, Pondicherry and printed at Chaman Enterprises, Delhi.

Library of Congress Cataloging-in-Publication Data
The art of facilitating participation: releasing the power of grassroots communication / edited by Shirley A. White.
    p.   cm.   (cloth) (pbk.)
    Includes bibliographical references and index.
    1. Communication in community development. 2. Group facilitation. 3. Community development—Citizen participation. I. White, Shirley A., 1931–
HN49.C6A69   307.1'4—dc21   1999   99–16909

ISBN: 0–7619–9369–X (US HB)   81–7036–843–X (India HB)
           0–7619–9370–3 (US PB)   81–7036–844–8 (India PB)

Sage Production Team: Rochelle Pinto, Ranu Jain, N.K. Negi
and Santosh Rawat

Contents

List of Figures

Foreword

The words 'participation' and 'participatory' have been widely adopted by development professionals in the 1990s. For many, participation makes sense as a means: with participation, projects and programs become cheaper, more effective, and more sustainable. For others, participation is an end in itself: a set of processes and relationships that are inherently good. Whatever the mix of reasons, a new consensus has put participation at the center stage of local development. Therefore the World Bank and other donors have sought to mainstream participatory processes, while NGOs and governments have sought to spread participatory methodologies on a formidable scale.

The reality of participation though, has often differed from the rhetoric. Much development that is participatory in name has remained top-down in practice. Participation has been promoted without changes in bureaucratic imperatives or personal orientation. It has been commanded. Targets have been set, methods routinized and then appearances of achievement contrived. For its part, facilitation has been seen as something people can be told to do, not as a skill to be learnt or an art to be practiced, still less as part of a way of being in the world. So it has been quite a challenge to understand the art of facilitation better, and to share more widely what this entails in method, in personal behavior, and attitudes.

This book contributes to that understanding. To an unusual degree it includes authors who are honest and open about their experiences, their failures as well as successes and what they have learnt. Readers will find much material for reflection. Each may wish to make her or his own collection of insights and lessons. For myself, four aspects of good facilitation stand out in this book.

The first poses the question: who participates? The words 'community' and 'community level' can obscure deep divisions. These include differences of gender, age, wealth, and social and religious grouping. Good facilitators are sensitive to these differences, and are usually committed to empowering those who are weaker, more vulnerable, marginalized, oppressed or otherwise disadvantaged. The cases presented here are about particular places and groups, but they provide insights that bear generalization. The attitudes, principles, and practices at work with, for instance, street children in a city, or women in a village, can be examined for application elsewhere, and hold lessons for all facilitators who seek to empower the excluded and victims of discrimination.

Second, to be a good facilitator entails unlearning. This starts with recognizing and countering disabilities of orientation. Often these have been imprinted or inflicted on development professionals in the name of education and training. Typically, they are embodied in attitudes and behaviors of superiority. Often, too, these disabilities are expressed in the old sense of communication, as being from development professionals who know, to local people who do not know. As this book suggests, a communication professional has to unlearn those old ideas, attitudes, and behaviors, and learn a new set. She or he has to become a facilitator, a person who enables others to express themselves. It is easy to underestimate what this shift means in personal terms: how threatening and radical it can be for some development practitioners; and how immensely rewarding it can be through the new experiences and satisfactions it opens up.

Third, good facilitation is itself a continuous learning and development for the facilitator. In chemical usage, a catalyst promotes a reaction without itself undergoing permanent change. A facilitator catalyst is different. Several contributors describe their own learning and change through the processes they have facilitated. The key is often 'letting go'. They hand over to local participants who then take the initiative, accept responsibility, make decisions on when and where to meet, on what and what not to discuss or record, and come to their own conclusions. This is more than the triumph of the broken egg when the chick breaks out. A good facilitator, like the egg, gives up control, but unlike the egg, learns and grows through the experience. A good facilitator learns by facilitating, by trying things out, taking risks, making mistakes, and improving through experience.

The fourth insight underpins the first three: it is to do with the primacy of the personal dimension. Good facilitation flows from personal commitment, attitudes, and behaviors. Whether it is with street children in a slum, women in a male-dominated village, or bureaucrats in an international agency, the key is understanding and honoring the realities of others. The central theme in development, as illuminated by this book, is personal change. For what happens in development depends largely on what sort of people we, development professionals, are, and how we interact with others.

This then becomes a personal journey on which each can help others. *The Art of Facilitating Participation* includes contributions from authors who freely and honestly describe their journeys, their failures, and successes. They describe how they themselves have changed. Their openness and transparency doubly help the rest of us, for we can learn not only from what they have learnt, but also from the example they set of critical self-awareness in sharing their experience.

Robert Chambers
September 1, 1999

Acknowledgments

The title of this book, *The Art of Facilitating Participation*, is highly symbolic both from a personal perspective and in regard to the contents that have been crafted. Perhaps your reading can be more meaningful if I share with you how the idea for the book originated and how the vision for the book emerged from a participatory process.

In the Fall of 1994 two of my graduate students, Ricardo Gomez and Joanne Dvorak, convinced me to conduct a pro-seminar with students who were keenly interested in issues of participatory development communication and the important role a facilitator plays in the process. Ricardo and Joanne handled the logistics of organizing the sessions, involving about a dozen graduate students, all of whom were ready to share their own experiences and take the lead in exploring various topics. We agreed to meet each Friday afternoon and carry forth as long as our enthusiasm for dialogue prevailed. Everyone in the pro-seminar had previous experience with development projects in several countries—in Latin America, Africa, Asia, the Eastern Bloc countries, and in the United States.

I shared my experiences from India, Honduras, and rural America. At that time I was struggling with a suggestion that Robert White had made to me while I was in Rome pursuing a sabbatical leave. He encouraged me to put together a book on community communication. For many reasons I couldn't grapple with that task and I shared my frustration with the students. The group quickly concluded that such a book could emerge from our weekly discussions in which we planned to identify issues and share information and insights about them and volunteered to help me.

As the dialogue continued they shared personal stories about their own experiences with development. Before the semester was over we had a plan for a book with some of them eager to contribute their personal perspectives on the art of facilitating participation. Our goal was to recount experiences, share knowledge, and contribute ideas which a field level practitioner would find useful.

Our debates throughout the seminar often ended with the conclusion that 'everybody talks about participation, but few people can effectively facilitate.' We agreed that peoples' participation was easy to talk about, hard to achieve. Moreover, we concluded that those people who were regarded as good facilitators on the development scene had not been mobilized to share their insights and knowledge in order to help others acquire the tools of facilitation.

Some of these students—Ricardo, Anne, and Josh, all of whom have launched careers in development and communication—contributed some of the essays that you find in this volume. As the book plan evolved, other students like Erik, Ndunge, and Meredith were invited to share their experiences. As we identified issues, I thought of some of my colleagues (some of whom had been my students earlier) who certainly had a lot to share from their professional experiences in development—Sadanandan, Joe, John, Kathy, Don, Simone, Marilyn, Peggy, Renuka, and Ricardo (Ramirez). I met Jim Lees in Mumbai and after an exciting conversation about his involvement there, invited him along with his colleague Sonali to share their experiences. Silvia Balit led me to the Zimbabwe project and to Chike, Titus, and Paolo for their contribution. Joe invited Ilias to collaborate with him. It is indeed a diverse group of contributors. Finally, Robert Chambers, who is a frequent visitor to Cornell University, graciously agreed to provide a foreword for our collection.

The impetus for assembling the information, thoughts, and feelings expressed in these chapters appropriately involved a participatory process of dialogue, reflection, and sharing. Some of this was face to face, but a lot took place through e-mails. There has been continuous interaction and re-action among and between us as the manuscript progressed. Perhaps one of the most important outcomes has been the new professional linkages and friendships that have resulted from these encounters with the 'participation concept.'

Admittedly, this has been more of an undertaking than I originally anticipated. My partner in word processing, Michele Finkelstein would agree. My husband, Alvin White, has been totally supportive.

He has been involved for nearly twenty years with the Lansing Planning Board, so is appreciative of the problems which face local people as 'participators' in rural development. He was helpful in reading some chapters and providing feedback from a 'people's point of view.'

Tejeshwar Singh, my publisher in New Delhi, has been patient from the beginning. His immediate enthusiastic response to the initial proposal was a real compliment. After suffering through three other manuscripts with me over the past 5 years, he was still open to another!

A book, which I thought could come together fairly quickly, has taken substantially longer to produce than anticipated. But the process has been most gratifying and has resulted in closer links with development communication colleagues and new insights into the concept of participation and the art of facilitation.

Shirley A. White
September 1, 1999

1

Participation: Walk the Talk!

Shirley A. White

Human centered development is a means for enlarging people's capabilities in terms of skills, productivity and inventiveness. This necessarily implies an empowerment that allows them to participate actively in their own development. Development in these terms is something that is done by people rather than for or to them. And it is this essential of people's participation which defines the right to development in both its economic and political aspects.

From **Human Rights—The New Consensus** (Reoch, 1994), p. 125

The United Nations General Assembly adopted the *Declaration on the Right to Development* in December of 1986. Article One states that people are entitled 'to participate in, contribute to, and enjoy economic, social, cultural and political development....' This is further clarified as '...the full realization of the right of peoples to self-determination....' There is special concern regarding women, as Article Eight states that, 'Effective measures should be undertaken to ensure that women have an active role in the development process.' Furthermore, it is a responsibility to 'encourage popular participation in all spheres as an important factor in development and in the full realization of all human rights' (Reoch, 1994: 298–99).

Earlier in 1973, a development visionary, Fuglesang, put it simply:

One may think sometimes that development can come about only by people's own creative action in an effort to increase their

control over the environment—and themselves. I am inclined to
believe that this is basically a problem of applied communication.
If that is so, work can be based only on a complete belief in the
ability and integrity of every man and woman in the process. A
true communication professional does not express anything.
(S)he helps people to express themselves (1973: 17).

This statement embodies the focus of this book which is on the 'true
communication professional,' the facilitator. Viewing the facilitator
as a person who is first and foremost a trained communicator is a
perspective that I believe is legitimate and necessary. The charge
involves not only being knowledgeable and skilled in communication theory and practice, but also being an enabling adult educator
who can assist grassroots people to become skilled as communicators and to be able to access information necessary for learning and
acquiring resources.

Authentic participation of grassroots people may still be more an
ideal than a *reality*. Individuals and agencies actively engaged in
development are conscientiously struggling to move beyond just
talking in order to achieve this ideal. From my own assessment,
based on observation and inquiry, there seems to be an ever-
increasing, overt recognition of the need to involve oppressed and
disadvantaged peoples in the flow of decision-making and action
required for development. But it isn't as though that recognition
will facilitate participation of the people and make it happen. It
won't! For a development professional to *talk* about participation is
pretty simple. But, to 'walk the talk' with a commitment to *make* it
happen, and to possess the savvy and patience to *see* it happen is not
easy.

Anthropologist Jim Lees knows the reality of walking the talk.
When I met him in Mumbai and learned about his work that was
underway with street children, he shared his story of a struggle for
relevance, for space and time to enable children to engage in 'a participatory process of self-discovery.' He was at the time challenging
the working methods of his sponsoring development agency, and
the charge that had been given to him. He noted that challenging
given methods 'can have its perils' and that tenuous relationships
between field workers and sponsors are commonplace. The issue
becomes one of 'whom do I work for?' In his case, after face to face
encounters with children of the street, it was clear to him and to his

associate, whom they were working for: 'the street children of India.'
He believes that the power of the participatory process can transform relationships and the people in them. He does point out that
to walk the talk may be risky, perhaps to the point of being relieved
of your duties somewhere along the way.

But even if the facilitator has such convictions and provides a catalyzing force, participation is a two-way proposition. The people
must be open to making a response. Ordinary citizens, the oppressed, and the resource-poor, at any age, *do* want a voice. The desire
and will to become involved and gain greater control over their lives
is real, but before it can happen it is necessary to make fundamental
changes. Jim Lees would agree with that.

Such changes, we're constantly reminded, are highly 'contextual,'
bounded by socio-cultural, economic, and political forces within the
physical environment. The world over, local cultures embody their
own uniqueness, but across cultures, there is a universality of
human need for freedom, dignity, and equal rights, an opportunity
to change via self-determined choice.

I asked my colleague, Ndunge Kiiti, what accounts for the gap
between 'talk and walk.' She told me that one main reason is, that
for many of those involved, development has become a business:

> There's a stronger emphasis on the 'economic driven approach'
> rather than the 'human driven approach.' I've been reminded of
> that several times by people 'committed' to development. We
> quickly forget that 'development starts with the heart.' We often
> start with our heads—intelligence. If your heart isn't in it, it's dif-
> ficult to have the compassion, passion and commitment we need
> to make development a success.

Ndunge, who is a field worker for an international NGO, further
commented that many development organizations only pay lip-
service to people's development. This might possibly be accounted
for by 'differences in values and philosophy between the funding
agency, the implementing agency, and local people in participating
communities.'

Last spring I was impressed with a college baccalaureate speaker
who challenged the young graduates to 'walk the talk.' She brought
up an interesting point that is worth pondering: 'sometimes talking
itself is walking.' One might at least be encouraged when people

and agencies begin talking about people's participation. However, she continued:

> I think that for me, the hardest thing to deal with is that there is a cavern between what folks say and what folks do. And that gap seems to be everywhere: in federal and state governments, within the institutions where I live my life, and most important, in my own behavior. I wonder if this is a place where you and I might reach across our generations and touch each other.
>
> I suspect that there are people and institutions that knowingly and intentionally talk what they don't walk. And if you meet one—leave it! But first be sure you know what you are looking at, because I think there is another animal out there that resembles a hypocritical beast but isn't one. I think I've met that animal. I think I've been that animal.
>
> It's probably easier for individuals to narrow the talking and walking gap than it is for institutions.... My talking with you like this is an act of faith, in you and in your ability to narrow the gap between the talk we talk and the walk we walk as individuals in a world where the gap houses hungry people and rampaging injustice (Caruso, 1997: 4–5).

When I heard this address I was working on this book. It struck me that her challenge to young college graduates would readily apply to persons who read this book—the challenge to become a 'facilitative' person, personally and professionally. Reaching across the barriers of diversity, power, caste, and class to touch the life force of a person and lift them to a 'higher ground' becomes the objective of the challenge.

Organizing 'The Art of Facilitating Participation'

It is important to place this book within a wider framework. Not every chapter directly relates to the underlying assumption that _communication is the foundation of participation_, but all do contribute to the understanding of some aspects of the facilitator role and its importance to charting a path to 'walk the talk.' _Effective facilitation is an art that engages the creative forces within persons which_ *energize thinking and doing.* The book explores this art from three important points of departure: activation, technique, and community-building.

As the chapters came together, it became clear that these were in no way separate categories. Rather, they became simply a loose organizational structure for presenting the ideas of contributors. Originally, the three categories did encompass our intent to present the process of participation as a series of phases. The first phase is one of *activation of people*, engaging their interest, their thinking, their creativity, their understanding of participation. The second phase is one of *employing various techniques or approaches to enable participation.* The third phase is that of *community-building* which we would consider an outcome of participation.

When the contributing authors became involved in the participatory process from which this book emerged, it was agreed that we all had something to share from our own experiences with participation and as facilitators. We wanted to make the book a 'down-to-earth' presentation based on our own unique positions and backgrounds. A diverse group of contributors evolved; academics, practitioners, and bureaucrats, of different ages, from different countries and cultures, with a wide range of experience. Honest accounts of successes and failures were to be shared. But for the most part, the basis of content would reflect the personal perspectives and commitments to the development process.

But it was a struggle for each contributor to launch out to put their thoughts on paper. We found that in sharing our 'honest' accounts, we faced a certain amount of nervousness about telling it like it is! Selective perception and memory, discomfort in discussion of conflicts, fear of power figures, credibility worries, were just some of the traumas experienced as the stories were put on paper. My own frustration was due to a feeling of inadequacy in being able to meaningfully communicate my thoughts and convictions on the subject, and edit a book which would be readable, useful, substantive, and interesting! Just how successful we have been in achieving our aspirations, is yet to be seen.

While I perceive a continuity in the different sections of this book, you, as the reader, may or may not find it so. While the chapters do inter-relate, each also stands alone as a statement of ideas, insights, intuition, and inspiration.

The Art of Activation

This set of essays begins with a presentation of the important concept of a *catalyst communicator* (CC). This concept, we feel, is useful for thinking through the behaviors which provide a foundation for the *facilitator* role. White and Nair see mastery of the *art of facilitation* as necessary for bringing about people-centered development. Enabling an environment for ongoing learning, and honing communication competencies, is necessary to building partnerships for participatory planning and action. The matrix of CC competencies and phases of interaction will be a useful tool for sorting out the beliefs, knowledge, and skills required for facilitating participation.

Kiiti and Nielsen follow in Chapter Three with a clarification of the concepts of *facilitation* and *advocacy*. Their intent is to help the practitioner examine his/her own philosophy of development, and define roles and purposes in context. In order to depict the differences between these two concepts, they introduce us to two development field workers, one behaving as a facilitator and the other as an advocate. The conceptual matrix they present is a tool intended to enable dialogue about what one does in playing these roles. They caution that the development field worker must be able to interchange and/or separate these two roles.

No doubt there is an overlap of behaviors of facilitation and advocacy. In a sense, any individual who chooses to enter the development arena is an advocate for uplifting the quality of life in developing countries. Ndunge and Erik point out that advocacy often entails a specific agenda that many times is external to the community and for the most part reflects short-term goals. On the other hand, the process of facilitation begins where the community members are, and often leads to empowerment and mutual respect, ensuring sustainable development programs.

In Chapter Four, which takes a rather unconventional view of the facilitator as a 'synergizer,' Simone St. Anne offers us an appreciation of the concept of *creativity*. She points out that in order to participate and communicate with each other, people need to 'connect.' Understanding creativity can be an exceptional force in the toolbox of the facilitator for activating the process of participation. Simone explores 'creative collaboration' and 'teaming selves' as ways to go beyond an individual's capacity to bring about change and participatory development. The facilitator is depicted as a harmonizer, one who can integrate individuals into team action in a creative way and into a circle of constructive interdependence. This is the state of 'flow' which takes us beyond ourselves and 'we connect with a greater source—become part of a greater force.'

The desire for such experiences is described as 'participatory or self-transcending tendencies.' Associated emotions and insights motivate a sense of community, facilitate interpersonal trust, awaken the self, and impel a person to be continuously open to new undertakings. 'Synergy is the spark that triggers thinking and helps form innovative connections to allow others to see what they see— that's the essence of creative collaboration.' The facilitator must allow participation to become an internal creative force in order to induce synergistic collaborative effort and partnerships.

In Chapter Five Ricardo Ramirez shares his own creative learning process—his 'journey in search of facilitative communication.' He supports the notion that the facilitator must be a 'true communication professional.' He sees the mission of development as 'empowerment through communication.' He says that 'communication for development is focused on sharing of knowledge and insight about the process of enabling disadvantaged people to increase control over their own lives and environments.' In addition to sharing his own process of becoming a development facilitator, he discusses the enabling conditions of development communication which give voice to different stakeholders to negotiate their positions and common interests.

While Chapter Six isn't framed that way, the concept of *negotiation* might be considered as a major underpinning for Peggy in her 'confessions of an outside facilitator.' When I asked her to share her experience of the Dominican Republic, she had just returned from a three-year assignment there as an external consultant. The freshness and honesty of her stories made my more academic perspectives on the struggles of facilitating participation come to life. But on these points we strongly agreed: Facilitating people's participation is in no way an easy task. It requires cultural sensitivity. It takes a lot of time. It requires a measure of selflessness. And, it tests one's commitment, persistence, and willingness to take risks.

At my insistence, Peggy has elaborated in great detail about her personal experience, step by step, in implementing a health project that aimed to be a participatory communication process. She shares her frustrations, the lessons learned, and the 'payoffs' of her efforts over a three-year period. She has captured the essence of her experience in her written account, but I feel privileged to have crossed the pathway of her life at an opportune time to be a sounding board for her reflections.

In a sense, the same thing happened when I came across Jim Lees in Mumbai. The difference was that he was in the middle of an exciting and life-giving project with a group of street children. He told me how they tried to engage the children in a participatory process of developing learning material to be used to help street children cope with the problems posed by drugs and AIDS. After listening to his stories and sharing his enthusiasm for what was happening in his project, I knew that what he had discovered was something that needed to be shared.

In Chapter Seven Jim and his collaborator, Sonali Ojha, offer you as many insights as they can about the realities of such a project. I saw in them the deep commitment that is obvious when there is determination to focus on the people one is engaged to help. Perhaps at times in conflict with their donor's wishes, he and his associates managed to move their project from one of 'disseminating information' to one of a 'participatory process of self-discovery' that would transform the relationship between street children and the adults who work with them. Their account will not only give you insights into the process that they used, but it will simultaneously warm your heart and tear it apart.

The Art of Technique

The title for this section of the book didn't happen by chance. It seemed to me that technology and technical proficiencies had been viewed as the saving grace of economic development. But with a fresh focus on human-centered development, I thought it would be useful to examine the difference between technical proficiencies and technique. Possessing technical knowledge and skills is important to development and should not be underestimated. But, if we apply technology without plan or purpose, there is no direction for our work, nor is there coherence or relevance to the people affected by the action. The *art of technique* then becomes the thoughtful articulation and interpretation of the need for technology, and the culturally sensitive way people are involved in assessing, acquiring, and applying that technology to benefit their development.

Technique must serve the *content* of development, and be the *art* that effectively promotes learning and effective communication. Mastery of the art is evident when, through participation, we *feel* the impact of human dialogue and interaction, and find ourselves in the 'flow' of progress toward renewal and change.

In Chapter Eight we are engaged in a conversation with Orlando Fals Borda who is internationally recognized for his commitment to people's participation. We were interested in his perspectives and to learn more about how he viewed the future of participatory research that has become so vital as a tool for development facilitators. Ricardo Gómez interviewed Orlando in his office in Bogota, Colombia. The importance of this conversation is to emphasize some of the stark realities of employing the concept of participation and the unwavering commitment which must be made to the philosophy which undergirds the concept.

In a way, this chapter can give us a realistic picture of how we view participation. Ricardo is a young Colombian face-to-face with a widely acclaimed scholar. His countryman, Orlando Fals Borda, is winding up a career committed to facilitating participation of the people, while he, Ricardo, is just launching a career with parallel purposes. Some of Orlando's comments reveal stark realities:

'People's participation is being manipulated...;'
'we cannot sell ourselves and give in to the manipulation process...;'
'we have to be able to stay alive, and to make our ideas and ideals stay alive as well...;'
'there is really no one profile of a good facilitator.'

Ricardo found his interview with Orlando Fals Borda simultaneously a heartening and disheartening emotion-filled experience. Hope and hopelessness no doubt characterize the current Colombian context. But for Ricardo, it was assuring that Orlando's vision of the future was after all, optimistic. His pioneering work in *participatory research* alone has made a permanent impact on the development community. Involving people in all phases of research which has the potential to change the course of their lives, is indeed a relevant and revolutionary idea.

Kathy Colverson was profoundly influenced by the work of participatory researchers like Orlando Fals Borda, Rajesh Tandon, K. Sadanandan Nair and others. While taking a course in participatory research she became intrigued by the relevance in the method of working with women Campesinas and marginalized segments of society. She felt the Participatory Action Research (PAR) process could be used to assist the women as they examined the realities of their life and as an empowering experience that could lead to increased access to information and learning. Chapter Nine is an account of her research in Honduras. She shares the techniques she used for approaching women in two contrasting rural communities.

The focus of her research was to investigate how women receive and utilize agricultural information. But she wanted, in the process, to give something back to the women that would enable them to assume greater control over their identities as agricultural producers. It was my good fortune to be with Kathy and accompany her for a week as she gathered data. After sharing a long, hot, bumpy jeep ride back into the remote village areas, I *felt* her commitment.

And this was just one of her many visits to the Lencas' community. Her enthusiasm and sincerity was an immediate connecting force with the women. The women had identified several things they would like to learn. On this particular day her 'giving back to the women' took the form of a hands-on demonstration for making cabbage rolls. While they labored in the fields to raise cabbage to market in the big city, they had never eaten cabbage. Any gleanings from the fields had simply been fed to their pigs. (Kathy joked to me that the pigs were nutritionally better off than the people were.) There was no question in my mind as I witnessed the interaction, the excitement in the women's eyes, and the laughter over their struggles while handling the cabbage rolling, that Kathy had become 'one of them.' She had erased any apprehension they might have had about the questions she would ask of them in her research.

Chapter Ten also attests to the power and usefulness of the techniques of participatory research. Meredith Fowlie was witness to the efforts of agricultural researchers in Nepal as they set out to employ a *participatory model*. She believes that participatory research goes hand in hand with participatory development that can result in sustainable agricultural practices.

Enlisting genuine farmer participation has the potential to change the face of agricultural science and research. For the researcher, it implies working at a farmer's pace. And, it may mean a loss of clarity, a loss of control, and a loss of 'professionalism' in the traditional sense. But the scientist can only enhance his skills by employing new techniques including:

- adeptness in initiating interpersonal dialogue,
- building alliances and partnerships,
- using local language more effectively,
- handling gender issues,
- group facilitation, conflict resolution, and
- doing the needful in any given situation.

Thus, science becomes more nebulous and vague when a scientist capitulates a clean, orderly laboratory for a farmer's field.

The scientist forgoes quantitative, systematic variables for an untidy array of hard-to-manipulate farmer criteria, and relinquishes his/her license for absolute control over the research by allowing farmers to participate in, if not dominate, the experimentation process. Meredith points out that the scientist must be prepared to part with ownership of innovations and projects at an early stage, thereby forsaking the road towards a single answer in favor of innumerable paths that may or may not lead to less dramatic 'eurekas.' The personal rewards offset the sacrifices made to participatory methods. You will find this discussion of the processes of scientific revelation and reflection an inspiration for exploring the techniques of participatory research.

Chapter Eleven offers some ideas which could be useful to the researcher who wants to use participatory methods. Josh Galper hopes to remove the mind blocks related to quantitative research, and suggests that learning to use statistics can be an empowering force for grassroots people. He focuses particularly on economic indicators which are critical information for rural development.

The mind leap I make, between the story Meredith tells and Josh's story of preparing grassroots people to be partners with the scientist, is one which says that through training in research methods, and by sharing their own indigenous methods of research, grassroots people can indeed become equal status partners in the process.

The intent of Josh's chapter is to encourage facilitators to recognize the need to make their own command of statistical research comprehensible and encourage involvement. This seems particularly important when grassroots people become partners in research, such as that done through Participatory Rural Appraisal (PRA), or through the newer approach to appraisal described in Chapter Twelve.

Sound training is one of the most important aspects of development programs. Our African colleagues—Chike, Paolo, and Titus—argue in Chapter Twelve that training of rural development facilitators in an innovative communication research approach known as Participatory Rural Communication Appraisal (PRCA), can be the first step in providing suitable skills, techniques, and materials to enable them to perform their roles.

Interestingly, they employ the notion of the *facilitator as a catalyst* in their experimental program, which encompasses the South African Development Community (SADC). There is a definite parallel between their conceptualizations and that of the *catalyst communicator* concept. They endeavor to give us an understanding of the training methodology that is being refined in their project. The approach has an 'in-built' field practice, which gives field workers a chance to practice facilitation skills and develop attitudes appropriate for working more effectively with grassroots people. They believe that these field workers will be better able to assist rural people to articulate their opinions and perceptions as well as to identify and prioritize their problems and needs. Most importantly, they believe that people can learn to develop and implement their own programs and acquire communication strategies that can improve their livelihood in a sustainable manner.

Chapter Thirteen centers on the *discovery principle* as a more specific participatory approach to training. Renuka Bery shares her philosophy and techniques for training which demonstrate the transformational power of participation. She believes that learning through discovery creates the stimuli which people need in order to develop individual judgment and in turn enables them to freely decide and contribute to the most important issues in their societies.

Renuka shares specific techniques she has used in her training from several projects, and the response of people to the training. She shows how participatory learning environments allow people to experiment with new knowledge and try it out in a safe environment. Throughout her discussion it becomes evident that her training technique is an empowering force that tends to equalize relationships between facilitator/trainer and participant. Her emphasis on critical thinking and reflection cannot be underestimated. She introduces the technique of *critical appreciation*, which is intended to assess a participant's progress, using positive reinforcement. The positive feedback encourages an individual to change his/her ways of working through a task, and explore alternative methods. The details of her successful experience with 'discovery' learning will definitely encourage experimentation with this approach and with techniques for facilitating learning through practice and for action.

The next chapter can be thought of as a bridge to the last part of this book. The importance of access to communication technologies and public media cannot be overstated as an important force for a community's development. The presence of media structures which are owned and operated, or which have active participation of the public in programming, are a distinct advantage and source of strength to enable people to have a voice in their own development.

Mass communication connects people with the outside world, but it is equally important to facilitate the networking of people and organizations inside a community. Community-owned and operated media—newspapers, radio, television, and now Internet services—are important for empowerment and democratization. Francis Kasoma (1994) makes a strong case for participatory rural newspapers which, he says, can be a significant force for setting the development agenda. Media access and control is a global issue, and one must be aware that government control of media is a big factor which impairs freedom of expression which ensures freedom of information.

John Hochheimer pursues the issue of public access to community radio in Chapter Fourteen. He lays out the techniques and processes for developing community-based journalism. Those who conceptualize and plan democratic media systems must account for important issues of access—who speaks, who hears, and who mediates and interprets issues that impact on the community. These issues are pertinent to any media system, and are important tools for community-building.

In Chapter Fifteen Don Richardson describes techniques and processes used for establishing a FreeSpace network in Wellington County, Canada. His project began in 1993 and can be considered one of the pioneering projects determined to make Internet services accessible in poor, isolated, rural areas. Such areas, which may never have seen telephones, are now gaining access to digital and microwave telephone systems as well as to the Internet. Such systems are now widespread in countries such as Mexico, Peru, and the Philippines and are providing rural stakeholder organizations with a variety of new participatory communication applications and opportunities.

There is no question about the fact that we have moved into the era of global communication. Prior to satellite communications carrying improved telephone, video, and computer signals, people were divided by the unexplored communication frontiers. 'Today... communications technologies have woven all parts of the world together into an electronic web' says a communications analyst. 'No longer is a community or dialogue restricted to a geographical place.' This is no small factor in the emergence of a new kind of 'global community' (Frederick, 1993: 284).

When I first visited India in 1982, I recall being stranded at the airport in New Delhi trying to complete the last leg of my flight to Calcutta. I tried all day long to make a telephone call to Calcutta, but with no success. Upon arriving late at night in Calcutta, there was no one to greet me. My host, Sujit Basu, had returned to the village thinking I would not come. I spent the first night in the lobby of the Grand Hotel. It was three days before I finally reached Sujit by sending a telegram to the village. Telephone calls made internally and to India, from the USA, were problematic for the next ten years. Contrast this with the many facilities for communication today. I can call my colleague Nair at home and in less than a minute have an audible connection. I send a fax or an e-mail late afternoon and the next morning I can have a reply.

Communication relationships are no longer restricted by space. But *access* to communication resources is another matter. Frederick depicts access as an 'inalienable right,' that all human communicators should have:

> ...the right to hold opinions without interference and to seek, receive, and impart information and ideas through any media and regardless of frontiers. This Right to Communicate includes the right to be informed as well as to inform, the right to reply as well as to listen, the right to listen or to ignore, the right to be

addressed as well as to speak, and the right to use communication resources to satisfy human social, economic, and cultural needs (1993: 283).

No doubt communication technologies have given us the capacity to connect with the 'outside' world. It is now possible to build collaborative relationships between individuals and coalitions among communities, which can transcend the local culture. But the bad news is that these technological developments are not within everyone's reach. In fact, the information superhighways are actually increasing the gap between the 'information-rich' and 'information-poor' populations of the world—a gap which is quickly becoming so wide that perhaps it may never be bridged. These dramatic differences are a critical issue of community-building.

The Art of Building Community

It would be well to keep in mind that the concept of community is not necessarily commonly understood, or interpreted. So the 'art of community-building' is one which needs to be given a frame of reference. The over-arching idea for thinking about community in a way that is meaningful to a development facilitator, is that a community is a collection of people linked together by communication within a physical environment that can be altered by their collective action. In other words, it is communication that creates community. When overlaid with the structures of nation, state, and region, it becomes a defined area within which political and social structures become the boundaries for development.

The kind of communication that creates community must be that of active interpersonal communication, leading to a common sense of purpose and solidarity. It seems sufficient for our purposes to view the art of community-building as that of creating effective communication linkages. These enable people to define their own problems, set their own goals, come up with their own solutions, and optimize individual and group abilities to learn, resolve their differences, and to act on their own behalf.

The chapters that fall under Part 3 contribute to our understanding about building community by approaching communities from the inside. Two of these chapters describe participatory approaches used in projects initiated by two international agencies. Chapter

Eighteen presents a critical aspect of community-building, that of confronting conflict.

Issues regarding tree and forest resources are both global and local. The Community Forestry Unit of the UN FAO has integrated participatory dimensions in all projects around the globe. But opening the doors for people's participation has been a challenge to the agency's leadership. In Chapter Sixteen, Marilyn Hoskins tells her inside story of providing leadership to the community forestry program that was funded in 1978 and became a part of her responsibilities in 1984. She traces the development of this program and shows how the common goals of local forestry programs were a force for building community through the participatory approaches used. While her discussion is in general terms, the underlying message is that participation works to build community, but that it isn't always a simple matter to evaluate how it works, or how to train people to facilitate participation toward a specific goal such as preserving forest resources. Though they are not listed in her chapter, there are many useful publications available about the Community Forestry Program directly from UN FAO Rome.

Joseph Ascroft and Ilias Hristodoulakis discuss their experiences with another international organization committed to people's participation and community-building. The principle of participation officially came to be adopted by the United Nations and many of their bilateral and non-governmental partners in the late 1980s. The United Nations Development Program (UNDP), responding to growing calls for a more participatory system, finally impaneled a team of international scholars and practitioners of development and charged it with resolving these issues. What emerged was a new goal for 'human development based on capacity-building at the grassroots.'

Chapter Seventeen looks at the 'Child to Child' model of community outreach which was a part of reaching that goal. The details provided show how a focus on child health can be a force for bringing the community together for a common cause. The idea of involving children along with adults in the community-building process is indeed an empowering one. Joe and Ilias say that 'to participate in decision-making is to become empowered.' They point out that this process is indeed that of community learning if both children and adults learn:

'The art of tabling one's own views while respecting those of others;'

'The give and take techniques of negotiation in the search for consensus;'
'The civic responsibility of teamwork along with community elders and learned outsiders who have come to help the community.'

Another important understanding regarding community learning outlined by Anne Marie Johnston in Chapter Eighteen, is how to confront conflict through collaborative action. As communities face increasingly complex issues, it is easy for a community to become divided by their differences. Anne believes it is possible for communities to build the capacity to handle difficult issues through collaborative action. Networks of mutual respect and trust that are built can generate new norms of respect, tolerance, and reciprocity.

Consensus-based collaboration and search-based collaboration are highly effective approaches for handling community disputes, and are thus an effective tool for building community. The information which Anne shares from her research and her experience, will be helpful in a researcher's own pursuit of a better understanding of the dimensions of collaborative action.

Chapter Nineteen wraps up the book by positing some challenges to better 'walk the talk.' If people's participation is so widely recognized as a critical dimension of bringing about sustainable development, why is there not more evidence of genuine participation?

So... What's all the Limping About?

I point the finger at us, the facilitators. After taking a pretty strong stand that losing perspective, harboring fears and feelings of inadequacy, lack of preparation to play the role, and reluctance to 'grow with the people' are the principle reasons, I take a closer look at those considerations which are important for the facilitator. The limping will be minimal if you are able to confront 'self,' take risks, build a culture of cooperation, acquire appropriate tools and techniques, and have a vision.

A Final Point

Keep in mind that this book is about *sharing*. The contributors have all played the facilitator role in their respective development-oriented careers. I have urged them to be as candid as possible, and to share their own points of view based on their on-site experiences. We all aspired to put these ideas and accounts into useful and concrete form, and, for some of us, to step down from our academic perches. Information about each contributor is included in the book. Feel free to contact them and continue the dialogue, sharing and comparing your own concerns, perspectives, and most of all, experiences. My goal is for you, the reader, to feel the support of this group in your own development pursuits.

References and Select Bibliography

Caruso, B.A. (1997). The Words We Wear: Talking and Walking, A Baccalaureate Address for the Graduating Class of Earlham College, May 11, 1997. Richmond, Indiana: Earlham College. Unpublished.

Frederick, H. (1993). Computer Networks and the Emergence of Global Civil Society. In Linda M. Harasim (Ed.), *Global Networks: Computers and International Communication*. Cambridge, Mass.: The MIT Press.

Fuglesang, A. (1973). *Applied Communication in Developing Countries— Ideas and observations*. Uppsala, Sweden: The Dag Hammarskjold Foundation.

Kasoma, F.P. (1994). Participatory Rural Newspapers as Agents of Development. In S. A. White, K. S. Nair and J. Ascroft (Eds.), *Participatory Communication: Working for Change and Development*. New Delhi: Sage Publications.

Nair, K.S. and **White S.A.** (1994). 'Participatory Communication as Cultural Renewal. In S. A. White, K. S. Nair and J. Ascroft (Eds.), *Participatory Communication: Working for Change and Development*. New Delhi: Sage Publications.

Ramirez, R. and **Richardson, D.** (1997). The Global Baranga of the 21st Century. Concept paper, Municipal Telephone Project Office, Department of Transportation and Communication, Government of The Philippines, Manila, The Philippines.

Reoch, R. (ed.). (1994). *Human Rights—The New Consensus*. London: Regency Press (Humanity) Ltd.

Part 1

The Art of Activation

2

The Catalyst Communicator: Facilitation without Fear

Shirley A. White and
K. Sadanandan Nair

*One of the key concepts emerging from our Poona–Cornell collaborative development communication research of the 1980s was that of the **catalyst communicator**. Our research supports the notion that this concept is pertinent to understanding the role of facilitator, and more importantly, to enacting that role. The ideas we share in this discussion, we believe, can lead to effective facilitation—**facilitation without fear**. Our language and content are tentative, meant to be regarded as unmolded clay from which you can fashion your own 'works of art.' We do intend to put forth a practical and meaningful point of view that can be of immediate use to persons who aspire to develop the art of facilitation.*

If, in fact, we have a people-centered vision of development in the next century, then the art of facilitation will need to be mastered by all those involved in the development process. To operate fearlessly within that vision, a high priority will be given to capacity-building of people who, as Korten (1990) points out, can be in a position 'to take charge of their own lives, communities and resources and to participate in local, national, and global decision-making processes.'

This is a huge expectation, and is enough to scare any conscientious person engaged in development. Who is to determine what capacities are to be *built*, who will be the *builders*, and who will be *transformed* through the building process? The answer is: *YOU!*
And you say: *But...how?*
We say: *Prepare yourself*. And, as an important aspect of your preparation, learn the art of facilitation without fear by becoming an effective catalyst communicator!'

The Participatory Communication Idea

Those who conceive of development as a process of social transformation view *participatory communication* as a necessary instrument and condition for change to take place. Insight about the nature of *participatory communication*, its ideological, practical, and functional dimensions is useful for everyone whose job it is to 'bring about participatory development.'

Nair and White (1987a: 37) projected a definition of communication for development, which is adapted to reflect the role of a *catalyst communicator*:

> *Participatory development communication* is a two-way, dynamic interaction, which through dialogue transforms 'grass-roots' people and enables them to become fully engaged in the process of development and become self-reliant.

They note that this requires 'transactional communication' wherein 'a sender and receiver of messages interact over a period of time to arrive at shared meanings.'

They suggest that this interaction 'motivates participation' and can result in what may be called a two-way process of persuasion resulting from an exchange of ideas and points of view. They 'talk over their differences, giving and taking, and finally arriving at consensual agreement.' Nair and White point out that 'the environment for participatory development communication is expected to be supportive, creative, consensual, facilitative, sharing ideas through dialogue.' This is a highly dynamic, transformational scenario.

But the viewpoints on participatory communication, what it is and what it entails, differ widely. On some points there tends to be a common understanding: that it is a dynamic (continuously changing) process, that it is dialectical and dialogic, that it brings about a transformation in communication competencies and social behaviors among those who engage in the process. Participatory communication for development begins with the premise that all people have a right to voice their views and become active partners in the development process. As a human interaction, it is both a process and a product; it is both a means and an end; it is both a right and a need. As a dialogue between power holders and the powerless, it is both empowering and disempowering, i.e., the dominance of power holders is reduced.

And...What is a Catalyst Communicator?

Sadanandan has a degree in chemistry (really!) and he remembers well many experiments that took place inside a beaker. For instance, simply dropping chips of dry ice into water created profuse bubbling and a fast rising vapor. That the dry ice catalyzed such a stunning reaction was surprising. But what about mixing a concentrated acid such as hydrochloric acid with water? If you pour the acid into a beaker of water, it simply dilutes the acid. But, *if you pour water into the acid*, a violent splattering results. Chemical reactions are catalyzed, but the outcome of experiments is determined by the intent and level of knowledge and understanding of the chemist who keeps in mind the goals of the experiment. Some dramatic changes can take place with very simple inputs and combinations.

This small example captures the essence of the concept of *catalyst communicator* (CC). If we split the concept into two parts—*communicator* and *catalyst*—then the communicator is the *role* to be played, and the catalyst characterizes the *actions* or behaviors within the role. You can immediately see the parallels between the role of the chemist and the catalyst communicator. Prior to coming into a laboratory or into a community, the chemist or CC has substantial knowledge gained through academic training and experiences. While in the role of enabling others to learn, they may be focused on the work to be done but their goals *may* or *may not* be explicit. The sharpening of the goals depends upon the specific needs of those who participate. As the people make inputs into the planning process, the pathways for learning will vary, but throughout, the chemist in the laboratory, or CC in the community provides the resources and framework for experimentation and learning. Ultimately the participators will be prepared to launch forth on their own to apply what they have gained from the experiential process in whatever way they choose.

You, as a catalyst communicator, will similarly bring a combination of knowledge, commitment, and capabilities to bear on your role in the context of development communication. In a sense you enter into a living laboratory where people are the elements, and through a myriad combinations, specific social outcomes result. Combining people, however, requires a different perspective for the catalyst communicator than that of the chemist. Within the people-centered vision of development, and with the focus on participatory processes, it is not appropriate to 'experiment' on people. Rather, grassroots people become full partners in crafting the development experiment, in its implementation, and in determining the worth of the outcomes.

Thus the *catalyst communicator* acts as a development facilitator putting people together in order to make things happen, to catalyze thinking, motivation, interaction, action, reaction, and reflection. Over time the CC role will change, and ideally will become a role that participants learn to play in daily dialogue and interaction among themselves. Through partnership and participation, people will build the capacity to more effectively communicate among themselves and with other people, on their own behalf. They will be in a position to catalyze action.

Combining people, in all their uniqueness, is no doubt less predictable than combining known chemical elements. New combinations can be uncertain and surprising. Catalyzing interactions can produce outcomes ranging from the benign to the explosive. But as specific people become 'known' elements in the living laboratory of development, it will be easier to decide clearly, how to jointly formulate and pursue courses of action which the people themselves will define as beneficial to all persons involved and to the wider community.

A generalized knowledge and understanding regarding needs, aspirations, goals, and anticipated outcomes is assumed to be present before these human linkages are made. In simple terms, this means that we assume that anyone engaged in the development facilitation role is prepared to play it, and knows what he/she is doing from a process point of view. What's more, we assume that this person is responsible, well-intentioned, and committed to playing a facilitation role focused on the well-being and empowerment of grassroots people. Admittedly, these assumptions are idealized, but they are increasingly regarded as realistic within the framework of *sustainable* development.

The Role of the Catalyst Communicator (CC)

Creating an environment for dialogue, learning, and transformation becomes the first mandate for the *catalyst communicator*. The concept of 'environment' is not a static one, and should be recognized as dynamic, ongoing, and ever changing. The dimensions of the environment are in a sense physical, because the ambience of time, space, and place do provide stimuli for human interaction. But the environment is at least three-dimensional—physical, mental, and spiritual. Setting the stage for constructive interaction between people requires a consideration of all three. It becomes obvious that facilitating such an environment is a Herculean task for the CC, and that the urgent and immediate need is to identify, sensitize, and empower partners for creating and nurturing the environment.

Perhaps you are familiar with the 'animator' role, a descriptor that is used in the development context. Tilakaratna (1991) noted that the task of an animator in a community is to stimulate grassroots people to 'undertake self-reliant initiatives.' This simple straightforward statement encompasses an important expectation. But, if it is to be realized, a *catalyst communicator* must come into the local development scenario with a wide range of competencies and facilitation tools such as appropriate beliefs, knowledge, and skills. These tools need to be suitable to each phase of interaction with the local situation. The various phases include preliminary preparations, entry level dialogue, exploration of needs and aspirations of people in the community, assessing the issues, and identifying courses of action. This may be followed by investigating alternatives for action, acquiring resources necessary to support alternatives chosen and to take decisive action, reflecting on the success of actions taken, and finally a redefinition of needs.

It becomes obvious that enacting these phases requires flexibility and ongoing open-minded problem-posing and solving processes.

Throughout these phases the challenge for the CC is to unfold a partnership with the people which *transforms* the way they look at themselves and feel about themselves, the way they relate to their neighbors and friends, the way they view their community, and the courage they have to reach out to a wider, more global sphere of action. *The transformational goal of the CC is to unlock the human potential of individuals, increasing their capacity to think, to relate, to act, and to reflect from a foundation of communication competencies.* The courage to launch out on an expanded vision of their own quality of life and what it takes to achieve it, will be an important outcome when this transformation goal is reached. The interesting thing about this transformational process is that it also brings about parallel changes within the catalyst communicators.

Two of our earlier development communication models are pertinent to this discussion and can give more specific grounding to your thinking about the role and tasks of the catalyst communicator in the process of facilitation. If you examine the 'reconceptualization of the development communication process' which we first presented at the East West Conference on Communication and Change in 1987, it will trigger your thinking. The model is framed within a transactional perspective which emphasizes the 'dialectical and interactive nature of both the communication process and participation process' (Nair and White, 1993: 47–70).

The 'cultural renewal model' articulates a dialectical interaction between the cultural renewal process and the development process in a community context of socio-cultural diversity. The model is useful to the catalyst communicator in that it provides pertinent detail for:

- *The interfacing process*—interpersonal dialogue, confrontation of differing perspectives and points of view, searching for relevant or useful information and coping with the realities of interpersonal communication.
- *The diagnostic process*—asking systematic relevant questions regarding needs and alternatives for meeting those needs, framed within a problem posing/solving framework.
- *The participatory research process*—a methodology that promotes the production of collective knowledge, collective critical analysis, making connections between personal and structural problems, and linking reflection and evaluation to action.

- *The action process*—thinking through courses of action, pursuing action, evaluating and accounting for action projects implemented, and reflecting on the outcomes.

It should be noted that the cultural renewal model is fully presented in another publication by Sage, *Participatory Communication: Working for Change and Development* (White et al., 1994: 138–93). But beyond the Nair–White model, that book contains a wide range of theoretical and conceptual information worthy of study that can further inform the catalyst communicator and contribute to competence.

A Closer Look at Competencies

Recalling the phases of interaction with a local situation, it is apparent that the catalyst communicator needs a wide array of competencies which link beliefs, knowledge, and skills in order to carry out services, processes, and action projects successfully. Admittedly, it will be rare to find all the competencies needed in a single individual. Because of this, it is often necessary and desirable to put together catalyst communicator teams who can complement each other, or shift responsibilities from one phase to another. Because the effective catalyst communicator cannot be cloned, it is no surprise that individuals may have very different qualities that account for their competencies and their credibility as they relate to people in the community. After observing individuals who are considered successful in facilitator roles, it seems that they do have a special quality which synergizes their relationships, whether you call it charisma, a dramatic self-presentation, a warm personality, intensity of concern, an endearing sense of humor, or elements of all of these.

In an effort to move out of abstractions as much as possible and be more concrete, we have constructed a matrix of CC competencies and phases of interaction, mentioned earlier, in relation to the core of beliefs, knowledge, and skills (see Figure 2.1). The multiple roles played by the catalyst communicator throughout the phases of interaction, such as those of the facilitator, the motivator, the linker, the synergizer, the sounding board, the counselor, and the educator, undergird the structure of the matrix.

Using this matrix as a guide, you can expand the cells with more descriptive detail of what would be appropriate to a specific situation. For example in a preliminary interaction, the core group in the participation partnership could use the matrix as a basis of discussion and create their own matrix. This kind of holistic look at phases of a project and competencies necessary to carry out the phases, serves as a communication device to bring about shared understandings. At the same time it can provide the framework to identify training needs and resources necessary to support the project over time.

To be more specific about beliefs, knowledge, and skills it is useful to elaborate:

On Beliefs

- Attitudes are situation or context bound, but stem from broader 'core' or general beliefs.
- All people have a right to enlightenment through experiential learning.
- Diversity of individuals and communities is to be respected, understood and preserved.
- Development functionaries and others have a responsibility for the well-being of the downtrodden.
- Open-mindedness, honesty, integrity, and intellectual curiosity are basic qualities to be cultivated.
- It is important to have courage of conviction and take risks necessary to empower people.
- Developing communication competencies and access to information and technology is crucial to empowerment.
- Coping with conflict, hostility, rejection, avoidance, deception, suspicion, envy, and erratic behavior is a normal and constructive process.
- Trust-building provides the foundation for all interpersonal interaction and human capacity-building.
- The importance of the individual is recognized in relation to collective well-being.
- A humanistic value system is necessary for authentic participation based on democratic principles and social justice.

Figure 2.1: A Matrix Listing Catalyst Communicator Competencies

Phase of Interaction	Belief	Knowledge	Skill
Interfacing: • preliminary preparation • entry level dialogue with people and officials in the community • observe the physical environment to get a sense of people and place	people want to improve their community; they can solve their own problems; are willing to be involved	development process and theory; aspects of the host community and type of people who live there; risks of village living	interpersonal communication; investigative reporting; process observer; synthesizer
Diagnosing: • identify aspirations and needs • discuss needs and aspirations • diagnose system problems • set major goals	people are able to articulate their own situations; system is changeable; goals can be set and met	social/psychological needs of people; organizational development; small group theory; change theory	discussion and focus group manager; problem-posing/ solving; search conference-organizer
Investigating: • assess issues • brainstorming over courses of action • gather information • examine options • establish objectives	people can do valid research and assess data, set own objectives and priorities, learn skills necessary to do own research	how to address issues and alternative research methods; sources for data; proposal development	conduct Participatory Action Research projects; design and manage research tools and teach others

Figure 2.1 continued

Figure 2.1 continued

Phase of Interaction	Belief	Knowledge	Skill
Acting: • thinking and planning • acquire needed resources • implement projects • monitor projects • make adjustments as necessary	people will take lead in projects and solve problems as they arise; all conflicts are resolvable, people can work together	guidance and counseling; trouble-shooting; risk and conflict theory; how to acquire and access resources	intervenor; mediator; counselor; adapter; monitor; media liaison
Evaluating: • reflect about outcomes and relationships • gather data, analyze, make interpretations for application • account for project resources • prepare and present needed reports • redefine needs/wants, new efforts	unity will be increased in the community; indigenous talent and leadership will emerge; the people will be uplifted/empowered	participatory evaluation methods; how to help people apply what has been learned; open new ways to learn, new roles	adult education methods; network and resource linker; report writing; participatory media development; do long range plan

On Knowledge

A grounding in development communication theory and practice, framed in a broader context of the social sciences and the discipline of communication, is required, as is:

- familiarity with theory and practice of political systems, organizational behavior and organizational communication and change;
- an understanding of adult education theory and practice as well as principles for designing experiential learning and access to learning resources;
- insight into self/other variables—esteem, prejudice, bias, motivation, confidence, identity, perception, reliance, evaluation;
- concept formation, organization, and integration; and
- awareness and appreciation of the interrelationship of belief systems, value frameworks, and attitudes in the context of the specific culture.

On Skills

- *Communication skills*—listening, questioning, making observations of visual environment and non-verbal cues, writing, speaking, participatory message-making, designing media, and production.
- *Training skills*—constructing learning experiences, facilitating intellectual and emotional growth, generating new ideas, and enabling critical reflection.
- *Counseling skills*—assisting others to pose and solve problems and make meaningful choices in the decision-making process, mediate, and negotiate conflict.
- *Interpersonal communication skills*—trust-building, team-building, supportive communication techniques, consensus-building, sharing thoughts and feelings.

There is little doubt that when you think about the competencies we have identified here, it can be a bit intimidating. Many people would agree that to be a successful facilitator, it does take a person with an unusually broad range of capabilities. These accrue with each added bit of experience and search for knowledge. And it isn't necessarily a matter of years. For example, we have several contributing authors for this book who, in their twenties, are well on their way to matching the competencies we have identified through our research and first hand exposure to development efforts. All are actively pursuing careers in development stemming from a deep concern for those who are marginalized or without a voice or measure of control over their lives.

If we keep in mind the CC roles which we pointed out, they would provide the underpinnings for the more specific competencies we have listed in our matrix—the facilitator, the motivator, the linker, the synergizer, the sounding board, the counselor and the educator—we can visualize how the catalyst communicator would proceed. There would be specific activities in which the CC will engage if 'self-reliance' of people is realized. For example, from the initial contact with the community, the CC would initiate discussion and talk directly with the people. The CC would provide technical training when needed. The CC would show people how to do things along the way, while looking to the people for their methods as well. In the case of organizing participatory data collection, media planning, production, dissemination, and project implementation, you, the CC, would very often be in the role of educator. In addition, the CC will encourage knowledge sharing and assist community leaders who emerge out of the sharing process to manage communication media and produce their own messages.

When confident, self-reliant, empowered people emerge through the initiatives of a process, they generate many options for future development. But most importantly, the *catalyst communicator* will withdraw from the field when the process is institutionalized, when resources are found and provided by the community. Ultimately the process can be sustained through the leadership within the grassroots community.

The activities of the catalyst communicator outlined by Nair (1994) in relation to participatory communication provide a good summary. This is discussed in the following sections.

Activities of the Catalyst Communicator

- Understanding the realities of village life,
- assisting the villagers in forming groups,

- putting together democratic organizations,
- creating a context for critical appraisal and reflection,
- providing technical assistance as and when needed,
- encouraging group action for problem-solving,
- fostering self-confidence and self-reliance,
- creating an environment which encourages internal 'animators' or 'catalysts' to emerge.

This suggests the characteristics or qualities of a person who can perform the CC role in relation to grassroots people. Nair (1994) notes the crucial ones as discussed in the sections below.

Characteristics of the Catalyst Communicator

- Socially committed,
- Culturally sensitive,
- Empathetic in interpersonal interactions,
- Democratic in communication relationships,
- Motivated by the desire to contribute to ecosensitive, sustainable development,
- Psychologically prepared for social action,
- Trained in participatory planning, and evaluation methodologies,
- Knowledgeable about participatory processes.

At this point, we would like to put forth some additional ideas, which can provide a kind of framework for our subsequent efforts to establish the importance of the catalyst communicator concept. The process, which is fostered by the CC, is the key to opening the door for people's participation in development. After a period of time in partnership with the CCs, people will no longer be afraid to speak out. Their basic insecurities will have been rooted out, confronted, and eliminated. Feelings of rejection, ridicule, embarrassment, and self-incrimination will largely be overcome. The CC addresses the core of the problems and when fears have been allayed, people are then prepared to participate.

In other words, the CC prepares the people to participate in the communication processes necessary for sustainable development. It is useful then to look at how participatory communication as a process of participation interrelates with empowerment and transformation.

On Empowerment and Transformation

Participatory communication then is conceived of as a process methodology that involves people in an interactive way, making communication resources accessible to them directly. In turn, grassroots people acquire the knowledge and skill that enables the formation of partnerships for making progress. Through that process, a person experiences self-awareness and becomes conscious of social issues that impair or enhance their lives. The transformative dynamic of communication exchanges, acts as a *catalyst* for identifying one's own problems, recognizes possible routes to empowerment and reliance, and builds a sense of *in*dependence through *inter*dependence. Participatory community communication aims to construct opportunities for dialogue in a context of commitment and concern about development, which has the potential to generate self-confidence, self-esteem, self-respect, and self-definition in relation to community. Behind the scenes is the *catalyst communicator* playing the roles necessary for transformation and empowerment of the people.

The outcome of participatory communication for the people is consciousness-raising through critical reflection about their own condition, which will lead to a significant voice in social action. Additionally, people develop communication skills, acquire new knowledge, contribute indigenous knowledge to development decision-making, and learn how to assess risks and opportunities. Ultimately, the participation process can lead to resource acquisition, which will enable them to reach common goals within the community where people live and work harmoniously. Above all, those who control the resources for development seek the input of people in the development process—an input that is valued and sought through interaction, involvement, patience, trust, and confidence-building. At the same time, grassroots people have to believe that their own individual efforts can make a difference and that they can become equal partners in development.

So bringing about 'self-reliance' requires people to become critically aware of those social forces which have brought about their current downtrodden condition, by reflecting on their life and living conditions. Through participation, developing trust in partners, and expanding their own communication knowledge and skills, they will gradually build confidence in themselves and others. It is an important realization to believe that through their collective action they can bring about positive change in the form of social action which leads to opportunities for an improved state of health, state of knowledge, access to resources, and ultimately to a more positive quality of life.

Empowerment is often conceived of as an individual's sense of confidence, which has perhaps resulted from a self-realization of oppression or lack of freedom and opportunity. While this is a valid aspect of empowerment, the framework of participatory communication would conceive of empowerment in a more holistic sense, as an outcome of establishing and strengthening interpersonal commitment and trust, and as alliances of groups of diverse individuals who share a similar sense of helplessness and lack of control. A growing sense of interdependence enhances feelings of self-worth, trust, and common cause. Out of this sense of interdependence can come a sense of excitement, adventure, and hope which motivates and renews faith in self, other, and community producing cohesion of purpose. When a sense of possibility based on a collective vision for the community's future emerges, true empowerment becomes reality.

If the people at the grassroots are transformed into self-sufficient actors in participatory development communication, then their partners must attach equal importance to the contribution of indigenous knowledge (as well as external expert knowledge) and local solutions within a culturally sound context for specific action. Traditional information or knowledge sources are one part of the participatory development equation. But in addition, the process of accessing indigenous sources is one in which the people themselves exert control, not only over decisions relating to internal and external communication messages, but also over the tools for media production.

Therefore, participatory communication places emphasis on the *process* of communicating as a means for releasing an empowering force within which people can reinforce their own communication skills, develop analytic and reflective skills which uplift levels of self-esteem, and lead to increased self-reliance and trust in others. The outcome is a strengthening of knowledge and decision-making abilities enabling co-equal, collaborative relationships, which transform individuals from a position of powerlessness and a voiceless existence to the point where they become active communicators. Courses of action which will shape their future are now worked out independently and by themselves, rather than by external power figures.

Through thinking about development approaches that can be mutually beneficial to both the people and to power-holding, decision-making functionaries, mutual dependency, that is, interdependency, is created. This interdependency recognizes micro-level needs, but also acknowledges that people at the micro-level do not live in isolation from broader development contexts at regional or national levels. Linkages among development units, as well as linkages among subgroups at each level are necessary and are dependent upon a willingness to communicate, participate, and create. The transformation puts emphasis on the value of the individual and the imperative to meet needs and enable personal growth. But the affirmation of the individual, as valued by others and in a position to shape the future in a broader sense, is a critical aspect of empowerment.

The stage is set for a new way of thinking about participatory communication for development, and a more meaningful involvement of people who presumably are to benefit from the development process. Most importantly, the lead actor in the drama is the *catalyst communicator* who is enthusiastic about sharing the stage with a cast of thousands.

References and Select Bibliography

Korten, David, (1990). *Getting into the 21st Century: Voluntary Action and the Global Agenda*. West Hartford, Conn.: Kumarain Press, Inc.

Melkote, Srinivas R. (1992). *Communication for Development in the Third World: Theory and Practice*. New Delhi: Sage Publications.

Mody, Bella, (1991). *Designing Messages for Development Communication: An Audience Participation-based Approach*. New Delhi: Sage Publications.

Nair, K. Sadanandan and **White, Shirley A.** (1987a). Participation is the Key to Development Communication, *Media Development, 34*(3), 36–40.

Nair, K. Sadanandan and **White, Shirley A.** (1987b). A Reconceptualization of Development Communication Concepts, Paper presented at *Communication and Change: An Agenda for the New Age of Communication Seminar*, University of Hawaii and East-West Centre, Honolulu, Hawaii.

———. (1993). *Perspectives on Development Communication*. New Delhi: Sage Publications.

Nair, K. Sadanandan, (1994). Participatory Video for Rural Development: A Methodology for Dialogic Message Design. Unpublished manuscript prepared for UN Food and Agriculture Organization, Rome, Italy.

Tilakaratna, S. (1991). Stimulation of Self-reliant Initiatives by Sensitized Agents: Some Lessons from Practice. In Orlando Fals Borda and M.A. Rahman (Eds.), *Action and Knowledge: Breaking the Monopoly with Participatory Action-research*, 135–145. New York, NY: Apex Press.

White, Shirley A., Nair, K.S. and **Ascroft, J.** (1994). *Participatory Communication: Working for Change and Development*. New Delhi: Sage Publications.

3

Facilitator or Advocate: What's the Difference?

Ndunge Kiiti and Erik Nielsen

In this chapter, Ndunge and Erik take a candid look at the facilitator and the advocate. How are their roles defined? How do these roles differ? Which role is most appropriate and in what context? They recognize that advocacy and facilitation do have points of overlap and similarity, but this chapter focuses on the distinctions. They have set out to articulate these differences so as to effectively guide field level workers in their own process of transformation and learning.

Facilitation and advocacy are concepts that have been extensively used in the development arena. We often hear phrases such as, 'we are going to *facilitate* a workshop on farmer to farmer exchange,' or 'they are *advocating* the use of contraceptives for family planning.' But what do these concepts really mean? We posed this question to individuals working in various development fields—education, economics, public policy, and communication—and their responses generated three main themes. From their responses, it was quite clear that both advocacy and facilitation were *viewed as either processes or part of a process.* A fine distinction was drawn between advocacy and facilitation by many. The most explicit distinction was that an *advocate is often driven by an 'external agenda' while the facilitator seeks to understand and help people determine their own agenda.*

This clearly reinforced the commonly shared perception that the philosophies, attitudes and behaviors which surround these two concepts vary. Advocacy and facilitation were often perceived as interrelated. There are situations or processes that call for one or the other and sometimes both, depending on the context. It is critical that one understand these processes and discern which is most appropriate in a given context.

Defining and Understanding the Concepts

Numerous development specialists have attempted to understand and define advocacy and facilitation. Paulo Freire, a well known educationalist, explains what he terms as the 'banking' approach to education and development, in which information or technology transfer is encouraged and promoted. This can be viewed as a parallel to the concept of advocacy. In this approach, the teacher determines goals and imparts knowledge and skills to students who are perceived as 'ignorant;' the teacher talks and the students listen. The whole process perpetuates the status quo. Freire (1972) contrasts the 'banking' approach with the 'critical thinking approach' or the facilitative process where the community members or learners are respected, determine their own goals, and ultimately control the process.

Tim Kennedy, well known for his community work with the Eskimos in the Sky River Project, and early pioneering with the use of video for empowerment, was driven by his conviction that people deserved a voice in the decisions critical to their own well-being. Based on his years of work in development programs and conducting research, Tim Kennedy, discusses his perspectives on advocacy and facilitation. He describes advocacy as the process whereby a person or persons acts on behalf of others for the express purpose of changing the attitudes or actions of decision-makers. Kennedy (1982) illustrates how this process often focuses on specific problems or issues as opposed to a continuum of sustainable change, thereby reinforcing dependency in development. He argues that in order to have genuine, long-term change in development, advocacy must shift toward facilitation. Kennedy defines facilitation as the process of change which takes place while organizing and mobilizing the competencies of the community members. He expounds on the definition by highlighting key components of this process. Facilitation ensures accountability, fosters the development of community-initiated solutions, and often leads to sustainable programs because the community members control all phases of the process.

Our own experiences and reflections in community development lead us to similar definitions as the ones both Freire and Kennedy have described. Advocacy is often perceived as a process where a specific agenda, external to the community, is promoted and achieved with short-term based goals in mind. In contrast, the process of facilitation begins where the community members are, and normally leads to empowerment and mutual respect, ensuring sustainable development programs. The ideas expressed and the issues we raise are based on these definitions of advocacy and facilitation.

Come! Share Our Journey

In order to illustrate more creatively the process that a facilitator and an advocate may follow, we have written a narrative which integrates key components of our joint background and experience. Join us on a journey toward a more complete understanding of the role of a facilitator and that of an advocate in community-based development. Our journey will take us to the Southern and Eastern parts of the African continent where, like in many other parts of the world, communities have struggled and engaged in critical reflection on how the facilitator and the advocate impact the development process. The debate continues today. We feel that all too often there has been far too little attention given to the differences between *facilitation* and *advocacy*. An understanding of how these differences and the unique aspects of each interact, is essential if we are to capitalize upon the strengths and challenges of each practice.

Our exploration will identify the main concepts and ideals which support each of these two approaches toward a more effective process of community development. Hopefully, the journey will be stimulating and useful to you as practitioners, as individuals and organizations directly involved in grassroots development. It will encourage and challenge you to critically explore the values, beliefs, and assumptions grassroots people have assimilated from the dominant culture, i.e., the culture of the power holders.

The Journey of the Facilitator

Our first visit on the journey took us to West Africa where we visited HOPE, a national people's organization with their main office in Banjul, the capital city of Gambia. Like most people's organizations, HOPE seeks to represent its members' interests, have member-accountable leadership, and is substantially self-reliant. HOPE's mission statement is to build collaborative relationships that strengthen and improve the local environment where rural peoples live and work. Their primary program focus is directed toward preventive health care and education.

Sera Musa was our guide. She has been with HOPE since it began and works as a field level practitioner in health programming and education. Sera provided a comprehensive and detailed overview of her organization's philosophy, approach, and programs. She tells us that her organization uses a grassroots, bottom-up oriented approach to development and has been working in the area for about three years. HOPE's philosophy and overall approach to development is one that is focused on the strength and solutions which lie within the people themselves. Though the organization does not encourage reliance on external financial or institutional support, HOPE does recognize the benefit of collaboration with others. HOPE seeks to identify and build upon the resources that exist within the Gambian community. Within this realm, HOPE prefers to engage Gambian organizations, and institutions, both locally and nationally before external assistance is sought. The cornerstone of HOPE's approach is that of long-term sustainability where they understand sustainable development as a process, encompassing the natural environment, social relations, education, production, and well-being of the community.

Sera narrates to us how HOPE got involved in this program. Specific members of a local community in the northeastern part of the Gambia began to recognize that there was a significant deterioration of general health and community well-being. However, the community alone did not fully understand the cause of the problems. Through local and regional networks, community members had heard about HOPE's involvement in health programs in other parts of the country. Recognizing that the situation was getting worse and health needs were on the increase, the community invited HOPE to help them address these problems.

As we walked around the village, it became clear that many members of the community were highly motivated to participate in confronting their problems. At the health clinic, we found a large group of women, both young and old, working side by side. During the morning hours, women brought their children for immunizations and to be weighed. In the afternoon, underneath the saba tree, a health trainer from HOPE, together with two of the community health workers (CHWs), provided health education on nutrition and breastfeeding. The following day, we attended an AIDS awareness seminar organized for youth and co-facilitated by HOPE and the local religious leaders from the mosque. We had the opportunity to talk to the Imam who described how HOPE had helped him identify and utilize his ability to take a key role as a community leader, in mobilizing youth to participate in AIDS education programs. 'Within our community, youth have been one of the groups most affected by the epidemic and we have had to actively provide education to slow the spread of this deadly disease,' he said. 'Much of the success of the program was a result of getting the youth involved.' The Imam continued to describe how the program was now completely controlled and directed by the youth: 'They meet and develop educational materials, organize plays, and provide peer education and counseling. Our role is only to support their efforts.'

The evening was a time of reflection and discussion with Sera. We asked her how HOPE had been able to create and promote the enabling environment, which was so evident within the community. 'It has not been easy and it has taken time, but a number of factors have been central to the success of the program,' said Sera. 'Obviously there is still a lot that can be done, but we have been encouraged to see how the community has come up and participated in solving their own problems.' Sera continued to explain this process: 'When we were invited to this community, we saw ourselves as no more than facilitators of a process. We recognized that the community members have ideas and knowledge, and, through a shared learning experience, we could identify a positive way forward. As I mentioned earlier, our philosophy holds that critical thinking is the most effective approach to learning and self-discovery. We encouraged the community members to determine their own goals and facilitated a process that helped them create their own realities. This process has not been easy but we feel that in the long run, it will empower the community members and create a sustainable program.'

We told Sera, 'It's great to hear that this community responded to HOPE the way it did. It is encouraging to see what you've done in this community in such a short time.' 'Oh no! It wasn't us. We recognized early on that giving people information is one thing, but engaging them to discover their own knowledge is another,' exclaimed Sera.

'How did you do that, because it sounds difficult? For example, the AIDS youth initiative: What do you hope will be the outcome of this process?' She replied: 'Basically, all the solutions to these problems have emerged from the community members themselves. For the most part, the youth have been empowered to participate and determine the process. This means that there is ownership, not only of the problems, but with a commitment to address these problems, which has led to locally appropriate and sustainable solutions. The youth, on their own initiative, have developed the AIDS educational materials, come up with plays and have been involved in peer counseling.'

'I also think the community has been empowered through the health education program. I have no doubt, that if HOPE were to leave the community today, the programs would continue. Local community members have taken up all the leadership roles in the program and we plan to phase out of the process. So our role was mainly to facilitate, enable and enhance the community's ability to identify their own problems, come up with solutions and participate in the process of enhancing and improving their own living conditions.'

The Journey of the Advocate

Our second stop was at Addis Ababa, the capital of the Ethiopian nation, which we visited along with the representatives of TEV International, a European headquartered, agricultural NGO that has offices in five continents. In Africa, and specifically in Ethiopia, the organization has worked with a variety of agricultural groups, ranging from local farmers to state level ministries for the last five years. TEV's global mission is to improve field crop yields for farmers at the grassroots level. To achieve this goal, TEV has focused and specialized in applied research, information dissemination and documentation, formal training and media promotion activities.

We were met in Addis Ababa by Chris Mutombo, one of TEV's principle agricultural field trainers, who brought us back to the organization's headquarters. Upon our arrival, we were introduced to TEV's management staff, including the directors of financial operations and external affairs.

After a good night's rest, we set out the next morning to visit one of TEV's field projects in the Western part of the country. As we drove to the site, Chris Mutombo shared a little bit about his personal background. His background is 'mainly academic' with little local level field experience. For four years, before taking up the position at TEV International, he worked in the capital investment section of a large international multinational organization.

During our ride, we posed a number of questions to Chris. We were especially interested in finding out more about TEV's approach to problem definition and situation analysis and their mechanism of engaging local level community members in the development process. 'What exactly is the problem in the community which we are going to visit?' we asked Chris. 'And, how was this problem defined?'

Chris began to explain: 'For TEV it is very important to base the definition of the problem on fact and scientific information. As you are aware, TEV is an agricultural organization and we rely heavily on information, not only from local farmers, but also from agencies and government ministries that work in agriculture. The problem in this particular community that we are going to visit today was known before TEV arrived.'

'Really? How so?' we asked.

Chris continued: 'We were contacted by the local level government and they informed us that these communities were experiencing low crop yields, due to poor agricultural practices. We were asked by the municipal government to conduct a situation analysis and needs assessment on behalf of the community. When we completed this evaluation, we determined two other key areas that needed to be addressed immediately. These were poor human nutrition status and a lack of inputs including technical resources, skill development, poor information and dissemination methods, and capital inflow.'

As Chris continued to elaborate on TEV's approach to development, we arrived at the local training center where TEV's field office staff is based. Jenny Smith, the head of the center, met us. She greeted us with great enthusiasm and welcomed us to Musoma village: 'You have arrived in good time. I have arranged for you to meet with some community farmers whom we have trained. But before we go out, let's sit in the conference room for a cup of tea and discuss any questions you might have for me.'

'On the way here, Chris provided us with a general background to TEV. However, we would be interested to hear more about your approach in Musoma. We are familiar with one of your other agricultural programs in Los Baños, Ecuador.'

'Oh, it's interesting you mention South America as I have just returned from a trip to Bolivia,' she said.

'And, what were you doing in Bolivia?'

'Well, I was there for one month helping set up a training program in La Paz. We were implementing the model that we use here in Africa in the South American context.'

'How is it different or similar to the African context?'

'Surprisingly, there were hardly any changes that had to be made from the African model. We have found that our model is superior and can be applied effectively in all contexts. We feel that TEV has an effective methodology to address agricultural training and crop improvement, and therefore, we have used it in more than forty-five countries worldwide. We have used this integrated system from Mexico to South Africa, from Albania to Laos.'

'How does your approach encourage community members to participate and become more involved in the decision-making process?' we asked.

'Well historically, there has been a limited amount of information on agriculture available in the rural communities and this is one of our principal driving forces; to provide information to these areas. This reinforces the need for our training and our role in providing the most current information and technology available so that crop production can be maximized. At the same time, we are encouraging the local and national government authorities to integrate some of these new ideas and practices at the village level.'

'Thank you for sharing these insights with us. They have been very helpful in understanding more about your program and your organization's approach to development. I think it will also be helpful in putting things in context when we talk to the farmers.' We quickly finished our cup of tea and were on our way.

After speaking to Jenny, we arrived shortly after, at one of the nearby village farms. We exchanged pleasantries with three local farmers who grow field crops and walked over to the green fields. Chris asked one of the farmers who had been working with TEV to show us his experimental agro-forestry plot. The plot had been designed and planted under TEV's training program. We asked the farmer why he had planted those particular species. Before he could respond, Chris answered that this was decided upon not only because of the high nutritional value for local people, but the high demand and value of the crops on the export market. Chris continued to describe the extensive research that had gone into this process. He also highlighted the fact that identical research plots were being introduced and implemented in sixteen other African countries.

A Matrix: Facilitator and Advocate

The 'journey' has exposed us to two different countries where two development agencies have applied varying approaches and philosophies to community-based development. In order to better understand the differences between them, we devised a matrix that highlights these approaches, comparing and contrasting the facilitator and the advocate. The matrix should not be viewed as one which merely lists either/or options, but rather as a tool to illustrate the principal differences between a facilitator and an advocate. Clearly, there will be an overlap at times. This matrix is in no way considered a definitive model, but one which will enable dialogue as to what one *does* in playing the roles. Importantly, it can help you recognize the roles you do play and reduce confusion of behaviors.

From our discussions with practitioners and researchers engaged in community development projects, we generated six criteria. We used these six criteria to elicit and understand the two contrasting philosophies toward community development. We believe that an essential component of understanding the development process in a given situation is to understand and articulate one's *own* philosophy. Each of the six criteria can serve as a guide or a beginning point for defining one's development philosophy as well as one's role and purpose in a specific development context.

Context

The context refers to the situation in which a particular process takes place. It is critical to understand all the different aspects of the environment in which the development process will occur, so optimum effectiveness can be achieved.

Problem

Personal and institutional backgrounds are instrumental to defining and understanding a given situation. The 'problem' criteria were explored in the matrix to ensure that the most appropriate person or group defines the problem to be addressed. Though this is not always the case, often, individuals external to the situation or context are responsible for defining a problem, whereas it is frequently best understood by those directly or internally associated with the context. This is not to say that external viewpoints and impressions/perspectives are not valuable or legitimate, because they do have their place. It must also be recognized that simply because an internal member or organization defines a problem, it does not mean that they are the most appropriate party to do so.

Approach

In reference to the approach, the matrix highlights the philosophical basis of the idea of community development held by the advocate and the facilitator. This category is particularly relevant in shaping the overall process related to problem definition and subsequent strategies and outcomes.

Strategy

The strategy refers to a series of mechanisms or techniques designed to stimulate effective outcomes; these outcomes may not always be tangible. Within this framework, the process, depending on the role of the facilitator or the advocate, can range from formula or prescription oriented to a more fluid and malleable strategic process.

Outcomes

This category highlights results that are expected from either an advocate or facilitator's process and approach.

Attitudes

This category is central to the overall understanding of the dynamics of the facilitator's or advocate's process. It is the attitudes and values held by an individual or organization that often dictate or guide their approach to community development (see Figure 3.1).

Figure 3.1: A Matrix Contrasting Facilitator and Advocate Behavior

Criteria	*The Facilitator*	*The Advocate*
1. Context	• Generally associated with organizations, groups or institutions that are fundamentally committed to people-centered development.	• Generally associated with organizations, groups or institutions that have predefined goals and objectives and their own predetermined agenda.
	• Principal areas of focus include capacity building, empowerment, training and facilitation, collaborative relationship building, and reciprocal learning.	• Principal areas of focus and specialization include research, documentation, training, and media activities, adoption of ideas and practices.
	• Process is the important focal point.	• Product is the focal point, usually predetermined.
	• Agenda is defined by the process.	• Agenda is defined by desired product outcome.
2. Problem	• Problem defined by the community.	• Problem defined (predefined) by external parties.
	• Facilitator assists in the exploration, understanding, and definition of the problem.	• The advocate often informs community members of the problem which has been defined.
	• Encourages the community to seek own information by stimulating critical reflection and discussion.	• Promotes the dissemination and transfer of knowledge derived from 'expert' and/or external sources.
3. Approach	• Process begins with the community people.	• Process begins with external organization or institution.
	• Fundamental belief is that community members have the capacity to collaborate and solve their own problems.	• Fundamental belief is that a solution is necessary from external sources.
	• Solution to problem emerges from local context.	• Solution is not tailored or adapted to local context.

Figure 3.1 continued

	Facilitator	Advocate
4. Strategy	• Facilitator stimulates critical reflection and dialogue for sustainable community development.	• Unilateral information transfer and communication from the advocate to the community.
	• Encourages people to find and use their own voice and evaluate information.	• Filter and control information dissemination to the community.
5. Expected Outcomes	• Locally appropriate action leading to increase in local capacity.	• Outcomes are not necessarily appropriate since they were preconceived and based on predetermined agenda.
	• Improves local decision-making capacity.	• Weakens local decision-making capacity.
	• Strengthens commitment and sense of local community.	• Sense of detachment and complacency among individuals
	• Sustainable, locally managed and directed activities.	• Not sustainable because of dependency.
6. Attitudes and Values	• Respects learners' ideas and knowledge.	• Personal or institutional ideas often overshadow those of community members.
	• Sees himself/herself as a co-learner who collaborates in the acquisition of knowledge and skills.	• Does not see the need to collaborate since their role is one of information and knowledge dissemination.
	• Values learner participation.	• No consideration of learner participation.
	• Does not claim to have the answers to problems or preconceptions about what changes are needed, but rather helps the process of change to move smoothly.	• Makes knowledge claims and attempts to impose them on communities.

Discussion: Which Way Forward?

For development practitioners to be most relevant and useful in their work, they need to be involved in the discussion of the critical issues confronting their situation.

Furthermore, practitioners must become active participants toward seeking a long term and sustainable solution within the development process. Facilitation and advocacy are two mechanisms that have been used in education and communication planning to improve and enhance this process.

The Process of Learning

More recently there has been a movement toward a facilitative mode through which development practitioners are trying to critically engage participants in their own transformation and learning. This is in contrast to the traditional mechanism of advocacy where people were viewed as 'sponges' to 'soak up' information that was handed to them. Learning has traditionally been thought of as going hand-in-hand with teacher-centered processes, usually occurring in a formal structure or system. Freire (1973) likened learning to a process whereby a teacher deposited information in the minds of students, similar to the way we make financial deposits in a bank.

A focus on effective learning suggests a minimization of the teacher-centered approach. It allows for the emergence of a concept of learning where the processes are initiated, directed, and owned by the participants themselves. You saw an example of this in our journey when we visited HOPE's health program. The youth were engaged in critical learning because they determined what they needed to learn and participated in that process themselves. Learning, in this alternative mindset, is best characterized as a continuous, life-long, evolving process. A learner-centered attitude values and respects the experiences of each individual as building blocks in a transformation of personal and social development. Effective learning is a fundamental and necessary ingredient for sustainable health, agriculture, and rural development.

Sustainability

One of the principal goals pursued, hopefully, by any development process, is the long-term self-sufficiency and sustainability of the program or project being implemented. This enables individuals and communities to strengthen local level capacity and build social capital in a more concerted fashion. However, in order for these same groups to engage in a sustainable process, the overall driving force behind the development process which guides them, also needs to have a philosophical motive and nature to encourage, stimulate, and build sustainability. The role of the facilitator and the advocate within the development process may or may not establish sustainability.

In this case, it may be useful to compare advocacy and facilitation processes since both of these terms are often used interchangeably. As we pointed out earlier, the two roles can be significantly different especially in regard to long-term sustainability. An advocacy approach tends to encourage processes to take place on the advocates, terms, using their methods, and their timeframe. In many instances, as with TEV International, the issues themselves are those defined by the advocate, and not by the community. Although they claimed to work with the local farmers, the agency had complete control of the process. Everything the farmers did, was part of TEV's broader agenda for their program. No initiative was encouraged from the local farmers.

Advocacy often does not provide an opportunity for communities to learn and build their own capacity. It is this failing that leads programs developed on external advocacy approaches to collapse. Not often do advocates have the satisfaction of seeing an ongoing process of change continue to flourish and grow after their departure (Kennedy 1982: 38).

In contrast, a facilitator has a much stronger and more valid role in building and incorporating sustainability into their actions. An effective facilitator is one who encourages full participation of community members by attempting to draw out peoples' ideas and opinions without imposing her/his own external agenda. It is this process, where trust is established upon a foundation of mutual respect, which recognizes that community members can be the source and stimulation of their own action. A facilitator can bolster the self-confidence of the community by focusing on their competencies rather than on how the facilitator's own expertise can be imparted to the community. It is this recognition of existing 'resources' that builds the capacity for future activities and processes. Unlike with advocacy, Kennedy says that facilitation builds on existing strengths and mobilizes the community members to critically reflect on the capacities that already exist, instead of the resolution of specific issues.

Whose Reality?

Who defines the problems or the issues in development? It is very important to understand who defines the situation and the issues to be addressed and the consequent power relationship involved. From the advocate's perspective, the problem is often defined narrowly. Advocates tend to think that they must advocate things on *behalf* of the rural poor, when in fact the perspective from which it needs to be addressed is that the rural poor are not ignorant. The poor have a voice and it simply needs to be heard, understood, and respected, which an advocate does not often recognize. Freire refers to this relation as the culture of silence.

From the perspective of the facilitator, people have ideas and are able to engage in critical reflection. This perspective thrives on the fact that if people are given the opportunity to understand and express themselves, they can offer solutions. Freire argues that this process of critical reflection, dialogue, and conscientization ultimately leads to awareness-raising among individuals and the community. It is the process of the facilitator which embraces the true reality of the community.

So What?

You have traveled with the advocate and the facilitator, exploring each approach toward development, and in many ways the two roads have been similar but more often than not, quite different. It is not always easy for development practitioners to know which approach to embrace. However, the cultural and socio-economic context of the environment in which development practitioners work, will often suggest which approach is best suited. Each approach will look different to different practitioners, based on their own personal experiences and background.

What is clear is that those working in development must take the journey which empowers both individuals and communities to find their voice, and move toward enhanced autonomy and sustainable actions which can be supported in the future. Those of us involved in the development process must challenge ourselves to understand individuals and their communities, and identify with their problems. Ultimately the effective community development practitioner is a *catalyzer*, an *encourager* and a *partner in progress*.

References and Select Bibliography

Freire, P. (1970a). *Pedagogy of the Oppressed*. New York, NY: The Continuum Publishing Corporation.

———. (1970b). *Cultural Action for Freedom*. Boston, MA: Harvard Educational Review, Monograph Series, No. 1.

———. (1973). *Education for Critical Consciousness*. New York, NY: Seabury Press.

Freire, P. and Shor, I. (1987). *A Pedagogy for Liberation: Dialogues on Transforming Education*. South Hadley, MA: Bergin & Garvey Publishers.

Kennedy, T. (1982). Beyond Advocacy: A Facilitative Approach to Public Participation. *Journal of the University Film and Video Association*, XXXIV, 3.

Korten, D. (1990). *Getting into the 21st Century: Voluntary Action and the Global Agenda*. West Hartford, Conn.: Kumarian Press.

Moyo, S. (1992). *NGO Advocacy in Zimbabwe: Systematising an Old Function or Inventing a New Role*. Harare, Zimbabwe: ZERO Publications.

Schneider, H. and Libercier, M. (1995). *Participatory Development: From Advocacy to Action*. Paris: OECD.

4

Synergizing Participation: Are you Able to Enable?

Simone St. Anne

Simone suggests that creativity can be an exceptional force in the toolbox of the facilitator for activating the process of participation for development. She advocates 'creative collaboration'—a method of working together modeled on the ways of the creative artist, scientist, discoverer—as a powerful way to create the team dynamic that is so vital for productive and satisfying participation.

Participation: People Connections

Participation for development is a 'people thing.' It holds to democratic ideals: of the people, for the people, by the people. It advocates that the best way to develop is intrinsically, from the inside out. People are the center, the focal point, the beginning, the middle, and the end of participation. Participation evolves through the efforts of people who are in turn transformed through the process. People make participation happen, of this we are certain!

Participation as a tool for development is rooted in a sound, valuable, and plentiful resource of human talent and energy. But how do we *mine* this precious resource? If a facilitator is to discover how to unleash the power and potential of the participation process, we need to understand the essence of the 'resource': our humanity.

Long before participation was purposefully advocated for development, people had formed collectivities in order to survive, to grow, or even to destroy. Human history is a story of participation. But in this contemporary world, why do we enter into collective relationships? Two reasons stand out: to achieve that which cannot be achieved individually and to transcend the limitations of the *self* through the experience of human interaction, i.e. relationships with the *other*, thus becoming part of a larger entirety. The *sense of belonging* is a strong need within the human species. It draws us into participation relationships time and again.

Participation is not just about getting together with a common goal and the desire to make it happen. Witness, for example, a bus-stop: a group of variously skilled and well-intentioned people with the same direction in mind, are gathered. They *are* sharing time, space, and a common path, but no participation takes place unless they connect with each other in the experience they share. The *sense of belonging* and feeling related to a larger whole doesn't happen when each person remains within a separate *self-reality* even though the physical circumstance is shared. *To be able to participate and communicate with each other, people need to connect.* We can hopefully conclude that people connections cause participation and that these connections forge a shared reality. This joining together, this binding, is fundamental to achieving the goals of participation. So we *team up*. Teaming up invites participation as people connections are activated.

'Teaming Selves'—A Necessary Interdependence

Forming teams is essential for participatory development. Teams can attain goals beyond an individual's capacity, and in doing so can enhance the individual. For this reason, the team approach is a chosen mode of operation to bring about change. Its prevalence can be seen everywhere—from the corporation to the classroom, the operating table to the field. Yet, in spite of its popularity and proven success, teamwork has earned the reputation of being difficult and stressful. Many teams have become 'committees committed to going nowhere.' Not all teams seem able to generate participation. Why do some teams work, and others struggle? What makes for team chemistry?

The research of Wendy Williams and Robert Sternberg found that the single most important factor in a group's success was their ability to create a state of internal harmony. Daniel Goleman (1995) explains:

> Whenever people come together to collaborate there is a very real sense in which they have a Group IQ—the sum total of the talents and skills of all those involved. And how well they accomplish their task will be determined by how high that IQ is. The single most important element in group intelligence, it turns out, is not the average IQ in the academic sense, but rather in terms of emotional intelligence. The key to high group IQ is social harmony. It is this ability to harmonize that, all other things being equal, will make one group especially talented, productive and successful, and another—with members whose talents and skill are equal in other regards—do poorly (1995: 160).

It is *selves* that make up a team and, it is a *facilitator* who becomes the harmonizer. Internal harmony within a team is directly related to internal harmony within the *self*, in its experience on the team. To achieve this harmony it is necessary to satisfy what the self is seeking from the team.

What draws a self to a team is its need for participation, for belonging, and for the opportunity to go beyond personal limitations in the achievement of goals. Harmony within the team would depend on the needs of the self being satisfied. Will the team give the self what it needs? Harmonizing the self into the team and the team into the self enables the team to find what it needs from the self and the self to find what it needs from the team. This sounds like a vicious circle and in a way it is. Individual learning and capacity building is what is needed from the facilitator, to transform this into a circle of constructive interdependence.

So, teams that *work* go beyond achieving task goals and seek to satisfy the individual's need to participate. Ensuring that this happens is a function of the facilitator. It seems timely to reflect on this most important function as we enter the threshold of a new millennium. Our mood is unusually introspective as we seek out the roots of mind, body, and soul and select our pathways to happiness, and self-fulfillment.

Creativity as a Tool for the Facilitator

One of the ways that you, the facilitator, can harmonize *self* and *team* is through the understanding and catalyzing process of creativity. We can learn from history how creative people have collaborated in order to accomplish the extraordinary. Gaining better insights about recognized creative collaborations can provide clues as to how we can create the group dynamic so vital for productive and satisfying participation within the development context. We might say that the creative process generates valuable appeals that can become basic tools for the facilitator. The first is a state within the individual, one of personal appeal; the second is a condition within the team, one of interpersonal appeal.

Creativity and the Individual

We identify creativity through products, often through processes, and sometimes through personalities. We are attracted to creative people and the process itself. The word has appeal but its expression can be seductive. Advertising, for example, presents an *allure* that goes beyond the enjoyment of discovering new products or new technologies that in turn feed the market. Most people experience excitement or internal satisfaction from the creative new twist of an ad. This is not surprising, for many times these communication masterpieces become stimuli or a motivation for development of our own creative side. They can validate our uniqueness, our humanness, and our personal identity.

But why are we attracted to such creativity? What is this creative allure? The answer lies in how the creative process engages us, and how it makes us feel. Recall staring at a canvas covered with splattered paint, or listening to a piece of music which moved you. Do you remember spending endless hours with simple blocks, Lego or Crayolas, building your first model airplane, putting poetic words on paper perhaps for a parent, or making an interesting form from play dough or clay? As young children and throughout our lives, we experience such moments of creation, recreation, or creative transformation. Such moments have an impact on us not just because the product is unique, but because the process has been exhilarating.

In those moments, whether minutes or hours, we experience what it means to be in 'flow' as Mihaly Csikszentmihalyi describes it, or to be in 'rapture' as Diane Ackerman suggests. It is the sense of being united, undivided, plugged in, to that 'oceanic feeling' of cosmic unity—a complete immersion which blurs the boundaries between bow and archer, brush and painter, poet and pen. The emotion rendered from these states motivates us, by allowing us to go beyond our own self-perceptions. We connect with a greater source—become part of a greater force. Arthur Koestler named our desire for such experiences 'participatory or self-transcending tendencies.' (1964) Associated emotions and insights motivate a sense of community, facilitate interpersonal trust, awaken the self, and impel a person to be continuously open to new undertakings.

Creative Collaboration

In addition to this *lure* of the personal creative experience, I have experienced the enormous appeal of the creative process on an interpersonal level, in the almost mystical *synergy* it produces. This synergy induces a quality of collaboration that sparkles, both in process and product. I call this 'creative collaboration.' Synergy, from the Greek *Synergos*, meaning 'working together,' is defined as 'the interaction of discrete agencies, agents or conditions such that the total effect is greater than the sum of the individual effects.' Synergy, released in creative collaborations, makes working together more than just pursuing tasks or pooling individual talents and skills for a common purpose. It empowers the team to 'become more than the sum of its parts'—together we can achieve beyond our individual efforts. Ideas, thoughts, and actions of the collaborators are triggered into a circle of dynamic energy. Momentum builds, individuals put forth more effort, the group moves ahead, and a community can be transformed.

Mihaly Csikszentmihalyi (1996) tells the story of how the central theme in the life of Jonas Salk, discoverer of the polio vaccine, was to make visible the invisible. To this end, Salk brought people together from different scientific domains, believing that interaction would spark new ideas and bring to light more than was possible if each worked separately. For creativity to happen in this way, Salk said:

> ...minds have to harmonize. There's something of a think-alike quality, an openness, a receptivity, a positive rather than negative attitude. There's a mutual affirmation; it comes about as a kind of a consensus, a reconciliation of differences that exist when you don a new vision or perception. Any dialogue...is of that nature. There is a tendency to draw each other out, to bring out the best or the most creative aspect of the mind.... In this kind of interaction each person helps the others see what they see (1996: 284–285).

To help the others see what they see: that's the essence of creative collaboration. This creative orientation generates focus, making effort purposeful, and vision clear. Creativity stimulates emotional dialogue, which I regard as fundamental to creative collaboration. Ideas spark action with directed momentum and the energy produced in such encounters enables more profound outcomes.

Creativity as Emotional Dialogue

Emotion is an integral part of ourselves and our expression each day. Emotion and rationality are often seen as opposites. Either you are being emotional, or you are being rational. But, as with most other things, emotion is irrational only in the extreme. Emotion is actually very useful, and recently has been labeled an important kind of intelligence.

Emotion or affect, as it is technically termed, is central to the creative process. Emotion and rationality complement each other. Emotion can motivate reason and facilitate the cognitive processes important to creative thinking. Intrinsic motivation is necessary for the creative process and remains active throughout the process. Thus, creativity makes productive use of emotion—a positive force that refuels itself. This cycle is important in the dialogue which Nair and White (1994) see as necessary to motivate production. It is dialogue *plus* emotion which makes communication a two-way flow of ideas and understandings. Over a period of time, communicators simultaneously give feedback and arrive at shared meanings, building trust, making communication credible and useful.

Emotional dialogue creates resonance between two people, mind to mind, heart to heart, body to body. Resonance facilitates a 'tuning-in' which improves listening, intensifies dialogue, triggers new thinking, and firmly anchors the foundations for trust-building. To observe the *blossoming of trust* is a beautiful thing—openness, nonjudgmental attitudes, flexibility, sharing, commitment, inspiration, creativity, synergy, laughter. Through trust the facilitator can catalyze the awakening of the individual and realization of the group, which enables team productivity. Awakening personal creativity facilitates harmony through the *self* into the *team*. Emotional dialogue is a communication commitment—an unvoiced source of motivation; a reaffirmation of each *self* in the other. Which are the issues that need attention in such group dynamics? We will briefly examine three: resonant listening, chemistry of mind and body, and constructive conflict.

Resonant Listening

When asked what helps produce their remarkable group synergy (at the end of a concert that left both performers and audience vibrating), Edgar Meyer, jazz musician and composer, in concert with Yo-Yo Ma and Mark O'Connor, said that playing together makes them hear better, and this enhances the results. What do we hear when we listen? Do we hear only the words, or also the non-verbal signals? Or, do we mostly just listen to the responses forming in our minds as the other speaks? Supportive, active listening is vital for developing authentic understandings. A resonant, empathic listening, i.e. listening from the other person's perspective, is integral to an accurate assessment of how others think and feel. And how others *feel* when they think, as well as *what* they think, greatly influences the outcome of group participation.

Chemistry of Mind and Body

Creative energy and sexual energy stem from the same source. It is inevitable that in a creatively oriented synergistic team, there will be an aura of attraction between people. As Bennis and Biederman (1997) say, 'great groups are sexy places'. While such attraction is normal and beneficial to creativity (these emotions motivate, and enhance emotional dialogue), there can possibly be social disapproval and discomfort. Artists have sometimes managed this by being freer with social boundaries, but for the most part ignoring boundaries can be a major factor that inhibits the synergizing of effective teams. This may be the explanation for the fact that most creative male/female teams in the sciences are married or eventually marry. The facilitator needs to be aware and perhaps creative, to prepare accepted channels to express feelings of love which are very much a part of the creative process. Often these relationships are not seen as normal outcomes of close working relationships and thus, are not recognized in an open manner.

Constructive Conflict

Disharmony in a group is a source of conflict, so needs to be prevented insofar as is possible. The facilitator needs to be a barometer in order to sense changes in the emotional mood of each group member, and levels of disturbance, easing them before they explode. Emotional dialogue helps a great deal here, as does space for disagreement and differing points of view. Compromise as a way of dealing with disagreement is not an ideal option for participation because it pushes for an enforced consensus and negative emotion may be an outcome. Rather, creative new alternatives can be cultivated as an alternative to compromise and thus enable members to see opposites in a harmonious way. While compromise brings opposites to half their intensity, creativity combines opposites to new intensity. While creativity may open up greater conflict, the creative attitude has more openness to disagreement, and a tendency to battle with ideas instead of battling with persons.

Viewing conflict as necessary to change enables group members to resolve conflict and move on to higher levels of accomplishment. A facilitator can set the stage for a group to confront conflict for 'win-win' outcomes.

Awakening the Creative Self, Releasing the Creative Spirit

It may be somewhat difficult for facilitators to clearly see how they might become proficient in creating the ambience for synergistic participation. A key approach is to bring the group into the process from the beginning and make the relationship a joint discovery and learning experience. There are some simple practices that can cultivate a creative attitude in the group. These begin with practices that the individual can share with the group. Sharing can start with one individual and gradually include everyone. Some practices worth trying are discussed in the following sections.

Keep a Visual Journal

Put together a blank book or notebook, one that pleases you, and one in which you can enter a daily record. Become more observant of the world around you and people in it. Start with one entry each day—something that caught your attention visually or triggered your thinking or your emotions. Draw it, write about it, explore it, and replay it through visual recall. Opening the visual mind allows more information to be absorbed and enhances the *way* we see. How we see and how we remember influences how we make connections. We can say we become more creative as we become more observing, and recognize more paths or options for our self.

Meditate

Take a comfortable position (preferably with your back straight to allow for channels of air to flow through your body). Close your eyes. Breathe. Feel the air you breathe. Let the outside flow in; the sounds, the smells, the sensations, and then let them go. Touch each of the thoughts that you encounter and let them go, one by one by one. Making the conscious mind quiet releases the unconscious mind. Linear perception gives way to lateral perception, and lateral perception releases creativity. Clearing the mind of thoughts also helps produce the *tabula rasa*, i.e., blank state, needed for creativity.

Be Around Creative People

This has continued to be one of the most effective methods to awaken the creative self. Being around creative people, being inspired by them, absorbing their passion, learning creative behaviors. It is an effective training ground for creative tuning-in.

Be Curious

Ask questions. Don't be satisfied with what's on the surface, go deeper. Look for multiple answers, methods, alternatives. Be open to different approaches and retain the ability to be amazed, and an appreciation and respect of others. Information and sensory overload common to today's way of life can cause us to 'tune-out,' take things for granted, or become bored or numbed by the overload.

Play

Serious creativity needs play. Playtime can lead to relaxed attention so important for creativity. It allows the mind and the body to find harmony with each other without obligation. It can free the mind from *directed* control, and enable a person to make connections through fresh thinking. Play produces laughter that interestingly uses the same mind pathways as does creativity. The old saying that 'all work and no play makes Jack a dull boy,' makes sense.

In playing a facilitator role, it often becomes necessary to focus on individuals—their sense of self, their creative potential, and their comfort in the group—particularly in early stages of group formation and teaming. Awakening the creative self will need personal tools for this *awakening* and these ideas can be a start towards providing them. One can visualize individuals who have been exploring these practices coming together to engage in a group process. They would no doubt enter into their relationship with high energy and enthusiasm. The catalyst communicator has been described in Chapter Two by White and Nair as a person who can '*Involve, Enable, Catalyze.*' There is little doubt that a successful facilitator is indeed a catalyst communicator.

As a Facilitator—Are you Able to Enable?

Without doubt, people are the planet's most valuable resource. Lending their talent, intellect, energy, and commitment, it is people who mobilize other people. Ingeniously, through relationships, they create further resources. The facilitator recognizes that people connections are the foundation for collaborations, for teamwork, for working together—all essential for both personal and community development and for the progress of the world at large. People who manage themselves as a human resource hold the key to managing other resources, both economic and natural.

Beyond facilitating synergistic connections, a team needs to be connected to resources, filled with purpose, and protected (creativity needs protection). There is need also for maintenance functions of body, mind, and soul. Taking breaks, making people laugh, changing the ambience to affect a mood, are some of the many needs. The facilitator must be able to nurture an environment that meets these conditions.

Once the creative process is energized, and is 'in flow,' there comes a moment when the facilitator must let go and stand aside, allowing the process to establish its own momentum. This moment is not always easy to discover, to talk about, or to do. It needs an awareness, a clarity of mind, humility of spirit. The facilitator must allow participation to become an internal force to drive collaborative efforts.

At the same time, the facilitator must be ready to ease back into the process at any time, to clarify, to release blockages, between people or within a person, to help remove noise or negative emotions that the process may also produce, to restabilize harmony at any point throughout the process. For the most important task of the facilitator is to enable others to act and to release personal power in order to empower others. The most effective way to inspire, is by example.

So when is a facilitator effective? Above all it is when s/he can activate synergistic people connections, bringing about a fusion of minds which leads to extraordinary outcomes and significant consequences. I believe it is within the powers of the facilitator to awaken the creative self by catalyzing dialogue. This dialogue produces a force from within. It helps you trust. It makes you believe. It produces a sense of identity and belonging. It empowers you to participate.

The facilitator has a *vision* that centers not on goals which are predetermined but on the process of setting and reaching goals that he/she is in a position to catalyze. The facilitator has a *vision* that individuals can become creative in their group relationships. Thus, the group is enabled to set and pursue their own development goals. Within this interactive, dialogic environment the important outcome

[handwritten margin note: We need to find other ways to tap creative abilities.]

of empowerment emerges, and with it, a deep feeling of confidence, hope for continuing growth, connectedness and 'flow'!

References and Select Bibliography

Ackerman, D. (1997). *Creating Minds: Artistic Intelligence across the Disciplines*. A Symposium at Cornell University, Ithaca, NY.

Amabile, T.M. (1996). *Creativity in Context*. Boulder, CO: Westview Press.

Bass, B.M. (1996). *A New Paradigm of Leadership: An Inquiry into Transformational Leadership*. Alexandria, VA: US Army Research Institute for the Behavioral and Social Sciences.

Bennis, W.G. and Biederman, P.W. (1997). *Organizing Genius: The Secret of Creative Collaboration*. Reading, MA: Addison-Wesley Publishing Company, Inc.

Burns, J.M. (1978). *Leadership*. New York, NY: Harper and Row.

Csikszentmihalyi, M. (1996). *Creativity: Flow and the Psychology of Discovery and Invention*. New York, NY: Harper Collins.

De Bono, E. (1970). *Lateral Thinking: Creativity Step by Step*. New York, NY: Harper and Row.

Fromm, E. (1959). The Creative Attitude. In H. Anderson (Ed.), *Creativity and its Cultivation*. New York, NY: Harper and Brothers.

Gibb, J.R. (1978). *Trust*. Los Angeles, CA: The Guild of Tutors Press.

Goleman, D. (1995). *Emotional Intelligence*. New York, NY: Bantam.

Hunter, D., Bailey, A. and Taylor, B. (1995). *The Zen of Groups*. Tucson, AZ: Fisher Books.

Koestler, A. (1964). *The Act of Creation*. New York, NY: Macmillan.

Laing, R.D. (1969). *Self and Others*. New York, NY: Pantheon.

Meyer, E. (1966). *In Concert with Yo-Yo Ma and Mark O'Connor*. Bailey Hall, Cornell University.   .

Nair, K.S. and White, S.A. (1994). Participatory Message Development. In S.A. White, K.S. Nair, and Joseph Ascroft, *Participatory Communication*. New Delhi: Sage Publications.

Russ, S.W. (1993). *Affect and Creativity*. Hillsdale, NJ: Lawrence Erlbaum.

Tichy, N.M. and Devanna, M.A. (1986). *The Transformational Leader*. New York, NY: John Wiley & Sons.

Williams, W. and Sternberg, R. (1988). Group Intelligence: Why Some Groups are Better than Others. In *Intelligence*. New York, NY: Cambridge University Press.

White, S.A., Nair, K.S. and Ascroft, J. (1994). *Participatory Communication*. New Delhi: Sage Publications.

5

A Journey in Search of
Facilitative Communication

Ricardo Ramirez

The road to understanding the intricate human factors of facilitative communication is a less traveled one—rough, up and down hill, with sharp curves and sometimes detours. But a person who heads down that road experiences many breathtaking vistas not open to those who travel the main road. Such is the personal journey that Ricardo shares in this chapter. He traces his professional journey toward understanding what it takes to empower people in the development scenario, and his search for tools and skills needed to facilitate that empowerment via development communication. His focus is within the context of natural resource management.

'Communication for development' is focused on sharing of knowledge and insight about the process of enabling disadvantaged groups to increase control over their own lives and environment. Large bureaucracies and small organizations alike have experimented with 'communication for development' over the last two decades but results are mixed. Projects have included communication components in order to strengthen training efforts, to bring different stakeholders together to exchange views and negotiate agreements, or to disseminate information. Organizational, financial, social, and technical requirements for projects are rarely ideal and consequently, the results fall short of those desired. Nevertheless, it is agreed that facilitative communication is critical to effective development. The journey in search of facilitative communication is ongoing!

Three Roles for Communication

Pertinent to our search, we find the three different roles that communication can play in accessing resources necessary for managing and facilitating people's participation (Röling, 1994).

- **Make things visible.** This refers to explaining biophysical information. The trend today is to *transfer information with the aim of creating new perspectives* rather than transferring prepackaged solutions.
- **Foster policy acceptance.** This includes enacting and promoting policies. The trend towards *interactive policy-making* thus moves away from persuasive advertising approaches.
- **Facilitate platform processes.** This *gives a voice to different stakeholders* to engage in relations where negotiation among different parties can take place with regard to competing as well as common interests.

This third dimension of communication for development is central to my own 'professional journey' as a facilitator. This is the communication role which public and international development institutions struggle to embrace. However, this role is often marginalized because at times it leads to unexpected outcomes which are beyond bureaucratic control and difficult to respond to. This role empowers people to voice perspectives and negotiate on an equal footing with other actors in the development scenario. It is this role that embodies the uniqueness of communication as a field which integrates art, science, and practice. In order to comprehend this uniqueness, I focus my discussion on this important third dimension of facilitative communication.

My inspiration comes from those early pioneers of the last twenty-five years—Don Snowden, Manuel Calvelo Ríos, Erskine Childers, Luis Ramiro Beltrán, Andreas Fuglesang, Joe Ascroft, and Santiago

Funes. These professionals put communication to work for development against all odds and all succeeded in showing its unique role as a tool for people to acknowledge, communicate, and value their own wisdom. Within their framework, I would share my account as a practitioner following a humbler path in search of tools, methods, and institutional conditions which foster 'facilitative communication.'

The Journey Starts: Practice

Drawing with Campesinos

My own journey began in the field working with Colombian farmers in the early 1980s, through Fundación Educadora San Nicolás, a Colombian NGO. I produced illustrated printed materials with the campesinos who collaborated in the developing of ecologically sound technologies for subsistence farms in Urabá and the central province of Antioquia. What started off as an attempt at producing extension materials became a means of expressing a common learning process. The farmers were very keen to express their wisdom and perspective using pen and ink in harmony with the local consteño dialect; the product was a proud statement of common learning. It was a rough, unstructured, yet purposeful, process of participatory research (see Figure 5.1).

Methods and Media in Community Participation

It was through drawings that we shaped common meaning from the work on the farms in Columbia (Ramírez and Villa, 1985). The work in rural Colombia paved the way for my interest in the field of adult education because I felt common learning was at the heart of communicative action.

Producing illustrated printed materials with campesinos also became a case to be shared with communication practitioners from around the world, during the 'Methods and Media in Community Participation' meetings hosted by the Dag Hammarskjöld Foundation in 1984 (Fuglesang and Chandler, 1986). These gatherings were unique events where practitioners of facilitative communication came together from the fields of health, rural development, and

Figure 5.1: A Campesino Concept

La Bregadera

GRANJA DEMOSTRATIVA COMUNIDAD por los NIÑOS

Boca del Rio San Juan (Urabá). Arboletes, Antioquia, Colombia, S.A.

agriculture to share experiences and approaches. Our supportive exchange of ideas was a source of personal confidence building and motivation to forge ahead.

Training Agricultural Communicators

My journey continued in Jamaica and southern Colombia in the mid 1980s through short-term contracts with NGOs. In Jamaica and Colombia I was faced with the challenge of training 'agricultural communicators.' I chose that label expressly to separate their role from the information function which then dominated the jobs of public extension workers. Engaging young people and professionals to assume the facilitative role of communication required trainees with a sensitivity and commitment to working with rural people, and an eagerness to explore the use of methods and media for joint learning.

The most promising candidates came, not from a background in media production, but from the practice of community development. Skill and commitment to facilitation, matched with a skill in producing simple graphic materials proved to be essential qualifications. Few professionals were amenable to 'learning with farmers,' and still fewer institutions offered incentives for this kind of approach. Overwhelming odds face facilitative communication when few institutions are willing to embrace and reward the humble process of providing learning opportunities for farmers in their own community.

Illuminative Evaluation

During the same period I explored the potential of participatory evaluation in the context of urban development projects in Bolivia. I was greatly influenced by the notion of 'illuminative evaluation' which relies on documenting the perception of 'beneficiaries' who illuminate the outsider about the impact of a project (Richards, 1985). The Bolivian and Jamaican experiences became the case studies I used in my study of adult education.

I was then faced with the challenge of bridging the fields of agricultural communication and participatory evaluation. I was able to tie these seemingly disparate experiences together by distilling the concepts and theories of adult education which provide their foundation (Ramírez, 1990). Since then, the principles of self-directed learning and development have served as a compass for me as I have pursued facilitative communication work. It is this perspective, I believe, that underpins a communication for development approach committed to empowerment, and which sets it apart from the other functions of communication.

The Journey Continues: Institutional Affiliation

Development Support Communication

At the end of the decade, I joined the Development Support Communication branch (DSC) of FAO. This group is embedded within the United Nations, Food and Agriculture Organization (FAO), which had played a pioneering role in the evolution of this field. Many of the pioneers mentioned earlier were able to articulate their vision under the umbrella of this small unit. Early on in my tour of duty there, we convened an informal Roundtable for Development Communication in Rome, bringing together the major players in the NGOs, UN system, universities, and some donors. It was evident that while the DSC branch enjoyed a good reputation in the international arena, it was struggling to gain recognition within the FAO. Not only was its mandate matched with insufficient resources, but it was also perceived in different ways by other units within the organization. This was the result of its historical evolution as a media production unit within the Information Division. Other technical units in the FAO member governments recognized its media production expertise, but only as functional in the first two roles of communication: technology transfer and policy delivery. But the commitment of the DSC branch staff was to a systematic inclusion role—giving stakeholders a voice by facilitating communication linkages among people and organizations at the grassroots.

Sharing Knowledge

In the early 1990s 'people's participation' and 'sustainable development' became the slogans for the decade. We in the DSC branch, had the methods and tools to demonstrate successful applications of media to enhance the voice of rural people to express themselves. Early on, we produced the video, 'Communication for Sustainable Development,' and soon after the documentary, 'Communication: A key to human development.' These two informational videos contained examples of creative experiences from three continents where communication for development, in its fullest sense, was put to work. In project design and implementation, we endeavored to introduce training and activities to introduce the 'facilitative role of communication.' We learned that producing information materials for rural audiences could best be done in a collaborative manner. Active participation by the user in developing, testing, adapting, and applying information products proved to be a key ingredient for success in this experimental approach. Conditions that enabled these experiences are difficult to recreate, but they can be analyzed so as to enable future practitioners to take advantage of favorable conditions in a serendipitous manner. Figure 5.2 lays out my assessment of enabling conditions.

Figure 5.2: Enabling Conditions for Communication for Development

Condition	Desirable Context
Policy Environment	Open, exploratory approach committed to gathering multiple perspectives for participatory planning and consultative project implementation.
Project Design	Flexibility, learning-oriented, project design with qualitative as well as quantitative outputs.
Institutional Framework	Flexibility and openness to embracing interinstitutional collaboration. A realistic projection of institutional sustainability beyond the project finances.
Communication Function	Embracing all three functions (roles) of communication and/or explicitly addressing the facilitative one. Communication assigned a role and resources a priori as a partner in project formulation, implementation and evaluation.
Human Resources	Adequate numbers of skilled or trainable staff. A minimum of professional incentives and rewards.
Financial Resources	Adequate financial resources allocated from the start (an indication of recommended figures for different types of projects in 1991 are available with the FAO).

Structural Adjustment Impacts DSC Units

Inevitably, the issue of sustainability comes into question. One of the most critical dimensions of the issue is the institutional one. When structural adjustment programs hit many of the Ministries where DSC units had been installed, the survival of these project-funded units came under threat. The immediate tendency was a shrinking of funding, staffing, and mandate. The feasibility studies commissioned for the DSC units in Mexico, Dominica, Nicaragua, Nepal, and Mali all recommended formulae that were practically impossible to apply. The developmental role of these units was costly to maintain, especially in terms of producing materials for the benefit of rural communities. The pressure on unit managers to generate revenue came from other clients who had different priorities: international projects in search of promotional and information and training products, private urban clients in search of production and editing equipment, or governmental departments in search of promotional materials. The facilitative role of communication is expensive and time consuming and its clients tend to lack the means to access and control it. Therefore, I came to the stark realization that it is a function not likely to survive in a policy environment which depends on market forces.

Who Pays for Communication?

In an age of structural adjustment and liberalization, communication services may be perceived as an unnecessary subsidy. Governments can no longer sustain the recurrent costs of communication units and the trend is to privatize them. Communication for development may be used as a tool to fulfill social objectives targeted to disadvantaged groups, but ultimately it becomes a marketable commodity for the creditworthy sectors of rural society.

Cost-effective alternatives, such as sub-contracting production from the private sector, while keeping small teams of communication professionals able to service different sectors, have been explored. The development of national development communication policies in several countries is one example of an enabling environment whereby resources are concentrated on a communication unit, servicing many different parts of government.

Internet is the newest promising communication channel for enabling development. The extent to which innovative arrangements and newer communication technologies may nourish the facilitative role of communication remains to be seen. Large NGOs with an international presence, such as Environment et Developpement Alternatif (ENDA) Tiers monde, based in Dakar, have maintained a commitment to grassroots learning and facilitation. It is encouraging to see how these institutions have matured into respected lobbies and they now collaborate and negotiate policies and action with governments.

The Journey Focuses: Participatory Approaches

The Informal RRA/PRA Network

The facilitative role of communication is a natural ally to participatory appraisal and research approaches which make use of multiple tools to visualize people's perception of their lives and their relationship with the environment. I was therefore keen to participate in the shaping of the informal RRA/PRA Network at FAO headquarters. Over eighty professionals at FAO headquarters from many disciplines, maintained an informal network focused on learning about participatory approaches for over six years. This experiment led to a tightly knit group that offered training sessions to colleagues and to managers within the organization, exchanged information electronically, and served as a clearinghouse to identify literature and expertise. This sub-culture within FAO was a rewarding experiment, even though it may not have changed structures in the organization.

Participatory Appraisal of Communication Network

I was able to explore the role of communication as part of a rapid and participatory appraisal in the Philippines and Ethiopia. In the Philippines we gathered an interdisciplinary team and improvised a method for mapping farmer communication networks which has since been applied elsewhere (FAO, 1995; Ramírez, 1997; den Big-gelaar, 1996; Lawrence, 1995). It was immensely rewarding to enable farmers and researchers to work jointly. We identified, mapped, and visualized the actors and institutions that had influenced their farming over the last ten years. The key linkages were analyzed systematically so as to explore new relationships that could allow different actors to interact more effectively towards fulfilling shared objectives.

This merging of facilitative communication with other tools of action research and appraisal is strategically important; it is a map for a continued journey. Visualizing complex relationships among institutions and between people and their environment is an important step. It shows that communication for development need not always be equipment-dependent nor do high financial inputs need to be invested into (unsustainable) institutions. It shows that participatory communication has a fundamental role to play different from that of 'top-down' approaches based on social marketing techniques. Facilitative communication is fundamentally different from that point of view, in that its underlying focus is to empower people and enhance their self-directed learning (Gumucio-Dagron, 1991).

Marketing in NGOs

After leaving FAO I joined ILEIA in the Netherlands to manage the information and communication dimension of this sustainable agriculture project. I felt very strongly that we needed to shift the project's information activities from a broadcasting mode (information dissemination function) to a communication mode where users of our information were closely involved with producing it and evaluating it.

My contribution was to devise a simple marketing approach to get to know the readers and match information products with their needs. This effort was aimed at introducing the strategic side of communication planning in an NGO. The outcome of the marketing effort is an understanding of different audience preferences for channels of communication, and their projections into the ones they hope to access in the future. It also allowed us to rationalize a multimedia effort to ensure we could communicate with different users. I felt that effort was unique in that not many organizations have data on the projected communication channels which over 10,000 stakeholders, active in sustainable agriculture hope to access over the next 3 years (Ramírez and van der Brom, 1997). This experience is an example of a global communication strategy for a small project. As such, it should be seen as a contributing effort to enable facilitative communication activities.

The Journey is Just Beginning

New organizations that are small, flexible, and able to adjust to change in a fluid manner are a hope for the future. The new civil society is already showing itself to be pluralist and complex. Actors come together to negotiate interests with regard to the use and maintenance of natural resources. Bringing actors together with different worldviews involves communication activities. I am convinced that the journey into facilitative communication is just beginning, because small, virtual, dynamic organizations are finding their niche.

It may be futile to keep pushing for *facilitative communication* within large bureaucracies, without finding a specific niche for this approach in a global arena. In my mind, the role of the bureaucracy is to endorse and legitimize these methods while delegating their implementation to a multitude of smaller localized groups that are able to embrace this participatory approach. A partnership where actors are exploring complementary roles is desirable.

I am now part of a group of professionals which is committed to exploring this type of approach further, in close collaboration with many stakeholders. We have created an international association with this goal in mind. The International Support Group (ISG: Linking local experience in agroecological management), is that organization. We are embarking on a search for new tools and techniques which can enable a wider practice of facilitative communication in development. There is room for many others to join in such journeys by creating similar new organizations that have the capacity to embrace new methods. But participators must have the patience and time it takes to learn how to work in collaborative ways along with other professionals and the people of rural communities.

References and Select Bibliography

den Biggelaar, C. (1996). *Linking Actors in the Agricultural Knowledge System in Embu District*. AFRENA, Report No. 103. Nairobi: ICRAF.

FAO. (1995). *Understanding Farmers' Communication Networks. Communication for Development Case Study 14*. Rome, Italy: Communication for Development, FAO.

————. (1996). *Communication for Rural Development in Mexico: In Good Times and in Bad*. Rome, Italy: Development for Development, FAO.

Fuglesang, A. and **Chandler, D.** (1986). *Search for Process: Report from a Project on Methods and Media for Community Participation*. Uppsala, Sweden: Dag Hammarskjöld Foundation.

Gumucio-Dagron, A. (1994). *Development Communication Report*. Roundtable of Communication for Development. Lima, Peru: IPAL.

Lawrence, A. (1995). The Neglected Uplands: Innovation and Environmental Change in Matalom, Philippines. AERDD Working Paper 95/11. England: The University of Reading.

Ramírez, R. (1990). The Application of Adult Education to Community Development. *Community Development Journal, 25* (2).

———— (1997). *Understanding Farmers' Communication Networks: Combining PRA with Agricultural Knowledge Systems Analysis*. IIED Gatekeeper Series no. 66.

Ramírez, R. and **Villa, I.** (1985). Where the Campesinos are Consultants. *CERES*, 107 (September–October).

Ramírez, R. and **van der Brom, M.** (1997) Do you Read Me? ILEIA's Efforts at Communicating with its Readers. *Information Development Journal, 25* (2).

Richards, H.C. (1985). *The Evaluation of Cultural Action: An Evaluative Study of the Parents and Children Program*, Programa Padres e Hijos (Parents and Children Programme). Ottawa: McMillan Press and IDRC.

Röling, N.G. (1994). Communication Support for Sustainable Natural Resource Management. In IDS Bulletin. *Knowledge is Power? The Use and Abuse of Information in Development, 25* (2), 125–133.

6

Confessions of an Outside Facilitator: Developing Educational Materials in the Dominican Republic

Peggy Koniz-Booher

In this chapter I would like to share, as honestly as possible, some of the challenges, obstacles, frustrations, pitfalls, lessons learned, and ultimate 'payoffs' experienced during the course of a three-year assignment as the Resident Information/ Education/ Communication (IEC) Advisor—an outside facilitator—for a reproductive health project supported by the United States Agency for International Development (USAID). This story is told entirely from my perspective as an expatriate professional living abroad for a contractual period of time. I fully recognize the many other people with differing and legitimate perspectives who were simultaneously involved and deeply committed to the project as well.

Although every situation has unique elements, I believe that many of the difficulties encountered and rewarding moments experienced are 'in common' for outside facilitators. If you are a specialist living and working abroad, an external consultant involved sporadically, or for short periods of time, in international projects, or a local professional struggling with donor agencies and the challenges of program development and management, I hope my perspectives and the lessons learned from my experiences will be relevant and useful to you.

In January 1994, I transplanted my family (husband and two boys) and most of our worldly possessions, from the suburbs of Washington, DC to the Dominican Republic, a country located just a few hours south of Miami, Florida and a culture vastly different from, but strangely similar, to that which we had left behind. Our new surroundings were lush and tropical. Spanish was the official language. The people on the streets and my professional colleagues seemed to be warm and friendly. Everyone we encountered, both young and old, seemed to be moving to the rhythm of meringue, a traditional and rather addictive music and dance form popular in that region of the world.

Despite the fact that the per capita income is less than $1500 a year, driving through downtown Santo Domingo with its population of several million, one could easily feel like you were driving through any metropolitan city on the 'mainland.' American brand-name products were advertized on billboards, American films played in every theater, multi-national fast food chains were blossoming at every major intersection, and fancy cars and 'Jeepetas' of every make and model crowded the urban highways. It was not until you hit the outskirts of town near the rivers or got out into the rural areas, that the differences were more evident. Thatched or cardboard houses, dirt floors, bare light bulbs running on stolen or 'borrowed' electricity, latrines or open trenches for sewage are the rule, rather than the exception, in much of the country.

Slicing through all economic and social strata, however, is an almost passionate fascination or addiction to baseball, a national 'adhesive.' Dominicans—rich or poor, urban or rural—are always talking about baseball. Other imported aspects of American life are also incredibly popular topics of conversation. Miami and Nueva York (New York City), are discussed as if they were the promised land. Obtaining a United States visa appears to be a driving goal among all classes. This impression is substantiated by the fact that the United States Consulate in Santo Domingo is the second largest in the world. Most Dominicans have family or friends in the States and are hoping to at least visit, if not immigrate some day soon.

It seemed somehow ironic, therefore, that I had come to explore all things Dominican, and to build a life in *their* country, with a *dream* of somehow making a contribution, albeit small, to the health of the Dominican population.

My Mission

The proposed scope of work for my mission was initially shared with me back in Washington. It seemed straightforward and precise—coordinate the design, development, production, and distribution of a series of educational print materials to promote family planning, breastfeeding, and other aspects of reproductive health. This was to be pursued in close collaboration with several non-governmental organizations (NGOs) throughout the country, under the auspices of the Family Planning and Health Project, supported by the local USAID Mission. I was told that my role was to *facilitate* the materials development process and to *build a team* of local expertise in this area which would continue to function after my three-year contract ended.

The goal was to produce sets of educational materials to be used with a wide variety of audiences by the three major NGOs selected by USAID to participate in the project, and potentially, by several other designated agencies. The stated mandate of the Information-Education-Communication (IEC) component of the project was intended to achieve wide distribution of technically accurate and consistent information by better utilizing the technical and financial resources made available through USAID, while avoiding duplication of efforts related to the production of any new materials. Historically, each of the participating NGOs had formed their own IEC departments and created limited quantities of relatively low budget materials for distribution only within their respective program areas. When we first reviewed existing family planning materials, for example, outdated technical information, and conflicting messages were prevalent in the materials produced by one NGO and another.

The IEC focus was consistent with the overall objectives established by USAID for the project as a whole: to strengthen the institutional capabilities of the designated private sector family planning and health NGOs, improve their ability to deliver services, address unmet client needs in both rural and urban communities, improve the coordination of family planning and maternal child health programs throughout the country, among others. On paper, the IEC mandate and overall project objectives looked great! Clearly, I felt that this Resident IEC Advisor position was an ideal assignment for someone like me, with an academic and experiential background in developing educational materials, and a tremendous personal interest in promoting a team approach. I was *committed to both building creative partnerships and strengthening community-based programs* and could not have imagined a more wonderful opportunity to put into practice what I so strongly believed in.

Facilitating the IEC component and meeting the goals of the project, however, proved to be much more complicated and frustrating than I had anticipated. Despite almost ten years of international consulting—predominantly in Latin America, I found myself uncomfortably ill-prepared for the challenge of total immersion in day-to-day project implementation. Working within a distinctly different culture, under an unfamiliar set of professional and social norms, was something for which my theoretical communication training at Cornell University and previous consulting experience had not adequately prepared me. In my previous work as a short term, external health-related communication consultant, I had always played an 'in and out' facilitative role—helping to outline the objectives of a project, developing work plans and budgets, leaving trip reports and recommendations behind for others to actually follow through on. However, I was never *fully involved* in the actual execution, that is, the day-to-day 'maintenance,' of the projects I helped launch. Although hard on my professional ego, I must confess that as the project's Resident IEC Advisor I soon felt as if I had as much to learn as I had to contribute.

The Challenge of Being an Outsider

The Dominican Republic and its people caught me off guard. On the one hand I felt extremely comfortable—at home almost immediately on the streets, in the supermarkets and shopping malls of Santo Domingo, the nation's capital. On the other hand, I was struck with a sense of insecurity, wondering how and when the anti-Yanky (anti-outsider) attitude that I had been warned about by various colleagues might surface. There was, after all, a long and complex history of American political, commercial, and development involvement in the country. There was no denying the fact that I was a Yanky, often struggling to understand the characteristic idiosyncracies of the Dominican variation of Spanish.

I was an outsider in every sense of the word, brought in to do a development job that I suspected that some of my Dominican counterparts felt they were capable of doing equally well, if not better, and for a fraction of the salary and none of the high-priced fringe benefits associated with my position. (Our housing, electricity, private school for my two children, and home leave were all paid for by the project.) I had prepared myself for some inevitable resentments, jealousies, and perhaps some professional backlash, but was uncertain of the form it might take, when it would surface, and how I would handle it. To be honest, there were moments on and off, especially throughout the first year of the project, when a nagging insecurity, even guilt feelings, made me wonder whether or not I was just another high-priced, government contractor.

Within the first few weeks on the job, I realized that my intuitive reaction was rooted in reality, and that the situation was more complex than I had bargained for. I found myself caught, almost immediately, in some kind of indirect crossfire or feud between the IEC-related technical staff of the three private sector NGOs that had been chosen to participate in the project. I also sensed tremendous tension between 'our' NGOs and many other NGOs operating in the country, and between 'our' NGOs and the public sector or government agencies that I was introduced to as part of my initial tour and orientation. It was months later before I confirmed the fact that the public sector and many NGOs were indeed resentful of USAID, Development Associates, and the whole Family Planning and Health Project in general. The fact that many groups had been essentially 'cut out of' the new project from the beginning accounted for that resentment.

For reasons I didn't initially understand, and so could not explain to those who asked, a distinct funding differentiation had been made at least five years earlier between private and public agencies. The United Nations Population Fund (UNFPA) provided support to the public sector agency known as CONAPOFA, which coordinated the national family planning program. USAID supported only the private sector, i.e. a variety, but as I said, not all, of the NGOs in the country involved in delivering family planning and health services. As I discovered, but not until several months into the project, USAID could not support the government program because of some serious fraud that had occurred within the Ministry of Health in the late 1980s. At that point, the US Government had shifted their technical assistance programs and financial resources to a small, select group of NGOs.

Arriving with little or no historical perspective, however, I was definitely in an awkward position during the first few months of the project. I found myself wishing that I had done more homework or that someone I trusted would pull me aside and fill me in on the major players and the evolution of the private and public sectors, as well as USAID and UNFPA's involvement in the country. I also needed more background on the individual agencies that I was working with, not just the institutional statements that were provided to me in the 'project paper.' I soon regretted being an outsider, arriving with such total naïvetè and idealism about the facilitation role to which I had committed three years.

I had no concrete knowledge of the complex socio-political issues that had influenced earlier population and health-related policy and programming. It was difficult to know whom to turn to for unbiased information and support in sorting out who was who, and how the pieces really fit together. Everyone seemed to have a different perspective, and I soon became aware of a number of institutional attitudes and behaviors revolving primarily around 'turf.' Subtle battles were being waged between donors themselves and also between potential recipients of donor funding. There seemed to be a constant 'positioning' by many members of the NGO community in particular—each jockeying to establish themselves and survive in a fragile economic environment. Technical control and limited project resources often seemed like carrots that donors dangled in an effort to move program objectives in one direction or another.

The Challenge of Team Building and Donor Coordination

Further complicating my role as an outside facilitator was the fact that the three participating project NGOs had no real history of collaboration. I did not think to ask, and no one mentioned at the time of my recruitment nor for weeks after I had arrived, that these NGOs had essentially been thrown together for the first time, and apparently against their wishes. The project's new, somewhat experimental, umbrella-type structure was designed to streamline the management of USAID funds and technical assistance in the country. Adding to the obvious difficulties associated with an experimental approach of this nature was the unspoken rejection of, and disguised antagonism toward the project's collaborative mandate. Because of my highly visible role, I sometimes felt targeted or 'blamed' by the participating NGO directors and their IEC technical staff for 'having to' collaborate on, and share responsibilities for the development of the educational materials and other components of the project.

It soon became obvious to me that it did not matter how wonderful the project goals looked on paper to USAID, many of my technical counterparts were far from committed to a *team approach*. Consequently, *team motivation* became a major focus of my work during the first year, although it never formally appeared in my job description. I will never forget how physically uncomfortable many of my Dominican colleagues appeared during some initial team meetings—finding it difficult to even sit together at the same table, let alone discuss successive steps in the collaboration. It was literally four months into the project before someone outside of it helped me understand the background of some of the problems that faced the project in general, and me personally. Armed with this information, however, I was able to begin to move the group toward becoming a cohesive working committee. It was close to a full year before I felt as if the group was truly functioning as a team.

As if the interpersonal and inter-agency relationships were not complicated enough to start with, the three NGOs participating in our project, were also simultaneously receiving financial support from UNFPA, but not *equal* support. Having multiple donor support required that these organizations also participate in other IEC activities under their UNFPA-supported programs. As timing would have it, just as our project kicked off, UNFPA launched a major, potentially complementary but apparently conflicting initiative— the establishment of an inter-agency IEC coordination team whose stated purpose included the development and execution of a national IEC strategy for reproductive health. UNFPA was making

[handwritten in left margin: Not all development work is well executed— be careful + do your research.]

a substantial technical assistance investment in promoting the development of national IEC strategies throughout Latin America and the Caribbean.

Unfortunately, given the fact that few local organizations have more than one or two people involved with IEC, both USAID and UNFPA were essentially dependent on the same technical pool for the execution of their respective programs. From my perspective, the fact that USAID had established a substantial budget for the development and dissemination of IEC materials over a five year period of time, required (no matter the price) that both Development Associates (me) and the project IEC team, contribute to developing and executing the national strategy. I felt strongly that establishing common goals and objectives was essential in order to maximize the impact of both USAID and UNFPA funds. I was convinced that coordination and collaboration would also help to reduce the otherwise almost 'certain duplication of efforts, and unnecessary overburdening of IEC-related human resources in the country.

You who have experienced any form of joint or multiple donor involvement in project development or service delivery will appreciate the conflicts that are often associated with competition between donors over the same limited human resources, target audiences, and even 'clients' within a limited geographic area. In the projects I have worked on in the past, I have rarely seen examples of good communication between donors. From my perspective, true donor coordination and collaboration—whether it be at the national or community level—is built on good communication. Unfortunately, I have grown to believe that donors often choose to limit their communication with each other for a variety of reasons, mostly related to issues of technical and financial control. This lack of communication is responsible to a very large extent for perpetuating the duplication of efforts, wasting valuable resources, and inefficiency in many development efforts.

The process of working out (negotiating) a positive relationship between the USAID-supported materials development initiative that I was responsible for coordinating, and the UNFPA-supported national IEC strategy initiative, was very complex. In retrospect, it consumed a lot of my time and energy! But, I believed that this first step in the process, although never contemplated in the design of our project and thus never formally incorporated into the time frame, was critical to the ultimate success and impact of the project. Although my role in promoting coordination between UNFPA and USAID is not the focus of this paper, and there is not space enough to go into more detail about it, I cannot make a meaningful summary of my three-year experience in the Dominican Republic without emphasizing its significance.

Unfortunately, there was a lot of internal disagreement initially about the value and long-term payoff of donor coordination and collaboration, and both Development Associates and USAID repeatedly questioned the wisdom of any investment, especially in terms of the design of our project's participation in the national IEC strategy. True coordination and collaboration, *not just lip service*, involved multiple planning workshops and meetings with UNFPA counterparts, especially during the first year, to discuss mechanisms for technical review and joint funding, etc. I was encouraged by Development Associates on more than one occasion to step out of the process, or at least reduce my level of involvement in what was definitely viewed as 'their' (UNFPA's) project. It was not easy to convince anyone at DA or USAID of the potential payoff, because from a management perspective it was risky. There was no way to *guarantee a payoff*. To my knowledge, there was no history of protracted donor coordination on any level in the country, no track record to lean on.

As highlighted later, successful donor collaboration and coordination, based on authentic communication, ultimately helped several donors achieve the unexpected and unprecedented goal of national-level distribution of a high quality set of learning materials on reproductive health. The ultimate proof that coordination and collaboration had paid off was the often-articulated sense of ownership of the materials by more than twenty institutions, both private and public. The printing and distribution of over five million copies of the various print products further justified the initial investments. This tremendously reduced the overall cost of the individual brochures, posters, and manuals that were produced, and ensured consistency of messages that were delivered by multiple agencies working at the community level. (No more conflicting advice between one agency and another working in the same small town.)

These concrete and measurable results were ultimately recognized by USAID as major programmatic achievements during the first half of the project. To my knowledge, few USAID-supported projects can boast this level of national impact. Clearly, the timing was crucial. Collaboration and coordination would have been less likely had UNFPA not been so committed to the process of developing and executing a national IEC strategy. As 'their' project unfolded, 'our' project found several ways to 'contribute' a number of significant elements to the overall process. The collection and technical review of existing educational materials on various reproductive health issues, mandated by both donors, was the first potential contribution that our team identified.

After much initial debate about the appropriate use of USAID funds, our project was *allowed* to spearhead the collection and organization of existing materials, and the development of a tool for evaluating education pamphlets and other print materials. We were subsequently *allowed* to support a serious technical review by both private and public institutions of the technical merits of the existing materials. The review was a major step in the overall national IEC strategy design. This successful collaboration marked a change in atmosphere in working relationships. Given the positive feedback about the collaboration, USAID *allowed* Development Associates to invite UNFPA and the public sector staff to participate in a series of technical meetings and training courses. These were organized under our project in preparation for the actual development of the materials, and included a contraceptive technology update and various workshops on innovations in training, quality control, materials development, and qualitative research techniques. UNFPA reciprocated with invitations to a variety of complementary activities that they were supporting. The *doors were opened for collaboration* on other components of the project as well.

By the second year of the project, the public sector agencies had become active participants in all aspects of the materials development process:

- Establishment of objectives,
- Development of draft materials,
- Technical review,
- Field testing, and
- Consensus-building workshops.

It was in the workshops that final decisions were made about the text, illustrations, and layout of a wide range of materials. The first 'set' of materials, a total of twenty integrated family planning pro-motional and educational brochures, a poster, and counseling man-ual, was formally presented, or 'launched' at a large public event toward the end of the second year of the project, shortly after the national strategy was placed in circulation. A second set of comple-mentary reproductive health materials—six additional brochures, a reference manual, and seven cloth training posters—was launched exactly one year later, about a month before my contract ended. Quantities printed varied from 100,000 to 450,000 copies of any given promotional brochure. Both the counseling and reference manuals, as well as laminated sets of the brochures, and a colorful storage box were provided to approximately 5,000 community health workers, both public and private, and other family planning coun-selors working throughout the country.

In my opening remarks at both 'launching' ceremonies, I made a point of emphasizing UNFPA's leadership in spearheading the de-velopment of the national IEC strategy that provided a wider justifi-cation and national framework for the materials that the project developed. In turn, UNFPA recognized the significant contribution of the project to the coordinated effort and praised the participa-tory methodology, particularly the involvement of the community during the field testing of draft materials, and the overall quality of materials produced. UNFPA supported the printing of over 2,000,000 of the brochures and almost half of the manuals from the first set of family planning materials for use by the public sector pro-gram and several NGOs, committing over $60,000 toward achieving national coverage.

During the next year, after many personal visits and much discus-sion, PLAN International, a major international NGO operating almost as a donor in the country, complemented UNFPA's contribu-tion by supporting the printing of over 1,000,000 reproductive health brochures for both the public and private sector. I believe that this inter-donor/inter-agency coordination and collaboration, although requiring much nurturing along the way, ultimately benefited the donors as much as the recipients of the materials. Each of the other donors claimed them as their own, deciding to affix stickers with their individual logos to each brochure, thus identifying the materi-als as their own tangible contribution to the communities in which they worked.

After reflecting on the evolution of the relationship between donors and their respective (overlapping) project technical teams, and on the quality of the products which were ultimately produced, I firmly believe that if I personally had not been so pigheaded and thick skinned when I first arrived, and that if USAID and Development Associates had not ultimately embraced the idea of collaborating with UNFPA and the public sector, our project's IEC component would not have had the impact that it ultimately did. Although the price was high in terms of the level of effort (physical and emotional energy expended), and in terms of unavoidable delays in the actual production schedule for the materials, I remain a strong, but more 'seasoned' proponent of this kind of approach. I also see, more clearly, the value of outside facilitation—bringing to the process an unjaded (albeit naive in my case) perspective and strong belief in the power of participatory communication.

Steps in the Materials Development Process

Having shared this general background on being an outsider, and various challenges and 'payoffs' associated with team building and donor coordination, I would like to share some of the actual steps taken during the materials development process. I will focus on the establishment of the methodology and objectives for both the IEC component as well as the individual materials, and lessons ultimately learned.

Establishing the Methodology

The initial technical challenge that I faced was 'selling' the idea that the entire materials development process should follow a rigorous methodology, rooted in the community to the greatest extent possible, from start to finish. I sincerely believe that establishing a step-by-step methodology at the outset, leaning heavily on the community for direction and verification that we were on track, defending each step along the way, and not allowing time and other pressures to dictate changes in the approach, resulted in a reshaping of attitudes toward the communication process in the Dominican

Republic. As I was recently reminded by one of my Dominican IEC colleagues, prior to this project, educational materials in the Dominican Republic were often developed in isolation, by individuals sitting behind a desk in their Santo Domingo offices. Brochures were occasionally taken to the field for 'testing' with the 'target' population *after* they had been printed. This blatant lack of consideration for the opinion of the audience is hard for me to understand, but evidently, this approach was the rule rather than the exception for many years. If, on rare occasion, a draft material was pretested, suggested changes were often not incorporated because the artist was not willing to make changes, or the text was too difficult to move around.

Although I had never totally embraced the neatly packaged health education and communication models promoted by some of the major international development communication firms, I found myself turning to them for 'ammunition.' Poring over the mass of reference materials on my shelves, I found several examples of theoretical communication models and other visual aids to present to my Development Associates colleagues, members of the IEC team, and the directors of their respective organizations. It seemed somehow ironic to me, but I knew that I needed the credibility of these large Washington-based institutions to justify the community approach and rigorous methodology that I knew would be required.

The 'P' Process, developed and refined over the years by Johns Hopkins University Center for Communication Programs (JHU/CP) provided the greatest support for my thinking. Armed with multiple copies of the Hopkins 'P' model, and samples of coordinated materials developed using this approach in Bolivia, I presented my recommendations to the group and reviewed the rationale behind each step in the process (see Figure 6.1).

The Hopkins communication process applies to materials development, and to communication campaigns as well. It involves five fluid steps: 1) analysis 2) design 3) development, pretesting, and revision 4) implementation 5) review and replanning. It loops back into the design step where the process continues looking very 'P'-like. It incorporates modifications to the materials or campaign, based on feedback from the community. Recently, a sixth step, planning for continuity, has been added to the model as well.

Our project approach evolved into a slightly modified 'P', a snail-like image (El Caracol in Spanish), which we half-jokingly used on

Figure 6.1: The Hopkins 'P' Model

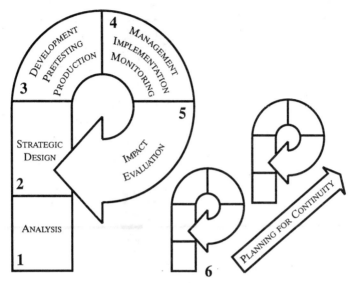

several occasions in defense of the rigorous and lengthy process that we had committed to. This modification of the model took place, not in avoidance of copyright laws, but rather as a logical reaction to the mandates and flow of our project in the communities (see Figure 6.2).

Our snail also reflected the reality of 'design by committee' and the challenge of responding to the national IEC strategy that was simultaneously evolving. After all, the 'P' is meant to serve as a model, not a mandate, and thus is open to adaptation given the local reality. Our snail model had fifteen distinct steps which we more or less grouped under six broad categories:

- identification of IEC objectives, audiences, appropriate imagery, and key message—steps, one through four;
- preparation of the objectives of individual materials and drafts of each material—steps five and six;
- field testing of materials, analysis of the findings, and development of consensus concerning the necessary steps—seven through ten;
- incorporation of changes, preparation of final art, printing, and distribution of the materials to the participating organizations—steps eleven through thirteen;

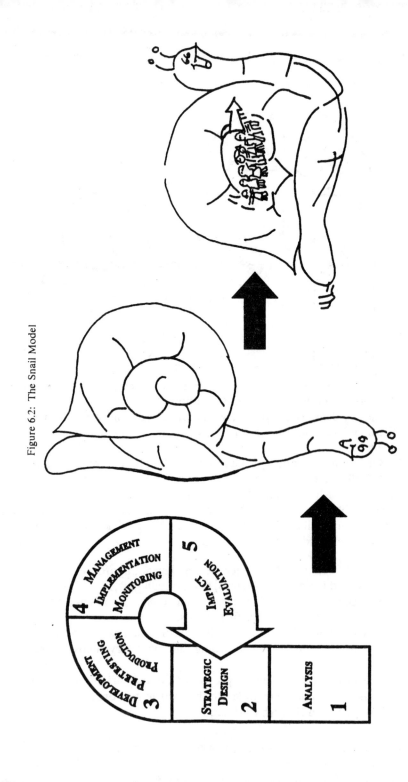

Figure 6.2: The Snail Model

- training of key personnel in the use of materials, distribution of materials at the field level, monitoring, and supervision—steps fourteen and fifteen; and
- evaluation of the materials, analysis of results, modification, and reprinting;—looping back to re-evaluate the original IEC objectives, audiences, imagery, and messages.

The fifteen step process is depicted in the graphic on page 108. This pictorial representation of the steps was useful in reminding the members of our IEC team of the activities that were taking place, each step along the way. The graphic also was a tool for discussion of the process, and was presented at both formal 'launchings' of the materials (see Figure 6.3).

Once again, as it isn't possible to go into great detail about all of these fifteen categories, I have chosen to highlight the establishment of objectives, both for the IEC component and the individual materials. Other relevant issues are briefly discussed under 'lessons learned.'

Establishing Realistic Objectives
for the IEC Component

After the proposed methodology and work plan was debated and accepted, the next technical challenge that the project's IEC team faced, was articulating and prioritizing a set of realistic objectives for both the IEC component as a whole, and the individual objectives of each material. Although IEC was one of many aspects of this relatively complex project, it was definitely viewed by both USAID and Development Associates as a cohesive element to the integrity of the overall project.

A number of vague IEC-related objectives were included in the 'project paper' which had been designed a year or so before I got involved in the project, but unfortunately, the objectives that were outlined gave little concrete guidance to our team. For example, the project paper referred to the development of seven 'sets' of education materials over the course of three years, but did not specify the content or the components of each set, nor did it prioritize audiences or messages. Luckily, we were able to convince USAID that this goal needed modification.

Figure 6.3: The Snail Model—15 Steps

Although establishing overall IEC objectives was, in my opinion, a very critical step in the process, it did not proceed in a smooth and logical manner. Indeed, some of the objectives were not articulated until almost a year into the project, and many were modified during the second year, as project priorities shifted and the national IEC strategy took shape. In hindsight, if I ever have the opportunity to coordinate another project of this nature, I would devote whatever amount of effort it takes, as early in the process as possible, to establish consensus among all collaborating organizations (directors and technical staff). Of course, we would allow for some degree of flexibility along the way.

Establishing the overall objectives for the IEC component of the project not only helped to determine the intended audiences and key messages for the print materials, but also helped to justify the proposed methodology, and define the coordinated 'look' of the end products. Ultimately, after much discussion and debate, the overall objectives focused on:

- The creation and technical training of an inter-agency team of IEC professionals.
- The development of an integrated set of promotional, educational, counseling, and training support materials related to family planning and other aspects of reproductive health.
- Ensuring systematic, national-level distribution of technically correct, audience-specific messages, consistently delivered by both public and private health care professionals and volunteers working throughout the Dominican Republic.

To meet these objectives, designated IEC personnel participated in technical updates on contraceptive technology, maternal and child health, and the prevention of sexually transmitted diseases (STDs) and AIDS. They also received training in community-based, qualitative research methods and key elements of materials development, and participated in reviews of audience research and evaluations of existing materials. This technical training and direct participation in research and materials review laid the foundation for determining the audiences and defining the key messages and objectives for each of the individual materials that were produced.

Building this foundation, however, also included:

- Securing commitment of the participating agencies to the proposed materials development methodology and the formalization of the IEC team.
- The development of a set of family planning norms by the project's technical committee which served as the guideline for the technical content of the materials.
- Conducting research on imagery for both the 'ideal' Dominican family and community promoter (as part of a technical training in qualitative research methodology).
- Selecting a talented artist who was willing to work within the parameters of the methodology and incorporate feedback from the community.
- Opting for a new material design and layout approach based on state-of-the-art computer technologies that allowed flexibility in the manipulation of illustrations and text.

From my perspective, all of these elements were essential to the process, and the time and money dedicated (although criticized by many), to consensus-building at the technical and donor levels and field testing with urban and rural population throughout the country, was completely justifiable.

Establishing Objectives for the Individual Materials

The complete set of full-color print materials developed by the project ultimately included eleven individual promotional brochures on all family planning methods. Seven informational brochures were prepared for users of specific hormonal and clinical methods. A poster and brochure summarizing all methods available, a brochure on appropriate methods to use after delivery, and a set of brochures on reproductive health including prenatal and postpartum care, STDs, HIV/AIDS, breast self-examination, and pap smear were all completed. An orientation manual for counseling individuals and couples, a reference manual designed for the community-level volunteer, and seven cloth training posters for both training and group discussions were also produced. The individual and collective elements of the coordinated set were designed to achieve a wide range of specific objectives as discussed below:

- *Promote the use of family planning methods in the Dominican Republic, with an emphasis on temporary methods.* Female sterilization, a permanent/irreversible method was by far the most popular among Dominican women when the project began. Many women were bearing two, three or four children, closely spaced, and then seeking sterilization in their early twenties.

- *Contribute to a positive attitude toward family planning.* The cover of all of the promotional brochures reflected images of 'ideal' Dominican families interacting in a positive and healthy environment. It was hoped that both the images and the information in the brochures would provide a strong counterbalance to the negative propaganda about family planning disseminated by various groups in the country.

- *Promote the image of community health volunteers as part of the family planning 'team.'* The imagery used in the materials to depict the volunteer was deliberately chosen to increase the volunteer's self esteem and recognition of the important service delivery role that he/she (a total of more than 5,000 volunteers nationwide) was playing. Also, having access to a set of high quality, full-color educational materials gave volunteers new status in their communities.

- *Contribute to the improvement of family planning service delivery.* By improving the training and technical competency of both health care professionals and community health volunteers, and by improving the quality and availability of educational materials (a critical service delivery tool), it was hoped that the quality of service would improve.

- *Promote the Lactational Amenorrhea Method (LAM) and other appropriate postpartum methods of family planning for breast feeding women.* The project included the introduction and promotion of LAM as one of its overall objectives, given the fact that this method had not been included in family planning service delivery programs in the past. A separate material was also developed to outline all of the postpartum family planning options, including LAM, and to encourage couples to think about child spacing and discuss postpartum contraceptive options during the pregnancy.

- *Contribute to an increase in client satisfaction with their chosen method and decrease abandonment of methods after short periods of time.* By clearly explaining possible short and long-term side effects of all methods, how to handle certain common side effects, and when a medical consultation is required, it was hoped that client satisfaction would increase and method abandonment would decrease.

- *Contribute to a decrease in the incidence of adolescent pregnancy.* Although the materials were not specifically designed for adolescents, nor were they a primary target audience, the materials were distributed in the communities to adolescents because of the fact that women under 18 years of age contributed to more than 25 percent of all births.

- *Contribute to an increase in the use of condoms in addition to hormonal or clinical methods for 'double protection.'* All of the materials contained messages about the fact that only the condom offered protection from STDs and AIDS. Use of condoms was recommended in order to prevent pregnancy and reduce STDs/AIDS.

- *Contribute to an increase in the period between pregnancies.* The project focused on temporary methods and encouraged both women and men to space pregnancies for the sake of both the mother and her children.

- *Promote the active participation of men in family planning.* Although increasing male involvement in family planning and other aspects of reproductive health was not a specific focus of the initial IEC component of the project, all of the materials contained positive imagery, or, images of men as husbands and fathers, clearly encouraging their participation.

- *Promote awareness about the importance of prenatal and postpartum care.* Given many problems with the public health system in the Dominican Republic, the average number of prenatal visits was less than three when the project began. Few women returned for check-ups after delivery. Consequently, a decision was made to develop two materials to help explain the importance of prenatal and postpartum care, and also what was involved. Danger signs were emphasized so that women would know when to seek emergency care. Ways in which a woman could personally contribute to a better pregnancy outcome were included, as well as information about how to take care of a newborn baby.

- *Promote awareness about STDs and HIV/AIDS, and the possible chain of infection.* A growing concern in the Dominican Republic is the incidence of HIV/AIDS and its high correlation with the incidence of STDs. Consequently, one material was developed to help focus attention on STDs, to encourage both men and women to recognize signs and symptoms of STDs, to seek treatment as a couple, and to follow through on treatment. Another material was developed to help explain the chain of infection of the AIDS virus.

Lessons Learned

The lessons learned throughout the development of educational materials under the Family Planning and Health Project are many, ranging from adequately preparing oneself for the role of outside facilitator, to ensuring the greatest possible participation of the community throughout the process. Although some of these lessons are more personal in nature, all had organizational implications and impact on the outcome of the overall project. Given obvious constraints, I have made an attempt to highlight key issues and organize concrete recommendations in what I hope is a useful manner.

Prepare Yourself for the Role of an Outside Facilitator

Get a good orientation and historical perspective as early as possible concerning the political and development environment—who is currently active in terms of donors, private and public sector programs, and key professionals. Learn as much as possible about the history and culture of any country where you will be working for an extended period of time. Local colleagues appreciate the extra effort that is often involved. Never presume that you, as an outsider, understand a culture. Remain open and honest about your naïveté.

Find someone who can provide you with concrete insights concerning valuable cooperators with whom to align yourself—the real 'doers' or movers and shakers, versus the big 'talkers.' Since there are often many biased and competing interests in the developing world, it is always best to seek out a variety of sources for this information so as to better ensure that you obtain an accurate picture.

Familiarize yourself with the objectives of any existing projects or programs related to the subject area(s) in which you will be working. Identify, predict, or be aware of potential 'turf' conflicts. Recognize the potential for competition between donors or between NGOs for future funds or technical control as you map your initial strategic planning. This is likely to ensure better coordination and collaboration.

Address the Challenges of Team Building

Building a team whose members are expected to collaborate on projects for an extended period of time is similar to raising a family. For optimum results, a lot of nurturing is involved, especially at the beginning during the formative stage. Take the time to find out as much as possible about potential team players, not only in terms of the organizations that they represent, but also their academic background, professional experience, and personal strengths and weaknesses. This understanding will give you a better perspective and help you understand the group dynamics that are bound to evolve. Find out to what extent, if ever, people have worked together in the past.

Recognize the institutional constraints, as well as the personal constraints you are working with on your team, but don't be afraid to 'push the envelope.' Most development-related organizations generally have a finite number of staff, a strict budget, a relatively short time frame for the projects that they conduct, and frequently competing priorities. It is essential to orient the directors and other program decision-makers about the objectives of the communication components of the project, and the recommended methodology. Make a realistic estimate of the time and energy required and the programmatic implications for each individual and/or institutional member. One needs to achieve consensus (from administrative leadership to technical staff to community health workers associated with a given institution) concerning the value of a given communication activity, as well as the most essential elements and order of priority. When this is done, there is greater hope for avoiding conflicts along the way and building commitment and enthusiasm for the project from start to finish.

The early steps in establishing the team and encouraging a spirit of collaboration often takes time and may require some kind of facilitated team building exercises, planning meetings and/or retreats. Although some project managers might find it difficult to justify an early retreat, others will understand that the long-term impact is worth the investment.

Budget the time needed in your work plan and ensure opportunities that allow and encourage true participation by all members of the team. Design by committee is notoriously slow, but has tremendous 'payoffs' in terms of ensuring technical accuracy of key messages, securing consistency in message delivery to a larger audience, reducing the overall cost of printing given the increased volume, and by ultimately developing a sense of ownership of the materials by a greater number of organizations. Projects always have time constraints, but if a concerted effort is made to budget an adequate amount of time for each element of the process that requires the participation of the team, you can avoid unnecessary frustrations and prevent having to skip essential methodological steps along the way.

Avoid, to the greatest extent possible, imposing communication-related objectives established by outside 'experts.' If there is no way around it, then validate these ideas with members of the team responsible for executing the program. Objectives established by a donor agency may indeed be valid, but need to be presented in an open forum in order to give stakeholders an opportunity to discuss, debate, refine, build upon what has been proposed, and/or explain why they reject an idea.

Recognize the possibility that the team usually takes on a personality and life of its own, occasionally exhibiting all of the positive and negative personality traits and mood swings of any living creature. Prepare yourself for inconsistencies in the performance of the team, and keep your spirits high despite occasional internal bickering or setbacks in work plans. This is to be expected.

Identify an artist and/or graphic artist who understands and agrees to the methodology to be used by the team in terms of developing, pretesting, and finalizing artwork, text, and layout of graphic materials. Many artists, perhaps most, feel uneasy when they yield their artistic license to other people who are involved in defining and executing a given image. He or she may quickly resent the team and/or the participatory community approach that recommends changes based on focus group and interview findings. A project artist can make or break the final execution of media products because of the undeniable importance and visual impact of an illustration to the overall layout.

If at all possible, involve the artist and/or graphic artist in team planning meetings, training workshops related to materials development, field testing and analysis of findings, and presentations of final products. This involvement will ensure increased understanding and appreciation for the methodology, and at the same time the team will often benefit from the artistic perspective that the artist potentially contributes to the process.

Establish Donor Coordination and Collaboration

Familiarize yourself with the range of members of the donor community (not just the USAID and UN variety), and the history of their involvement in the country. Explore all donor-driven programs that are related to the subject area(s) in which you will be working, both in terms of identifying potential allies, but also, as with the NGO community, in terms of avoiding potential 'turf' conflicts. This information will help in your initial strategic planning and open the doors for discussion of future opportunities for coordination and collaboration.

Be physically and emotionally prepared to face many solid arguments about why donor coordination and collaboration will not work and/or is not worth the effort. Understand that the words *donor, coordination, and collaboration* are viewed by many as being contradictory or incongruous by nature. Recognize the fact that examples of good communication and sustained coordination and collaboration within the donor community are rare. Be prepared to make supportive counter-arguments. Acknowledge the fact that it is difficult for donors to consider any kind of joint initiative for a wide variety of reasons ranging from:

- differences in project goals and objectives,
- conflicting funding cycles,
- difficulties in coordinating scopes of work,
- other responsibilities,
- real or imagined barriers to communication at either the technical or administrative levels, and
- inability to share the credit or blame for positive or negative project outcomes.

Donors appreciate it when other donors, or the projects that they support, take the time to study their donor strategies, and their short and long-term work plans. Even if minimal efforts are made to avoid duplication of programs or scheduling potentially conflicting activities such as training or other programs that involve the same technical people, they are appreciative. Such professional courtesies are often reciprocated, and, if nothing else, help to create a positive collegial atmosphere at both the headquarters and field staff levels.

If you are hoping to build a collaborative relationship between donors related to funding the printing and distribution of educational materials, involve (or at least invite) an appropriate donor representative to take part in planning discussions. Give them an active role in establishing objectives for the materials. Have them participate in conducting technical reviews of the proposed educational messages of the materials, and in reviewing drafts of materials, no matter how time consuming the commitment. Estimates of the cost of production that you expect a given donor to share should be presented as early in the process as possible. This will allow the donor the time needed to adjust budgets and/or allocate the necessary funds. Should a donor decide not to participate, extra time is always useful for exploring other options.

Recognize the fact that all organizations, both donors and the programs that they support, need recognition for their financial and technical contributions to a project. Identify opportunities to publicly thank a donor for collaborating. Public relations articles and reports can emphasize the role of collaboration. If at all possible, the logo of the contributing donor(s) and/or the program(s) they support should be included on the material. Logos can be printed directly on the materials, or prepared in the form of a sticker that can be affixed to individual materials.

Ensure Participation of the Community throughout the Process

Active participation of the community at key intervals throughout the entire materials development process is essential to ensure the success of your project. It is important to emphasize the value of participation and to fight for a participatory process if the idea is not immediately embraced. It is essential to budget the time and other resources needed in your work plan to allow true community participation to occur.

Setting realistic communication-related program objectives and specific objectives for materials requires knowing and listening to the people that you are trying to communicate with, rather than trying to manipulate them in any way. Getting to know your audience may begin with a review of the finding of both qualitative and quantitative studies that have been conducted involving the intended audience. It may also revolve around conducting formative research in order to understand the way people think and feel about the relevant issues and how they are actually dealing with them.

The participation of the community is fundamental in choosing the most appropriate or effective style of illustration and/or the actual images of key 'personalities,' especially those that may emerge repeatedly in your materials. Developing an image for a community volunteer or clinic health worker, for example, may require some creative formative research. Alternative styles should be prepared whenever possible so that the community actually has an opportunity to choose from a variety of options rather than just 'rubber stamp' a pre-selected image.

The role of the community needs to be clear in everyone's mind. It is not the responsibility of the community members to correct technical errors. It is important, therefore, for draft materials to be reviewed with appropriate technical experts, (and suggested changes incorporated), prior to field testing at the community level. A distinction should be made, however, between the technical accuracy of the text and illustrations, and the most appropriate presentation of concepts and visual material for a given audience. Technical experts often have difficulty simplifying the language and imagery that they use. Therefore, experienced communication professionals need to guide the ultimate presentation to the community, taking into consideration, of course, any technical feedback they offer. Thus the community shapes the final product.

It is extremely rewarding to bring printed material back to a community where it was originally pretested and share a final product that reflects the contributions of that community in the design of the material. When the production team participates in a feedback session with the community, it underscores the importance of bridging gaps between professionals and the people that they serve. Evaluation of the materials with the intended audience is an essential step in the whole, all too often, snail-like process, and brings the experience full-circle, or wraps the snail back into itself. Feedback would answer such questions as:

- How were the materials received?
- Were the intended messages understood?
- Did the community value the materials?
- Did they serve the purpose that they were intended to serve?
- Did they stimulate interest in obtaining more information?
- What changes are recommended in the future?

Let go of Your Role as an Outside Facilitator

Perhaps the hardest lesson of all to learn, at least for me, is *how to let go of your role as an outside facilitator.* I have always believed in the saying that you will have done your work well if you have worked yourself out of a job, by the end of a particular project. But, in reality, the process of letting go can be extremely difficult and almost painful at times. Given the level of personal involvement required in a team building situation, and the amount of time and energy dedicated to every step of the process, it is difficult for many outside facilitators to separate themselves despite the end of their contract. I believe that a close analogy to this would be the situation of a parent forced to set his or her child free, to move through the rights of passage necessary to reach adulthood.

It is not unusual for outside facilitators to be forgotten. Recognition of their exact roles or contributions may be short-lived. Therefore, I think that it is important for people like us to take personal pride in our 'offspring' and to continue to keep our own contributions in perspective. We should never, however, *expect* public recognition for our achievements. Institutional and individual memories will fade, but if at all possible, it is useful to maintain contact with at least some members of the core team of a project. Keep track of materials that are produced or campaigns that are launched by the technical people that you worked with. Although it's not the same as being there, it is personally satisfying to watch from the sidelines as projects mature and people grow professionally.

In the case of the Family Planning and Health Project in the Dominican Republic, the IEC team has evaluated, modified, and reprinted many of the original materials over the last two years, and has also expanded the set to include new materials on STDs and AIDS. The project's IEC team also worked in close coordination with other organizations to launch a national-level media campaign to involve men in reproductive health. Donors are to be thanked for a strong technical foundation and for having commitment to continued funding of the project. The agency directors recognized the key role that communication plays in education and behavior change and ultimately in improving service delivery and program quality. The IEC team continues to play a striking role in reproductive health in that country.

References and Select Bibliography

Johns Hopkins University Center for Communication Programs, Population Communication Project (JHU CCP/PCS). The Hopkins' 'P' Model. Baltimore, MD: Johns Hopkins University.

Nolasko, V. (1995). 'The Snail Model', a graphic. Santo Domingo, Dominican Republic.

7

Listening, Respect and Caring: The Heart of Participatory Work with Children

Jim Lees and Sonali Ojha

We began our work in India charged with making use of two video productions on HIV and drugs, putting them in the hands of adults working with street children in Mumbai. Early on, the team of eleven of these children convinced us that it was important to move beyond interpretations of the videos, beyond AIDS and drugs. They convinced us that the real subject of our work was children's lives, and that sense cannot be made of drugs or AIDS without understanding how they fit into their lives. It became a question of meaning; what HIV means and what drugs mean to street children. Understanding children's lives meant asking the team to teach us how they interpret their own lives and how they understand their own behavior. It also meant learning how street children interpret the world of adults who they see every day.

'It doesn't matter how much you know about AIDS or drugs. If you don't care about yourself, you're still going to get HIV or use drugs.' This statement was disturbing. It was from a 12-year-old boy, a child of the streets living without his family on the streets of Mumbai. We had gathered a group of these children together for an afternoon to help us in our work with HIV, drugs and street children. Immediately, the voices of the other dozen or so boys in the room rose in support of the 12-year-old's statement.

One of the boys began crying, asking through his tears why we were not doing something about the older men who force young street boys to have sex with them. He had witnessed his parents' murder during the Mumbai riots of 1993 and was immediately gang-raped by his parents' assassins. For the following two years, from the age of 11, he had been living alone on the street. All the boys agreed; they wanted to know why older men rape them. They told us that if someone did not stop it, they would some day end up doing the same thing to younger children. That, they told us, is how it works on the street.

Drugs? 'Well,' they said, 'how else can a child survive?'

Our work in India was to distribute two videos on drug use and HIV that had been created specifically for street children. The videos were designed as universally applicable pieces to be used throughout the globe and were to be accompanied by a training workshop for their use. Curious about how children and adults would respond to the videos in India, we showed them to the group of children. We were ready with our questions. What messages did the children get from the videos? What scenes did they feel were most important? Were the messages of the videos the right messages for children? Would the videos make a difference in children's lives? But we were not ready for the children's response. What began as an attempt to learn how the videos could best be used with children in India, became an experience that surprised and frightened us. Videos designed to trigger discussion, triggered memories as well, the results all too clear in the children's tears which flowed before us.

Our afternoon with the group of boys was upsetting beyond the experience of hearing of the children's horror stories of how they have been treated and what they must endure daily. The foundation for our work, which had been pre-established, seemed to slip from under us. Our videos were about HIV and drug use prevention. They were ostensibly designed (and liberally funded) to educate and protect the child viewers from AIDS and drugs. We now had more questions. Could the ideas alone meet such a goal? Was it

Good questions!

realistic to think that children's behavior would change with the viewing of two short videos? And did the videos' messages blame children
for behaviors that were out of their own control? These children obviously knew a tremendous amount about HIV and drugs, perhaps
more than many of the adults who work with them. But the trauma
they expressed upon viewing the videos could not be ignored. It did
explain, in part, why the HIV video, which had first been distributed
five years earlier, had not been successfully used in India. The claim
was that people did not know how to use it with children or how to
answer their questions after they watched the video.

By the end of that significant day, we were convinced that we
could not proceed with our training and distribution project as
planned by our employer in North America. We needed to re-think
what it was we had been hired to do. We had to re-examine the
assumptions our employer held about street children—assumptions
upon which the two videos, the training and our 'work plan' had
been created. It was clear to us that the children in the room that
day did not need any more messages about HIV and drugs than they
had already received. Rather, they needed options to HIV infection
and drug addiction. We needed to understand how these children
understand HIV and drugs, and what meaning HIV and drugs have
for them, in their lives. We were impelled to address the haunting
statement: 'If you don't care about yourself, you're still going to get
AIDS or use drugs.'

We proceeded in a manner that involved children and the adults
who work with them, to understand the role and meaning of HIV
and drugs in street children's lives. Our primary focus evolved away
from HIV and drugs and onto street children's lives. Our 'product'
evolved from two globally distributed videos to a participatory process of self-discovery that would transform the relationship between
street children and the adults who work with them. Working side-
by-side with a team of street children, following their directions and
believing that they were leading us on an important journey, was a
remarkable process of faith and discovery—faith in the children,
discovery about ourselves. The children, the street educators, and
we, as facilitators, all experienced repeated moments of self-
introspection. Participating openly and honestly with each other, we
all learned and we all grew.

In the following pages, we would like to take the reader to what
we believe to be at the core of the art of participatory work with

children. We would like to fuel thinking on what it means to undertake participatory work with children, what this means for the involved children, and what this means for the adults. And we would like to fuel thinking on what it means not to participate with children in addressing the issues that affect their lives. Ultimately, we would like our readers to see that adults are the ones who should participate with children as they work to figure out their lives. It is not that adults should ask children to join them. It is that we, as adults, should learn how to join children and assist them in doing what it is they are already doing: living, learning, and growing.

The Mumbai Street Child

In a nation plunging headlong into the global economy, Mumbai occupies a unique position as the financial center, shipping center, and video center of India. For many of India's 950 million inhabitants, Mumbai's opportunities are intimately wrapped in the images and illusions of a false prosperity generated by the 'Bollywood' movie industry (a film industry that far out-produces Hollywood). For children throughout India, familiar with its larger-than-life images on celluloid, Mumbai is a place to go when the present is intolerable, or opportunities for the future are few.

'Street children' arrive in Mumbai at an average age of 6 to 7 years old. They are about 35,000 in number in a city of twelve million. Street children must be distinguished from 'pavement children' who live with at least one relative, 'slum children' with some kind of roof and family, and 'beggar children' who are born into families which put their young to work asking strangers for money. Street children are *alone* on the street, away from their families, many with no chance of ever returning home. The risk of their encountering physical and sexual abuse is extraordinarily high, drug use common at age 8 or 9, life expectancy far lower than the national average, and the possibilities for their futures, few. While 75 percent of the girls who come to the streets of Mumbai unwillingly end up in the city's notorious brothels, street boys face their own daily threat of physical attack, hunger, and homosexual rape.

In his description of the New York life of the heroin-addicted character Sonny in his brilliant short story 'Sonny's Blues,' James

Baldwin unknowingly captures children's lives on the streets of Mumbai. I was sure that the first time Sonny had ever had horse (heroin), he couldn't have been much older than our Mumbai street boys. They were growing up with a rush and their heads bumped abruptly against the low ceiling of their actual possibilities. They were filled with rage. All they really knew were two kinds of darkness: the darkness of their lives which was now closing in on them, and the darkness of the movies which had blinded them to that other darkness about which they now, vindictively dreamed. They were, all at once, more together than at any other time, and more alone.

Together and alone. Rage. Darkness. Dreams. Who are these children? And by what right or seemingly good intentions could we enter their lives?

The Indian novelist, R. K. Narayan, in his work *The Malgudi Omnibus*, writes about the somewhat eccentric headmaster, Gajapathy:

'(These children are) wonderful creatures! It is wonderful how much they can see and do!' says the headmaster. 'I tell you, sir, live in their midst and you will want nothing else in life. These are the classrooms,' he points out. 'Not for them. For us elders to learn. Just watch them for a while. We can learn a great deal watching them and playing with them. When we are qualified we can enter their life.'

Challenging our assumptions about street children, why they use drugs, what puts them at risk for HIV, and why, in general, they do what they do, we began to define the values that would guide our own behavior throughout our work. Our first value seemed that of basic respect, that the time and values of all organizations, individuals, and children will be respected and protected. Many NGOs and individuals with whom we had already been in contact, expressed strong feelings about how they had been treated by western development organizations in the past. They were discontented with the large number of foreign organizations visiting their centers, taking workers away from direct work with the children for long periods of time. Several referred to AIDS and drug abuse tourism, where 'visitors walk away with their heads and arms full, their camera film

exposed with unauthorized shots of children, and leave little of
practical value behind.'

We agreed that we would recognize children as the knowledge
base about situations that affect their lives, and see street children
not simply as recipients of services but as conscious actors. Children, we believed, have the ability to perceive their needs, organize
solutions, and make rational decisions about their behavior within
the context of the choices and resources available to them.

We knew that substance abuse and HIV/AIDS risk reduction and
treatment, present street educators (a term referring to those persons who work directly with street youth) with new and difficult
problems. We saw that street educators had a critical role to play in
the ongoing process of risk reduction among street children. Substance use and HIV/AIDS work by educators elicits their own reactions of fear, anxiety, powerlessness, frustration, anger, and sadness
due to death, loss, transference, counter-transference, and burnout.

We were aware of how little is done to support and develop the
skills and effectiveness of street educators, though they account for
the majority of any organization's face-to-face time with the children they serve. Since street educators would be the people using
the two videos we represented with children, we felt it imperative
that street educators themselves must be valued and supported to
address their personal issues and attitudes, and to attain the professional skills required to sustain their work through time.

Throughout our participatory work with children and street educators, we looked to these values to guide us. While at times we
were tempted to impose our own beliefs on those with whom we
worked, or to direct discussions toward a place more comfortable or
easier for us, constant reference to our values prevented us from
doing so. Stating our values and having them written on paper also
helped us to represent ourselves and our project, making the decision to participate with us easier for the three organizations, seven
adults, and eleven children with whom we eventually worked.

It was through our last value that the next step in our project
became clear. The leadership role in developing intervention strategies, aimed at reducing risk behavior related to HIV/AIDS and substance use, we believed, must be given to children. This did not
mean involving children in what we as adults were doing, but rather
it meant that we became involved in what we found children already

doing: trying to understand their lives. It did not mean culling information from children about drugs, HIV, and their lives, developing 'interventions' on our own and returning to the children to 'test out' those interventions. It meant having faith that, with adequate support and resources, children would be able to find their own solutions to the problems that plague them, including the threat of HIV infection and drug addiction.

Examining Assumptions, Challenging Beliefs

'They will come the first time because they are curious,' we were told, 'and some will come the second because you are paying them. But after that, they won't come.'

'These children have short attention spans,' someone else said, 'so you will have to keep everything short. They will never last three hours.'

Yet another person suggested that we must be entertaining and plan lots of physical activities. 'They will get bored and restless. You know how much energy children have.'

We had identified eleven street children in Mumbai and our plan was to gather them into a team to guide our work. The youngest child was 10 years old at the time, the oldest 17. We wanted to meet with the boys three times per week for three hours each session, (access to girls for the team proved, sadly, impossible at the time in Mumbai). We wanted to meet for four weeks. At the suggestion of the newly forming team, we arranged to meet at a neutral location away from any of the centers serving street children which these boys might depend upon in some way. At the boys' suggestion, we would meet late in the afternoons, after they had completed their work and earned what money they needed for food or shelter that day. Sixteen individuals had joined us, uncertain of any outcome of their efforts. That these individuals were willing to experiment with us, that they were willing to risk investing their time and experience in a participatory process whose outcome could not, at the time, be clearly defined, was to their great credit. We had already met with five street educators who were to be part of the team, but their bosses and ours seemed less than convinced that our plan would work.

Our first team meeting was in February of 1996. Our intent was to explain what it was we wanted to do with the group. The children's need, however, was to understand why we wanted to do it. What were our motivations? Could they trust us? Why were we interested in listening to them? Did we want something from them that we were not telling them about? Our answer to the boys' direct question of why we wanted to teach them about HIV and AIDS was a fairly generic explanation of the risks associated with HIV and the consequences of infection. The boys seemed restless and half-interested, until we said, 'And we don't want you to suffer with it.' The short but heartfelt statement changed the atmosphere in the room. The children later explained that here they sat with adults they did not know, who said, however indirectly, that they cared about their lives and had good wishes for them. These adults somehow cared enough to go to the trouble of arranging a place to meet, getting the boys together, and providing tea and snacks. In addition, the adults had taken direction from the children to schedule the meeting times for the late afternoon so their daily work activities to earn money for food, would not be disrupted. The boys were curious. Not trusting, no, but curious.

The weeks that followed were a powerful mix of learning and unlearning. Meetings we had planned for three hours regularly stretched to four. The boys insisted on meeting four days per week, and after five weeks of meeting, still wanted to continue. More than two years later, they still ask us when we can do another project together. Our meetings had neither entertainment nor 'fun' exercises. The children chose to talk, sometimes for four hours uninterrupted. The common adult assumption of children's 'short attention span' or 'need for entertainment' was proven false, and those assumptions replaced by honest discussion about difficult lives within a setting of respect and care.

Within moments of our first meeting, we recognized that the two videos on HIV and drugs would not be the subjects of our meetings. We thought, then, that the subject of our work must be HIV and drugs. It seemed logical to us. But the team of children quickly taught us that we were wrong. Without a verbal discussion, they showed us each day that the subject of our meetings, the focus of our work, was their lives—their lives, and the lives of the tens of thousands of children like them who live on the streets in cities and towns throughout India.

The Children Emerge

An 11-year-old boy sits on a curb outside a busy rail station. Anxious commuters rush to and from their trains. The boy is unaware of the furious human migration, looking only at the tattoo inscribed in the skin of his forearm. It is his mother's name. He has not seen her in three years. The tattoo is all he has of her. He looks at it intently, reading the faded ink again and again when he misses her. Her name gives him comfort, no matter how small. Her name, his tattoo, is all he will ever see of her again.

On the boy's other arm are scars. Hundreds of them. Perhaps he does not want his mother to know of them. When the reassurance of her name is not enough, when his hurt overwhelms him, he picks up a rough stone, a broken piece of glass, or a discarded razor, and cuts. Cuts himself, his arm. *Again and again and again. Not too deep, not too shallow.* Enough, just enough, to rid himself of the pain he is feeling inside. Some days, cutting is not enough. Some days, the boy feels the need to harm himself. It is a feeling he shares with most children on the streets. It is not comfort he seeks on these days, but a blotting out, a blank nothingness that will soak up every drop of his hurt, confusion, and hopelessness. Escape from pain.

The boy has a keen understanding of drugs. He knows what drugs exist, their affect and where to buy each one. He knows their costs and the different combinations of drugs with which he can get the maximum affect for a minimum amount of money. He knows what drugs can, might, and probably will do to his body. He has seen others only slightly older than him, die on the streets because of drug use. Death has not been a stranger.

The boy also knows a great deal about HIV and AIDS. By the age of 12, he is already tired of the AIDS lectures he hears at various shelters for street children. How it is transmitted, who might have it, how not to get it. He has been repeatedly informed of the facts. On days when there is to be a guest speaker about HIV, he avoids the shelter. No one ever asks the question he truly wants answered. Why do older boys and men force younger boys like him to have sex?

The rail passengers rushing by rarely notice our friend sitting on the curb. Thousands of boys and girls eat, sleep, work, wander, and play on the streets of large cities like Mumbai. It is the playing that the public seems to notice the most. 'These children are only interested in their freedom,' we hear. 'They are irresponsible;' 'They are lazy;' 'Look at them, running and laughing and shouting like that,' as if laughter in children was a bad thing. 'They are bad and worthless, the police should do something about them, running in and out of traffic all the time;' in and out of traffic because the police will not allow them to run, play, sit in, or even enter the nearby park. One American movie star, on her visit to Mumbai, commented on how 'joyous' these 'wonderful little children' are. She wanted to 'scoop one or two up' and take them home to Beverly Hills. The public, like the movie star, rarely sees beyond the darling or devil interpretations of who street children are. They never venture into darker alleyways or abandoned buildings to see the sick child being cared for by his friends. They do not know the dangers of the night when the rail station is empty, and children drawn into dark corners by adult men and raped. They do not experience the pain and stigma of a life alone on the streets, struggling with abusive words and physical violence.

As the boy outside the rail station gets older, as he understands how his past has handicapped his future, he will need more than the comfort of a tattoo or the pain of cutting. Lacking nourishment, his ability to care about himself will diminish. And he will learn through experience what the small group of boys told us so many months ago: 'It doesn't matter how much you know about AIDS or drugs. If you don't care about yourself, you are still going to get HIV or use drugs.'

How does this cycle end?

Interpretation: A Child's Eye View

Children interpret their own lives far differently from those of the adults who pass them by each day. Through their own experience and logic, they have learned to make decisions within the set of options that they see as available to them. Children will not reject or stigmatize a child with HIV. During the Mumbai riots of 1993, Hindu street boys were known for protecting Muslim boys from

attack by armed and violent bands of Hindu men. Children are for-
ever aware of their feelings, which are constantly under attack in a
life on the street. Though they may not understand what they are
feeling, they do know that hurt is the primary motivator in their lives
for their own behavior, and that sometimes their own behavior is
harmful to themselves. Harming themselves is a response to the
hurt that has been done to them. Feelings and tension need constant monitoring, with various efforts employed to cope with feelings or reduce tension. Feelings and tension explain behavior. A
child who is sad may sit for the day feeling low. But a child who has
been beaten or has lost his job will experience far greater tension
and struggle to cope with his emotions. He may use drugs. He may
beat a younger boy, cut his arm, sleep, or attempt to kill himself.
But, he must do something with his feelings and tension.

Children develop a logic that is not unlike that of adults, yet they
are often belittled for it. As boys reach puberty, visits to prostitutes
are not unusual. The boys explained that a prostitute charging ten
rupees (about thirty cents) will probably carry HIV or another disease and require the use of a condom. One charging forty rupees
will be 'clean,' making the use of a condom unnecessary. Tension
and feelings also influence their sexual behavior. 'If your tension is
low,' the boys relate, 'then you will probably use a condom. But if
your tension is high, then you need maximum relief. You can't even
think about condoms at a time like that.'

Adult interpretations of street children's behavior are far different from children's interpretation of their own behavior. Adults
take little time to move beyond their superficial impressions. Yet
street children are constantly trying to understand the behavior of
the adults who surround them, interpreting their behavior and trying desperately to anticipate their next actions, for it is the adult's
next action that could bring food and shelter, or abuse and rape.

Following the Children's Lead

Supporting and respecting the leadership role of the team of children and following their direction was hard work. Lack of daily
plans and weekly agendas for team meetings made our distant
bosses uncomfortable. We were constantly challenged not to jump

into the children's discussions and lead them toward what made sense to us as adults. How we asked questions was important. We were rebuked one afternoon for writing down the names of who said what in our daily notes:

'*Why are you writing names?*' we were asked.
'*So we can keep track of who said what,*' was our reply.

'*This is the first time you have hurt us,*' the children said. '*It does not matter who says something. The important thing is that it is coming from us, from all of us.*'

Following the children's lead forced us to dispel our false assumptions about children and brought us to a richer understanding of their lives. Challenging our own assumptions about the children with whom we were working was an essential and continuous part of our process. As adults involved in a participatory process with children, we did a lot of unlearning, letting go of what we thought we knew about children that proved false. Such 'letting go' is not always easy for adults vis-à-vis children. As adults, we certainly felt a sense of loss of our age-old (or, perhaps, old age) position of authority, along with the anxiety about not knowing when, or at what point, the team would succeed in its project. Our team could not have succeeded however, if we as adults, had tried to maintain a position of authority over the team's children. Though responses of 'I don't know' or 'I was wrong' to children's questions are not always easy for adults, the respect they communicate to children is tremendous. Slowly, as a team of children, street educators, and adult facilitators, we were learning to respect each other for our experiences and for who we were. The unique qualities of each team participant were being revealed. Working with the team of children in Mumbai, we developed a profound respect for our ignorance, for the more we were willing to reveal it to the children, the more children were willing to reveal the complexity of their lives to us.

Two weeks into our meetings with the team, the children clearly defined for us the primary task of their lives on the streets: *managing their hurt*. Using the term 'tension,' the children were able to talk about their mechanisms and strategies for dealing with their hurt. Drug use and sex took their places as examples of two of the many different coping mechanisms street children employ, two of a long list which includes sleep, hurting others, talking to a friend, damaging property, cutting on ones' own body with a blade or glass, crying, and suicide. While adults group some of these coping mechanisms under 'positive alternatives to drug use' or other 'risk behavior' (i.e., sex), the team was clear that street children *do not* place drugs or sex at the center of their conceptual understanding of their behavior. Rather, they experience their own lives and emotions as central to their behavior choices, of which drug use and sex are but two possible options. Drug use and unprotected sex are potentially harmful behaviors in which street children engage. But to focus on harmful behaviors or on drugs and HIV, in themselves, reduces children to the risks they take. And, it fails to understand the place that drugs and sex occupy in the range of behaviors, harmful or supportive, in which the street children engage.

'Fifty percent of the children on the street,' the team said, 'have so much tension that they are unable to hear any message you are trying to give them.' This revelation was a jolt for us. Our work had been focused on messages adults wanted to convey to children. We had been hired to begin with those messages, in fact to deliver those messages and move on. 'Should our starting point really be tension rather than drugs and HIV?' we asked the children. 'No,' they replied. 'Your starting point should be our lives, the lives of street children.' It was at this moment that our hope and faith that these eleven children would lead our project to its rightful place became trust in the children's ability, caring, and will to do so.

Children Creating for Others

Working with a graphic artist and a cartoonist, the children eventually developed a workbook to accompany the two videos through which children and adults can work together, to understand from street children, the complexities of their lives. The artists were immediately comfortable with our instructions that the eleven children were their bosses, not us. Being on time for each meeting and really listening as children spoke, was paramount to communicating our respect to them. As for the artists' drawings and all of our work, it had to reflect our care for the children and their lives. We would have to keep at it until we had successfully reflected this. The drawings had to be of the highest quality possible.

The artists responded well to our instructions and to the children. Each day, the children and the artists were engaged in drawing and creating characters for the workbook. The artists were continually willing to abandon characters they had developed with the children if the children felt the characters were not right. Such willingness to take direction and to be redirected by children strengthened the children's ability to express what they felt was important. By the end of our second week of team meetings, the children knew we were genuine in our commitment to them. They responded, unasked, with near perfect attendance, to the meetings in the following weeks. If they could not attend, they always sent word and apologies. Though we never made a reference to it, each time we met, the children's physical appearance was changing: they made certain their clothing was washed, replacing tattered shorts and shirts. They bathed before our meetings, washed, and cut their hair. No matter how early we arrived for meetings, we were never the first; a group of children was always waiting expectantly.

Some discontent was generated when we learned that a number of other children requested that they be allowed to join our team after hearing reports from the current participants. They were sad when we said no, but our resolve was clear. We recognized how vulnerable the team children had become, and we recognized our responsibility to assure them that in their vulnerability they were neither harmed nor exploited. No new members would be added. No visitors would be allowed. And all proceedings would be confidential, though the end product would be shared throughout India. Several journalists heard of our project and requested interviews with the children. Respecting what the children had already said about their lives being written about and photos appearing before the public, the journalists' requests were politely denied.

During the third week, something we did not expect happened: four of the five children who had been actively using drugs stopped their use. We had never spoken to them about their drug use, nor had they spoken about their drug use during team meetings. But they stopped.

From the first day of our meeting with children, we followed a rule that contradicts the cathartic approaches to working with 'troubled' children so common in the west. We never asked any child to talk directly about his own life. The children supported this group rule and developed it into a value: that all children have a right to decide when, where, how, and with whom they will reveal aspects of their personal life and feelings. Adults often ask questions of children that would be found offensive if asked of them. Have you ever used drugs? Do you use drugs now? Which drugs? How often? How much? Have you ever had sex? How old were you when you first had sex? Have you ever been paid for sex? Have you ever been raped? Children feel compelled to answer adults' questions, though not always with the truth.

The team children explained that they feared being evicted from organizations they depend upon for food and shelter if they do not 'tell their story' when asked. Telling one's story, however, is commonly a traumatic event for street children, one too traumatic to tell outside a relationship of trust with another. There are many children, the team said, who avoid all organizations because they are not going to answer the battery of questions repeatedly fired at them. We respected this value refined by the team, looking toward each team member to talk about the lives of street children in general, not their own. We were very surprised one day, then, after working again and again with the video on drugs, when the team of children said, 'Now we want to tell our own story.'

Adults Learning with Children

Telling their Own Story

We did not know what that meant. So, we watched as the team collectively created and told the story of two street boys' experience with drugs. (see Figure 7.1)

In the weeks prior to this, the children had directed the artists to illustrate ten pages about decision-making and harmful behaviors. Using the concept of life as a path, the illustrations represent various stages of the decision-making process that children go through relating to their behavior. Decisions and choices, the children maintained, are central to a street child's involvement in drug use and other harmful or supportive behaviors. Tension and feelings influence decisions and can put a child on a path he would not choose under different circumstances. On one's path in life, whether by desire or not, one will enter crossroads where decisions about one's path must be made. (see Figure 7.2) It is on these crossroads that

Figure 7.1: What is Our Boy Thinking?

Figure 7.2: Standing at the Crossroads

the children focused their attention. With the artists, they developed through drawings, a format where any child can discuss the influences on children's decisions, explore options and choices, understand the importance and consequences of decisions, and perhaps learn something more about him or herself. The ten drawings require a collective interpretation by children and allow them to make connections between feelings, tension, harmful behaviors, and the paths of their lives. It is, if you will, a collective self-inquiry into many individual paths in life (see Figure 7.3).

The illustrations, created and first drawn by the children, are free of all language. Though language is used in many non-formal education materials, the team insisted that the mere existence of words intimidates children who are unable to read them, removing them from participating in the process of learning. The drawings also had to make sense no matter where on the page one began 'reading' them. As literate adults, we were used to reading books and drawings from left to right, and top to bottom. Such is not the case with non-literate children.

When the team of children began to tell 'their story,' their own language and understanding was already steeped in the lessons they learned and concepts they put forth in their ten decision-making illustrations. They had already tested these illustrations with their peers on the streets throughout Mumbai. It was crucial, they said, that children be allowed to interpret the illustrations for themselves and share their interpretations with their peers. There were no right or wrong interpretations of the drawings, and the role of the adult using them with children should be to ask questions that prompt children's discussion and exploration. Adults should not, they stated, be interpreters of any of the illustrations.

What we had discovered by this point, was that by listening to children interpret the ten decision-making illustrations, we were learning more about their lives. Though by instruction, children were asked to talk about the lives of the characters in the illustrations and were not being asked to talk about their own lives, a dynamic was emerging before us that we had not expected. The children, it seemed, were very comfortable projecting their own experiences onto the drawn characters, though never revealing to one another that this was what they were doing. The children seemed freed to talk about many of the complex, hurtful, and dangerous and sometimes humiliating situations they face on the street—all covered by the cloak of projecting on their own experience onto

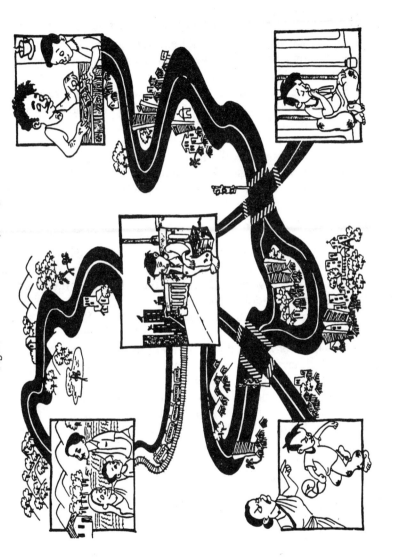

Figure 7.3: Where is Our Boy Going?

drawn characters. Stories, situations, and behaviors we had never heard before were shared and discussed by the group of children, and we listened. We thought that the illustrations and methods for their use developed by the children, were for teaching other children, but they turned out to be equally useful for teaching adults about street children's lives.

Nearly one year after our team's work was complete, we were still learning from the various children with whom we had participated, in the use of the decision-making illustrations. On one occasion, we asked how the boy in a particular drawing would feel about himself if he left the path of work that he was on and entered the path of stealing. We were pleased when the reply was that he would feel bad about himself, the move to steal being a blow to his self-esteem. One quiet child suddenly differed with the group's opinion. 'He would feel *better* about himself,' the boy insisted. We were taken by surprise. Shouldn't the boy feel worse about himself with his stealing? Isn't this the message we wanted children to understand? We had to make a decision ourselves at that moment: push this lone objector onto our belief path, or take the risk to enter onto his path and see where it would lead.

We entered his path with a simple question. 'Why?' we asked. 'Well,' replied the boy, 'this fellow in the drawing has been working for this man for almost a year. In that year he has been repeatedly beaten by him, forced to sleep on a filthy floor where the garbage is kept, gets paid only rarely, and has to fight off the sexual advances of the man's friends. He was constantly humiliated, and he had almost lost all of his dignity. He finally found the courage to leave the man. He knew that stealing is wrong and he did not really want to steal. But the only choice he saw for himself was to steal or to lose the last bit of dignity he had left.' The boy in the drawing was saving his self-esteem, not losing it. Once again, as adults, we learned a valuable lesson from a child.

And now, our team of eleven in Mumbai wanted to tell their own story.

A Participatory Learning Story

Most children who viewed the two videos we represented enjoyed the inspired animation and rapid-paced story. The last line of the drug video asks children to tell their own story. The Mumbai team found this invitation problematic. 'Telling one's story,' as they had said, can be a traumatic event for a street child. The video's request went against the team's stated values of the privacy, respect, and care that should be shown to children.

The team found a way, however, to tell their story. We believe they knew the value of the healing that can take place in the telling. What they created was a collective story, recorded through nineteen pages of drawings on paper, told collectively by each group of children who interpret the drawings. Again, no words exist on any of the pages. Children receive their own photocopy of the story, inexpensive and easily reproduced, upon which they may draw, write, fold, sit, or do anything else they wish. Sitting in a circle, page by page they narrate the lives of the two boys who wind through the nineteen pages. Similar to the decision-making illustrations, the story provides children the opportunity to anonymously project their own experiences onto the characters in the drawings. Listening to what other children say gives children the opportunity to compare their experience with others, or perhaps to see alternatives to their own situations. Telling their own interpretation of the drawings to the group, each child is afforded the respect of others as they listen. And in the collective and shared telling, children learn from each other and discover more about themselves.

The story as developed by the Mumbai team focuses on the lives of two children, Ravi and Baldie for our purposes here. When used with a group of children, the first task is for the participating children to agree upon names for each of the two boys, and the street educator who appear in the story. The nineteen drawings are an outline allowing stories to be projected onto them, drawings that illustrate people and situations familiar to most street children. The story begins with Ravi, a child of 10 or 11, leaving his village and family for the distant city. His head filled with more fantasy than fact about city life, his first days living on the street are difficult. Hunger, loneliness, and threats of abuse follow him everywhere. Ravi's life takes a turn for the better when he meets Baldie, a street boy several years older than he is. The boys become good friends and the story proceeds through pages of their exploits and exploration of the city.

One day, both boys are attacked by a group of older boys and their source of income, a small shoeshine kit, is stolen. Overwhelmed with anger and despair, the boys take to drugs. A street educator eventually enters the story, and Ravi enters a drug rehab program (though Baldie refuses to go). After successful completion of the program, Ravi is released to the streets and is reunited with his friend, Baldie. Baldie has been in tough shape since his friend went to detox, continuing with his drug use even while knowing the affect of the drugs on his body. But Baldie is unable to care about himself, unable to summon the will to change. Despite Ravi's pleas and the street educator's efforts, Baldie's life ends, dying on the streets, found by Ravi and the street educator in a busy crowd of passers-by who care nothing of the child's death.

As the Mumbai team created the original story, we objected to the death of Baldie. As adults, we simply did not want Baldie to die and questioned the value of having him do so. Despite our pleas, the team refused to back down in their insistence at Baldie's death. 'One child will succeed,' they said, 'but one must die.' So Baldie did die. And one year after his paper death, we have repeatedly seen the powerful grip on children's lives that Baldie holds. They recognize Baldie, they see Baldie on the streets, and they see Baldie inside of themselves. The adults who attended our workshops had equally strong reactions to the character, and we knew that the team had been right. Baldie's death was important, and it continues to motivate change in children's lives.

As with the decision-making illustrations, this story created by the Mumbai team provided the opportunity for children and adults to learn about the lives of street children. The story, eventually termed a *Participatory Learning Story*, allowed even more. If adults would participate with children in its use, if they would listen carefully to children's interpretations, they would be better able to understand their own role in children's lives and better see what they can do to support street children in their struggle toward the future. The learning story becomes *participatory* when the adults organizing its use are able to challenge their own thinking and are willing to learn from those whom they have been hired to teach. The existence of the street educator character in the *Participatory Learning Story* allows adults working with children to learn to ask street children what they can and should do, to best support children in their lives.

Participatory Learning Stories, we realized, can be created on many subjects with a variety of groups. The children with whom we were working asked if we could create other stories, one on the difficulties of returning home, and another focused on the relationship between street children and street educators. They wanted yet another on the relationship between the emotions children struggle with, and their attempts to build a life on, or away from the streets. The creation and use of each story would initiate and continue a process of mutual discovery involving targeted groups (in this case, street children) and those who are in a position to assist that group (street educators here.)

Through the story of Baldie and Ravi, street educators are presented with a powerful opportunity to examine their own role vis-á-vis children, and can better their ability to assist children by participating with them. Children are able to learn more about their emotions, their tensions, and the decisions they make. The team's children created a character who represents their fears, Baldie, and one who embodies their hopes, Ravi. Both characters are real, at times painfully so. Children recognize the potential they hold for living out each character's life. Through them, through two black and white characters on photocopied pages, one who continues toward the future and one whose end comes tragically early, they are able to communicate to the adults they depend upon, who they are and what they need.

Relationships

By truly listening to children's experience, we were able to see how adults' faulty interpretations of who street children are can limit supportive work with them. We saw that adults' explanations for a child's behavior can be very different from that of the child, and can potentially harm that child's chances for their future. And we discovered that for street children, filled as they are with information about drugs, AIDS, and other threats to their lives, filled with observations about their peers and the lives of the adults who surround them, their relationships with adults are powerful motivators of both supportive and harmful behavior.

Where do street children learn to care about themselves? It is a difficult question to answer. The Mumbai team believes children learn to care or not to care about themselves in their relationships with the adults who surround them. Through one adult having genuine care for a child, that child can begin to learn to care about him or herself. The child will believe in a future and strive to get there. A child who is abused, like Baldie's, struggles with his or her own sense of worth, and often destroys any possibility for his/her own future.

Street children are surrounded by a world that appears uncaring to them, a world that constantly threatens their physical and emotional well-being. Many adults look to exploit street children in numerous ways. Society's failures to provide safe places, education, employment, or even a basic meal, are all interpreted by street children as signs of their own insignificance and lack of value. And for most children on the street, their position of insignificance is emotionally compounded by the impossibility of a return home.

Street children, according to the Mumbai team and many other children throughout India, place special significance on their relationships with street educators. Hired to give children support, street educators represent a final source of hope, caring, respect, and possibility for many of those children. Children expect their relationship with these adults to be free of hurt. But the potential and reality of children being hurt by street educators, we discovered, is tremendous. Disappointment or hurt from one of the few adults left with whom a child might receive support, can be devastating to a street child. One child spoke of being hit by a street educator, an experience that is not unique. 'I left home because my father beat me,' the boy said. 'If I would not let my own father beat me, I certainly am not going to let some stranger beat me. I left that center and I will never return.'

One child of twelve years related a similar incident. 'I asked uncle (the term children use for male street educators) to get me into the drug detox program. I had decided that I had had enough of drugs, and I really wanted to quit. But when I asked him, he laughed at me and said he did not believe I was serious. He told me all that I really wanted was a free place to sleep and free food. He gave me thirty rupees (eighty cents) and told me that if I was really serious about quitting drugs I would come back tomorrow with the thirty rupees and he would take me to detox. Then he sent me away, saying that I would spend the money on drugs. I was so hurt and humiliated by him that I immediately bought some drugs, and I made sure that uncle saw me using them.' The child of twelve struck out at the adult who had hurt him by hurting himself. The educator simply reaffirmed his own belief that the child did not want to quit drugs.

Relationships between street educators and street children hold in them a tremendous potential for motivating change in each child. But, as the team pointed out, they are relationships that are fraught with problems. Street educators, like the children with whom they work, have very little status in India. Though they account for most of any organization's time spent directly with children, little investment is made to increase their skills and sensitivity. This potentially powerful relationship between street children and the adults whose job it is to support them, became the focus of the next phase of our work in India. The decision-making illustrations and the *Participatory Learning Story*, we hoped, would help transform these relationships so that their potential could become a transformational element and agent of change in more street children's lives.

One Year Later

The team's hard work eventually resulted in a companion workbook to the two videos made for street children. Using the videos and the materials and strategies developed by the Mumbai team, we conducted workshops for street educators throughout India. The workshops were divided into two parts, the first comprising three full days with a two-day follow up two months later. The street educators involved in the workshops were challenged to move beyond what they thought they knew about the children in their charge, and to learn how to learn from them continually. It was a difficult challenge for many. One year later, some of the participants have reported an evolution in their relationships with children similar to what we had experienced within our Mumbai team. Their language has changed with children, and they continue to learn where they are passing judgment and what that means to children. Most striking of all, the street educator's relationship to themselves seems to have undergone change. Some are able to speak of why they continue their work with children, their sense of their own value having increased. And a few have built on our experience and are creating new participatory learning stories on various subjects with team of children and adults.

Listening to children requires dropping assumptions about them. Adults throughout the world maintain a number of assumptions about street children; that they are lazy, immoral, corrupt, have no values, and seek only fun and freedom. Yet, street children are castigated for wanting what every parent wishes for their own child:

- Days of joyous play,
- Freedom from hunger,
- Freedom from the threat of physical abuse,
- Freedom from the threat of sexual abuse, and
- Freedom from the kind of hurt that damages the very spirit of a child.

Street children experience their unique position of stigma almost everywhere in the world, from the moment they set out from home (most, ironically, in search of a better life and a better world). And street children are aware of the stigmatized position they occupy in the world.

Like most children, street children respond to genuine respect and caring. We made an emotional investment into each child on the team, and the team clearly made an investment into all the street children of India who would use their workbook. The respect and care invested in the workbook the Mumbai team created, was recognized by street children throughout India. They recognized it as respect and care for them. Children have hopes and expectations of all the adults they meet. Children feel deeply. And every child is an individual, composed of their own unique combination of emotions, experiences, memories, decisions, and dreams. Every child looks to and responds to each adult in his or her own particular way. Truly listening to the team of children in Mumbai, showing them genuine respect and care, believing in their abilities, and trusting them led us to places we could never have anticipated. In the end, because we listened, because we participated with children as they tried to figure out their own lives, the children's lives changed and our lives changed.

Eleven street children in Mumbai developed an approach and a set of materials that transformed the passive viewing of two videos on drugs and AIDS into an active process of exploring their lives. They developed a way in which adults and children can participate together, can learn together, and can build children's futures together. We are no longer daunted by the children's statement, 'It doesn't matter how much you know about AIDS or drugs. If you don't care about yourself, you are still going to get HIV or use drugs.' We are no longer daunted because we learned from eleven children what matters. We learned from eleven children what makes a difference. To those eleven children we give our sincerest thanks.

Relationship is central to interpersonal communication.

Part 2

The Art of Technique

8

Facilitating Participatory Action Research: Looking into the Future with Orlando Fals Borda

Ricardo Gómez

*Internationally recognized for his contributions to participatory
action research, Orlando Fals Borda is a historian and sociologist,
born in Barranquilla, on the Caribbean coast of Colombia, in 1925.
Founder of the School of Sociology at the National University of
Colombia, he has been a guest professor at many universities in the
country, as well as in North America and Europe. Orlando has published many books and papers on the history and present condition
of peasants and farmers in rural Colombia, as well as acute reflections on the methods and implications of participatory action
research. He is today a professor and researcher of the Institute for
Political Studies and International Relations of the National University in Bogotá, where I met him to talk about the role of the facilitator
in participatory development.*

Orlando receives me in an office cluttered with papers and flip
charts, evidence of the ongoing preparation process for The World
Congresses he is coordinating. The Fourth World Congress on

Action Research, Action Learning and Process-Management, and the Eighth World Congress on Participatory Action Research are to meet together this summer in Cartagena, Colombia, and Orlando is the Chair of the organizing committee. The Congresses bring together scholars and practitioners from the four corners of the world, who are meeting to discuss the advances and perspectives of participatory action and research at the turn of the century.

The Idea of Participation

I begin our conversation by noting that after being considered marginal and alternative, the idea of participation has become very popular in development circles. It has even been embraced by international and multilateral agencies as an essential ingredient for sustainable development programs.

'Orlando, how do you feel about the popularization of the notion of participatory development?'

'There has been a growing trend to accept participation as a fashionable concept, but without much conviction on the part of the international and non-governmental organizations,' says Orlando calmly. He then points out that these institutions are now recognizing that their economic and social development programs have been defective. 'Their implementation is problematic, they are absorbed by corruption and mismanagement of resources, or they are administered by governments that are not very organized and cannot manage them. This happens because most of these projects are vertical, centrally controlled, authoritarian, and they are not very participatory.'

He continues: 'Traditionally powerful institutions, such as the World Bank and other multilateral organizations, began to realize that their projects were not being very successful or that they were failing. They have started to look for alternatives, and one of the alternatives they have found is the idea of the people's participation. It is a very appealing idea, one of those ideas that appears to be a lifesaver to institutions that need to justify themselves and their enormous budgets.'

'Participation has become a *life saver?*'

I then remark that it is extremely interesting to watch how participation has even become a requirement for projects to be funded by many agencies. Nevertheless, I wonder how genuine this concern for participation is. I have seen many people who think they are facilitating participation when they *organize* a meeting with the local population, but in this meeting project managers *tell* the locals what they intend to do and only ask for comments without an intent to act upon them. Many truly believe this is how one includes the local population in the planning and decision-making process of development programs. They are happy to call this participatory, but nothing happens beyond the meeting.

Orlando agrees that the notion of participation has been co-opted. 'Just as many other important notions in society have been manipulated: democracy, peace, justice—they all have become very relative,' he points out. Then he notes that the same has happened with people's participation, and with participatory action research (PAR). 'In the beginning when we first started to talk about it, PAR was considered dangerous and subversive, or at the very least, unscientific. Since we have passed our trial period, people now realize participatory action research is something worthwhile.' He points out that, 'traditional institutions have no choice but to accept it, even though they accept it only superficially. This is what seems to be happening now. Since they are not fully convinced about its strengths, and since they have never worked in a participatory way in the past, they end up co-opting the concept of participation, and adopt it only in its most superficial form and formal expression. This is an unavoidable process, and one about which we can do very little, because we cannot prevent them from spreading their ideas,' concludes Orlando, 'but there is no doubt in my mind that there is a manipulation process going on in the name of participation.'

In the course of our conversation there have been several interruptions: an incoming fax message that jams, somebody on the phone with an urgent comment, a question about hotel rates for the conference. Orlando patiently addresses each one as they come, giving his full attention to every detail, and returns to our conversation as if there had been no pauses.

'I wonder whether the popularization of the notion of participation cannot bring with it a positive side as well? Many activists have been struggling for a long time, struggling to promote more participatory programs in development in the whole world, but they usually face a concrete wall of opposition in the authoritarian procedures and practices of most funding institutions and agencies.' I point out that perhaps this is a good time to help many of these community animators and development facilitators since they now may be in a better position to defend and promote more genuine participation at a local level. I ask Orlando if there is any way he can synthesize some of the key elements that practitioners of PAR need to keep in mind, in order to help them take better advantage of the current interest in participatory approaches among traditional development organizations.

Orlando smiles and offers the cautious advice of an experienced animator, researcher, and professor: 'I believe we always have to take advantage of every opportunity that arises,' he says, 'but we cannot lose our soul. We cannot sell ourselves and give in to the manipulation process.' He is aware that this requires a certain degree of caution, and ability to survive in the rare atmosphere of the dominant capitalist system. 'Grassroots practitioners, development facilitators, and even university professors like myself, we all need to seize any opportunity that may help the cause of the poor and the marginalized.' Orlando sees no contradiction in receiving his pay from the state, since he works at a state university. He points out that his salary is paid for by money that belongs to the people of Colombia, and that as long as he can do his work in ways that will serve the people of Colombia, he is happy to be there. But, he insists that the important thing is to be able to adapt, to be cautious and to weigh the pros and the cons in each particular situation.

'The most important thing is to be able to promote one's original ideals, without losing them, and always forging ahead. This is many times extremely difficult, and sometimes dangerous. We have to be able to stay alive, and to make our ideas and ideals stay alive as well.' That's a very real observation because in the context of indiscriminate violence that Colombia is now experiencing, many people have been killed for far less than being PAR advocates. We both are sensitive to the reality and realize that one can never be overly cautious in the face of death.

Advice to Facilitators

My thoughts turn to the people who work with the community in the villages and in the slums—the local animators and development facilitators who are working in the field. They are the ones who need to be able to adapt to their existing conditions, as Orlando says. I wonder what kind of advice Orlando could share with them, to help them make the right decisions at the right time, in each particular context. 'Orlando, there needs to be a delicate balance between the personal capabilities and insights of facilitators, and the concrete conditions of the context in which they carry out their work. How do you think these two aspects need to be combined in order to help advance local participation in more genuine ways?'

'I believe if you are trying to do your work well, you first have to get in tune with the local population,' replies Orlando. 'You need to spend a lot of time in the field, because "tuning in" is not an easy process that can happen overnight.' He goes on to explain that you need to identify yourself with the local situation and the local life of the people, with their specific culture, values, and history. Only then can you start to help them generate solutions. But then, there are no formulae about what needs to be done. 'I cannot tell you that you need to do this or that,' he observes. Decisions have to be based on the particular circumstances in which work is being done, on the nature of the pressures that are perceived locally, and on the degree of support of the local people. 'There is no advice I can give on this. Each person has to be able to judge what is best.'

A great responsibility is placed on the shoulders of the facilitator. It is not an easy task, and I wonder what characteristics one must have to be a good participatory development facilitator. 'Suppose you were to recruit a group of facilitators to work with you in a region you know well, for example Cordoba, on the Atlantic region of Colombia, what would you be looking for in the potential candidates? What are the features you expect to find in a good facilitator for participatory action research?'

Orlando looks doubtful for a moment, scratches his chin, but then smiles and says: 'There is really no one profile for a good facilitator.' Young and old, women and men, people of all colors, even children can be excellent facilitators in participatory action research. 'In my opinion,' he submits, 'it all depends on the capabilities and personal values you have, on how serious you are in your commitment with the cause of the people, and on your persistence in carrying out your work.' He points out that the work of the facilitator requires great inner strength not to give in, to adapt in order to survive. 'In the end, it is the combination of many factors, but the most important ones are those that come from within, from the spirit, and from the attitude and values of the individual in his or her commitment to the people.'

'This must be something very difficult to teach in any school,' I remark. Orlando does not fully agree. He is confident that formal education can help to provide solid bases in this direction. 'What you can learn in school, in the university, is useful knowledge as long as you can assimilate it and use it in the context of real life,' he observes. 'In these institutions you can learn much about values and aptitudes. There is no doubt school can help to form you as much as to deform you. But if you have the inclination and the talent, formal training in school can be very useful.'

He points out that the theoretical and practical applications one can learn in school, such as social and economic research methods, statistics and history, as well as photography, video, and other forms of artistic expression, can all be very advantageous. They can all be combined into the fieldwork, where new lessons are also learned. In this way, the combination of formal, academic knowledge, together with the knowledge gained from experiencing life on the side of the people, is an excellent combination; one that can provide the tools that are needed for the work of the facilitator to be effective.

A new fax message comes in, and the old fax machine tweets and chirps out loud, bringing our attention back to the busy office and busy Orlando once again. His two young assistants rush in and out the door, shuffling papers and answering the phone, helping him with the numerous details of his research, the magazine he edits, and the preparations for the Congresses. I feel my time with Orlando is precious, but coming to an end. As soon as the fax machine is silent again, I pick up the thread of the conversation.

The Balance of Power and Trust

I mention that the work of the facilitator in PAR rests on the delicate balance of power and trust in the relations he or she establishes with the local people. 'How is this balance constructed?' I question. 'What is the articulation between trust and power in the role of the facilitator?'

Orlando confirms that it is inevitable that a power relation is established when you arrive in a poor or marginalized community, because you are easily seen as an agent coming from a different society, a rich and powerful one. But if you are effective, people will want you to take on a leadership role. 'Leadership can be earned, if you deserve it,' he remarks. But Orlando then explains that if the power relationship becomes too strong, the facilitator will need to make a choice between being a catalyzer—an agent for change with the participation of the community—or being a political leader. 'Perhaps as a political leader you will be better informed of what the people need and want, but you will no longer be a participatory researcher,' he declares and he explains that the role of the facilitator is entirely different from that of a political leader. The facilitator of the PAR process is a catalyzer, one who has gained the trust of the people and remains at their side in the process of researching their reality in order to transform it with concrete actions. 'In my experience,' insists Orlando, 'I have never seen a case in which you can be at the same time a participatory action researcher and a political leader. The two roles are not compatible and they have to be differentiated. Natural leaders may become spokespersons for the community and can continue to collaborate with the people, but that is entirely different from the participatory action research process.'

Recapping the conversation, I realize that even with an increasing interest in participation among traditional development institutions, facilitators need to be very astute in order to adapt and take advantage of every opportunity to advance genuine PAR processes. The contexts in which these processes take place are extremely varied, and there are no clear-cut formulae or profiles to ensure their success. Furthermore, the facilitator needs to be able to combine the knowledge of formal training with real life experience, and maintain a delicate balance between power and trust in the relationship with the community.

Is PAR Still Viable?

The complexity of the PAR task is magnified by the pervasive violence of the Colombian context, where Orlando has been working for half a century. I insinuate that the only way to keep on working for PAR in such a context is with huge amounts of hope for the future. 'If this is true,' I ask Orlando, 'what do you think needs to be done to keep alive the hope that participatory action research will help us build a better future?'

'Facts are definitive,' he immediately responds, 'and there are both positive and negative facts.' Orlando then candidly comments that if participatory processes are interrupted by massacres and political persecutions, and if they are severed by the death of the participants, then the processes will evidently not be able to continue. He points out that Colombian peasants have indescribably suffered the consequences of persecution and death in the last few decades, as a result of the actions of the political class of the country. 'But of course,' he retorts, 'hope is the last thing we can lose. We have continued with our work, although with much care, as long as we have been able to.'

Orlando observes that the fact that PAR was born out of the work in these communities in the context of severe violence and struggles is an indication that hope has persisted. 'For over twenty years now, the peasants have not given in, and those of us who are with them have not given in either. We have done what we have been able to do.'

'Uno hace lo que puede.'

Orlando looks at his watch once again, and I realize our conversation has to end. I tell him that as he has been working with PAR for several decades already, his contribution has been very valuable for many people. To wrap up, I ask him what are, in his opinion, the most important challenges that PAR advocates and practitioners face, for the decades to come.

He laughs heartily, and points at the flip chart behind my back. 'That, my friend, we will know for sure after the World Congresses that we are now preparing for. The central theme is *Convergence: convergence in space, in time, in knowledge, in disciplines.* That is the great challenge we have ahead of us.' He then briefly describes how we live at a time in which the traditional notions of state, power, and social organization are in crisis, and concludes that our task is to come up with new understandings that will help us confront the new century. 'This is what we will be discussing in Cartagena, during the Congresses.'

References and Select Bibliography

Fals Borda, O. (1988). *Knowledge and People's Power.* New Delhi: Indian Social Institute.
———. (1997). Personal interview in Bogatá. January.
Fals Borda, O. and **Rahman, M.A.**, (Eds.), (1991). *Action and Knowledge: Breaking the Monopoly with Participatory Action Research.* New York, NY: Apex Press.

9

Women in Agriculture: Participation and Access

Kathleen E. Colverson

This chapter addresses the issue of women's role in agriculture and the fact that they are not full participants in training to enhance that role. Kathy shares the insights gained from her research in Honduras. She interviewed rural women hoping to uncover the obstacles that limit their access to agricultural education programming. And, what is even more critical, explored ideas women have about how they can gain greater access to information.

The world over, women have always played an active role in agriculture, but their contributions have often been overlooked or ignored, their opportunities to access information and participate, limited. As a professional woman employed in the agricultural industry for many years, this situation always troubled me. While pursuing a doctoral degree, I took the opportunity to learn more about some aspects of this concern. I decided to investigate how women in developing countries receive and utilize agricultural information. While doing this, I felt I also wanted an opportunity to inspire the women I studied and enable them to take greater charge of their identities as agricultural producers. At the same time I wanted to encourage organizations to review their attitudes toward working with women in the field of agriculture. While doing research I would reach my academic goals, but the women I studied could also benefit.

Participatory Approach to Research

Insofar as possible, I aspired to employ a participatory research approach. I was struck by the relevance of Orlando Fals Borda's research framework used in Latin America:

> ...we view PAR as a methodology within a total experiential process (ensuring a satisfactory productive cycle of life and labour in human communities). Its aim is to achieve 'power' and not merely 'growth' for the grassroots population. This total process simultaneously encompasses adult education, scientific research and political action in which critical theory, situation analysis and practice are seen as sources of knowledge (Fals Borda, 1985: 2).

It was unrealistic to think I could initiate a full blown PAR model that, as Fals Borda indicates, should enable grassroots people 'to participate in the research process from the very beginning...and remain involved at every step of the process until the publication of results and the various forms of returning the knowledge to the people are completed (1985: 94).' However, I intended to employ as many of the elements of the model as was feasible. So I began the process and allowed each new insight to guide me through each phase of my research.

My first task was to search for, and scan research reports related to women's roles in agricultural work and their access to agricultural information. But where could I manage to pursue my research project? After some reflection (and having found grant assistance!), I decided to go to Honduras, a country about which relatively little had been written on women's roles in agriculture. I did find a study by Constantina Safilios-Rothschild (1985) which reported that 46 percent of Honduran women interviewed did agricultural work: sowing (39 percent), hoeing (41 percent), harvesting (39 percent), and weeding (22 percent). Another study by Buvinic and Yudelman (1990) determined that Honduran women comprise 40 percent of the wage labor force in tobacco, and 90 percent in coffee. So, before I visited Honduras, I had a preliminary idea about women's involvement in agriculture there. In conversations with several individuals who had recently returned from Honduras, or were Hondurans, I sought to explore their thoughts about the roles of Honduran women who were engaged in agriculture.

While taking a course in participatory research (PR) with Professor K. Sadanandan Nair, I engaged in spirited discussions with him and fellow students about the potential for using PR methods in the Honduran context. I was intrigued by its relevance to working with women campesinos and convinced that it could be an effective tool for securing data and could be beneficial to them as well, as Fals Borda believes. In developing countries, rural women are often the most marginalized population, and this is true in Honduras. If I could involve them in project design and implementation, I thought I would be more likely to encourage project continuity and at the same time leave them with more personal benefits.

Participatory approaches encourage an examination of existing social structures, and facilitate structural transformation (Hall, 1981). These characteristics are especially critical in developing sustainable programs for rural women who have little access to resources, and limited participation in community development. Since I hoped to ensure that the women would be left with positive outcomes when I left the country, I became even more convinced that participatory research was the most appropriate research method I could employ. The PAR process could be used to assist women in examining their existing realities, and bring about changes in the organizational systems whose purpose it is to provide agricultural information and assistance for their learning.

Initiating My Research

While I was producing an acceptable research proposal, I identified and contacted in-country research collaborators. One of the organizations in the United States with which I had worked previously, Heifer Project International (HPI), had invited my collaboration with them in Honduras. The other collaborator, the Pan-American Agricultural School, Zamorano, was affiliated with Cornell University and had expressed interest in researching rural women's issues. Prior to departing, I identified people to contact in each organization and obtained information from them related to housing, transportation, and about language skills I would need to function effectively. These contacts served as my entreé into the rural communities after I arrived in Honduras.

Arriving in Central America for the first time, at an airport with no lighting after dark, is a memorable experience (well, almost traumatic) for any traveler. We were fortunate to be met by friends, and whisked through customs, only after all luggage was 'thoroughly' inspected. After a short respite for my family and me to adjust to our accommodations, I learned that I would need to arrange my own travel to research sites, and provide for my own translation; I was stymied, but only temporarily.

A person undertaking research in a developing country must always be resourceful and flexible, I reminded myself. Within a few weeks, I dramatically improved my intermediate level Spanish and drained my reserve bank account to acquire a jeep. Transportation in developing countries is erratic once you depart from major highways, so the jeep was a real asset! With the assistance of my collaborators, I identified two remote research sites and was thankful to have made the vehicular investment. The 'Jeepeta' became not only a method of transportation but an important symbol of my willingness to work with local people. I routinely ferried campesinas (women farmers) to larger villages, carried feed bags to research sites, and picked women and children up, en route to meetings.

During the selection of research sites, I focused on identifying as many diverse locations as possible. With a limited amount of time in the country (just seven months), it was important to focus on few sites and learn as much as possible of what was related to the research question, in each site. Ultimately, the criteria that emerged for site selection included access to roads, the length of time the organization had been in community, women's agricultural roles in the community, and type of population and location in the country. Even though the communities I worked with were both in Honduras, a country about the size of Pennsylvania, they were remarkably different and each required a slightly different approach. I knew it was critical for a researcher to be sensitive to local cultural variations, and I discovered that Honduras had many.

About the Research Sites

Rural communities in Honduras have many things in common, like poverty, limited resources, and limited access, which tend to isolate their citizens. At the same time they have those unique characteristics which tend to bring people together. I kept this in mind before and after selection of village sites for my research.

One research community I selected in Southern Honduras, Corralito, is composed primarily of mestizos, people of mixed Indian and Spanish descent. The village is approximately two hours from the Capital City of Tegucigalpa. Typically, people migrate to the city in search of work. Approximately 100 families live in the village of Corralito (little corral). Village buildings consist of a two-room school, constructed fifteen years ago, and staffed with two teachers who instruct grades one to six. A 'pulperia' (small store) in Corralito sells soda, candy, and very basic supplies. Another woman sells candy from her house, but any other food must be grown or purchased in Guinope. There are approximately fifteen houses of adobe and tile construction in the village. Other families live scattered in the hills surrounding Corralito.

There is no church or community building, therefore training or meetings occur in the school or in someone's home. The bus service to Corralito terminated a few years ago due to poor road conditions. The nearest medical facility is in Guinope, a three-hour walk over rough roads. There is one truck in the village, owned by a 'coyote' (a person who sells produce outside the village). Zamorano extensionists had been working in Corralito for approximately two years, in mixed-gender community meetings. I found that Corralito's women did not perceive themselves as being actively involved in agriculture, although every woman interviewed raised small animals, and cultivated some type of home garden. Women in Corralito were strongly influenced by male migration, often becoming single heads of household. Contrary to the next research location I will describe, women also could migrate in search of work, and often did.

The village of Togopala is about one hour by vehicle from LaEsperanza on dirt roads. There is no regular bus service to the community but a truck from the potato cooperative comes through the area almost daily. Togopala includes six buildings, with the largest and best maintained being the church. There is no priest in the village, but a 'Delegado de la Palabra' (Celebrant of the Word) gives mass to the families that attend every Sunday. Other buildings in the village include the 'men's building,' a one-room structure with an earthen floor, that serves as the meeting house for men in the potato cooperative, and for training sessions with Corralito Community Development (CCD).

The 'women's building' is similarly constructed, but split into two rooms. The larger room houses a kindergarten for children of 5 and under, run by two women trained by 'Save the Children'. The smaller room is the 'tienda de consumo' (small store) staffed and run by women in the CCD cooperative. The kitchen, a separate facility constructed of native materials, is staffed by women belonging to a cooperative, who cook and feed children rice and beans. The 'tejadora' (weaving shop) is the third and final building associated with CCD. The remaining building in Togopala is a small storage facility for the men's cooperative. Houses are scattered in the hills surrounding the central village buildings. Togopala, located in the western part of Honduras, is populated by an indigenous group of people, the Lencas.

Heifer Project International entered the Togopala community approximately seven years prior to my arrival, and had single-gender groups working in numerous projects. Women participate in many aspects of production agriculture, including raising and selling crops, raising and milking cows, and cultivating small home gardens. Lencan women wear brightly colored, traditional dresses with hand-woven plaid scarves. And one additional notable contrast to the mestizo women, is that Lencan women wear shoes! The women in Corralito generally wore only flimsy flip-flops, possibly a correlation to their limited involvement in production agriculture.

Initially, I entered each community with a person equivalent to an extension agent from the collaborating organization. We attended a pre-organized community meeting, with men and women present, and I was introduced as someone from Zamorano who wanted to speak with the women about their daily activities. It was important for the men to attend the first session to avoid any suspicion, or concern about their wives attending meetings without them present. Women later confided to me that males were often an obstacle to their participation in organized events. The first few times I visited the villages with the extensionist, we would visit individual women's homes in the morning and invite them to attend an afternoon meeting. I was able to interview and ask questions of individual women during the morning visits, and hold group question and answer sessions in the afternoons.

After I became familiar with where the women lived and inquired as to the best time and location to meet, I arranged most of the remaining village visits on my own. Over the succeeding months I came to know the women, their lives and many issues directly and indirectly related to my research. As we discussed questions from the questionnaire I had developed, the questionnaire evolved till it more closely reflected the women's concerns. The notion of flexibility pervaded the entire participatory research process. Their issues drove the research. In addition to interviewing and observing the women's daily activities, I interviewed the staff and administrators of development organizations providing women's programs, and collected secondary data related to women's access to agricultural information. Approaching the research question from a variety of angles helped to validate the women's responses, and generate new questions.

During the individual and group interviews, a dialogue emerged about women's roles in Honduran culture, and what women might do to improve their status. Honduran culture is enmeshed in machismo, a male-dominated perspective that relegates women to being wives and mothers only, with no need to earn an income or assume independence. Women recognize machismo as an obstacle to their full participation in accessing any type of information. These discussions encouraged women to examine ways to overcome the effects of machismo, and assert their needs.

An interesting aspect of the participatory process I internalized was the growing desire to give something useful and meaningful, back to the women who were cooperating in the research. Each of these women voluntarily offered their precious time to interact with me, providing valuable data, and I felt the need to give something valuable in return. This was something I had *thought* a lot about but now I *felt* the need. Throughout the individual and group discussions, the women told me about the various areas in which they wished to receive training. As part of our developing reciprocal relationship, I then arranged for specialists in the desired areas to accompany me to the research sites to help the women. This aspect of giving was crucial as I sought to develop a trusting, open environment of communication. The women shared their thoughts freely. It enhanced my ability to achieve as much as I did, in a limited period of time.

While working with the Lencan women, I developed a close rapport with many of them, particularly the group leader. We shared many aspects of their struggles to create and expand the group's activities. In these discussions, the women indicated they wanted further training in a variety of areas. Some of these were areas for which I felt capable of providing training.

One such session involved demonstrating how to make the equivalent of play-dough from flour, salt, water, and oil. The women's group had a small kindergarten for village children, and they were responsible for purchasing their own teaching supplies. Purchasing any commercially produced item consumed a large percentage of their meager budget. The necessary items were already in the kitchen area, so I borrowed a small quantity one morning, and involved all the women in creating pliable figures. For many of the women, this was a return to a childhood they never had, as the kindergarten was only a few years old. The joyful expressions on their faces as they molded the damp balls of flour, were priceless. The training sessions I delivered also served to emphasize my commitment to a mutually beneficial relationship with the Lencans. On a number of occasions I simultaneously asked questions while demonstrating techniques in nutrition, composting, and animal care. Their needs were unending.

Certainly the time required for participatory projects is infinitely greater than non-participatory projects. This is a reality that is often underestimated by researchers. I believe that devoting time to developing relationships, along with utilizing the data collected from other sources, ensured my confidence in the quality of the overall responses I received.

What Did I Find Out?

After spending months meeting with the women individually, and in organized weekly meetings, issues began to emerge and were identified as relevant obstacles to their accessing agricultural information. The categories that evolved included: training issues, perceptions of women's work, obstacles working with women, women's access to resources, literacy, and organizational issues. I will detail what I learned about these issues. Each of these areas individually affects women's access to information but they often overlap in women's daily lives.

Training Issues

The *way* training of community or group leaders is handled, the *frequency and quality* of training and *who will participate* are important to how campesino women perceive and receive information. Women's groups (or the organizations they work with) often make the decision as to which individual from the village is selected to receive training in the regional office. This designee becomes important because she becomes the conduit through which information is provided to other members of her group. There can be a number of obstacles that prevent women from receiving information. The woman selected to pass on the information must be highly motivated, capable of attending regional training sessions, and committed to community development rather than simply seeking personal gain. Not only that, but how the women regard her, is important, i.e., with respect, acceptance, and credibility.

Gender *is* an important factor in training. Extensionists generally receive formal training in gender specific topics. Agents who provide agricultural information are generally male, and are trained in topics primarily related to agricultural production. Female extensionists receive training in the traditional assortment of women's topics, such as nutrition and health. Male extensionists are often unaware of women's roles, and routinely bypass women farmers and provide technical information only to males. The gender segregation seen in extensionist training is consistent with and symptomatic of a larger force in Honduran culture, '*el machismo.*' Women are enculturated from an early age to assume lower status positions as homemakers and child care providers, while men are encouraged to work outside the home, and earn an income. This status, maintained by male control of power structures, including development organizations, is difficult to alter even in professional fields. The subtleties of course, intimate that women are of lesser value, and they are thus devalued in the process.

A few organizations are beginning to challenge traditional extensionist training by mandating that both members of an extension team, male and female, attend identical training in certain topics, such as nutrition and agriculture. This 'cross gender training' encourages respect for women's roles among male agents and allows female agents the chance to receive agricultural information that can be transmitted to village women.

Organizations often deliver training in mixed-gender sessions. However, men tend to dominate mixed-gender meetings. Since rural women feel their lower status in Honduran culture, they hesitate to speak in public meetings where men attend. This hesitancy to speak out also affects their desire to interact with extensionists, particularly if they are male. In some organizations, single gender groups, both male and female needs have been incorporated so as to better address women's needs and create a more gender sensitive learning environment. Organizations are also beginning to 'conscientize' extension workers and community leaders about the many important roles women play in the agricultural enterprise and their contributions to Honduran society. These efforts, in addition to programs on self-evaluation, are enabling women to assert their rights to educational resources. If this continues, then women will need continuing opportunities to participate and experience ongoing supportive relationships.

Obstacles to Working with Women

Rural women have numerous home-centered responsibilities that often conflict with their ability to travel to meeting sites, or attend training sessions. Their husbands' control, or lack of support to attend meetings may also restrict them. Organizations that work with women find it necessary to use different strategies to circumvent a husband's lack of support. Sometimes they speak to him directly, confronting him, and asking that he be supportive. They sometimes work through a community member to gain wider support for a specific woman to participate. Linked closely to the issue of male control, is the image that a woman holds of herself.

When a culture marginalizes a woman's contribution, it is not surprising to find that many women have low self-esteem, and feel downtrodden, and unable to muster up the confidence needed to become involved. Some organizations I find, incorporate self-valuation and reflection as well as an examination of gender relationships into their training programs. Women are encouraged to explore alternatives to a male-dominated society. Thus, they are supported as they seek out avenues to increase their participation in knowledge acquisition. Obstacles, such as distance or lack of transportation, become huge factors when women consider the possibility of attending training programs. Small children also present a challenge. Daycare arrangements are rare in rural Honduras, children are often ill, or feelings of uncertainty about leaving them, interfere. These obstacles must be overcome, and training courses arranged in a central location, at regular times, in order to accommodate as many individual schedules and situations as possible. The women also suggested that training be occasionally shifted to a location that is convenient to reach out to women with small children.

Women's Access to Resources

Since rural women find themselves a part of the poorest stratum of Honduran society, they have little access to resources such as land, agricultural inputs, and credit that could improve their status. They experience greater restrictions in attending secondary school than men attend, which consequently reduces their literacy levels. Low literacy affects their ability to read extension materials, and in some cases, to attend training programs. One lack leads to another in domino-like fashion.

Various organizations and women's groups have worked to develop plans of action that propose to provide women with small loans, to lift themselves out of poverty. Rotating funds enable women to purchase land and jump-start small businesses. Fortunately, women pay nominal interest fees to borrow money. They monitor each other in their group for repayment—a supportive measure. Women who are on their way out of poverty not only need access to credit, they need relevant education to manage, and administer funds. A number of organizations do recognize this need and are providing courses that provide the knowledge and skills necessary to manage money.

A woman cannot utilize written materials if she lacks literacy skills. Organizations that recognize this limitation use more graphic materials and simplify texts in order to reach women with useful information. Other organizations offer literacy classes, or establish collaborative linkages with literacy organizations. Government radio programs are also a channel of information for rural women.

Organizational Issues

There is a big difference in the way organizations approach the people. It is a challenge to encourage rural people to involve themselves in development processes. Some distribute free items as incentives to 'buy' people's participation. Others empower rural people to contribute to their own development by facilitating involvement through catalytic approaches. The ability of an extensionist to create or destroy independence and self-reliance, is a determining factor in whether programs continue to operate and flourish after the organization leaves. An increasing number of organizations understand the factors that contribute to building independence in project participants, and effectively orchestrate them. Facilitating people's ability to solve their own problems and create long lasting solutions to community development, requires time and trust among all participants. The women I interviewed also point to the need to 'motivate participants from within' rather than use giveaways to attract involvement.

Only through a participatory approach that results in commitment, can we generate sustainable development, which survives and remains viable after the development organization withdraws. As Fals Borda (1985) noted, '...the intellectual and practical aspirations of all of us were rooted in a single and shared experience...we tested different techniques for creating and communicating knowledge, with the appropriate adjustments being made in attitudes and values.' He concluded that through his research:

'There was a real process of transformation and material and intellectual progress congruent with our personal and institutional aims. This process is still alive, and it has sometimes gone beyond our expectation.' (1985: 11)

Honduras is blessed (or cursed) with hundreds of development organizations. Unfortunately they compete for women's limited free time, and duplicate services that could be shared. Women must choose between training programs that compete for their time. Consequently they may attend those that offer 'acceptable' female subjects rather than face a less comfortable opportunity to acquire agricultural information. It is imperative that organizations explore ways to work together, not only to reduce waste and share precious resources, but also to integrate program offerings and reduce conflicting alternatives. In this way women can receive information not only on family nutrition, for example, but also on raising crops and marketing excess produce.

It is not uncommon for training programs to be guided by funding cycles. When funds expire, programs often terminate. This myopic view of training discourages rural people from investing much energy in short-lived programs. Women in my study voiced the need for *confianza* (trust) in training relationships that take time to evolve. They need to feel that the organization values *their* input and respects *their* needs. Organizations in order to do this must take a more extensive view of program development. Who are the project beneficiaries—the people of the community or the organization?

What Does This All Mean?

What can I tell you from insights I gained from Honduran women campesinos? Women need to feel valued if they are to have the courage to participate in training. The courage can stem from inclusion in designing, implementing, and evaluating processes of development projects. It is imperative to create an environment of trust, using honest and open communication. Organizations have to be genuinely committed to long-term relationships with communities in order to foster women's trust and create the desire to participate in training. Individual practitioners must have the conceptual knowledge about trust building and acquire necessary interpersonal and organizational communication skills to build trusting relationships.

In agreement with scholars I have read, the women indicated that organizations need to change the way they do things and reevaluate women's multi-dimensional roles. Development practitioners must see women not only as wives and mothers, but as agricultural producers and heads of households with important informational needs. They must be exposed to gender sensitive training to expand their personal and professional knowledge of women's roles. Cross-training of male and female practitioners (extensionists) can provide a venue for this. In addition, they need to recognize what problems are evident in gender restricted training. I observed that women prefer to learn in single gender environments until they have gained the self-confidence necessary to function in mixed-gender groups. Organizations that utilize mixed community meetings to maximize limited staff, should consider this learning preference when initiating projects. Both men and women must be comfortable in early training experiences, and be led into mixed gender environments carefully, slowly but surely. New levels of comfort will develop, and ultimately men or women can make their own decisions about participation without regard to gender.

As Korten (1990) suggests, networking and collaborative efforts are mandatory for successful programs. In Honduras, organizations must begin to network more effectively to minimize duplication of efforts, and allow women to actively participate in non-traditional female subjects related to agriculture. While organizations can work toward building independence in all participants to ensure project continuity, women must recognize the need to empower and motivate themselves (and each other) to solve their own problems. This is the only insurance for creating independence and project sustainability.

Rural women in Honduras must face and meet many challenges before they have equal access to agricultural information. But beyond that, they must be a force to renew their own culture, in order to make it more 'woman friendly,' establishing their individual right to be valued human beings. As women become active participants in their personal empowerment, they will acknowledge their individual and collective value. They will recognize their contributions to society, demanding and getting equal access to information and resources. Rural women will not chart their course without risk, but by beginning the ascent to equality, they will gain momentum in reaching their destination. Development organizations must be encouraged to assume a greater role in facilitating this ascent, and supporting women's access to information and resources through programs and government intervention.

References and Select Bibliography

Fals Borda, O. (1985). *Knowledge and People's Power: Lessons with Peasants in Nicaragua, Mexico and Colombia*. New York, NY: New Horizons Press.

Buvinic, M. and **Yudelman, S.** (1990). *Women, Poverty and Progress in the Third World*. New York, NY: Foreign Policy Association.

Chaney, E. and **Lewis, M.** (1985). Headline Series. *Women, Migration, and the Decline of Smallholder Agriculture*. Lansing, MI: Michigan State University Women in Development Series.

Cornwall, A., Guijt, I. and **Wellbourn, A.** (1992). Acknowledging Process: Challenges for Agricultural Research and Extension Methodology. Paper presented at the Beyond Farmer First Conference.   London: International Institute for Environment and Development.

Hall, B. (1981). Participatory Research, Popular Knowledge and Power: A Personal Reflection. *Convergence*, 3, 6–19.

Jiggins, J. (1986). Gender-related Impacts and the Work of the International Agricultural Research Centers. CIGAR Study Paper #17. Washington, DC: The World Bank.

Korten, D. (1990). *Getting to the Twenty-first Century: Voluntary Action and the Global Agenda*. West Hartford, CT: Kumarian Press.

Louden, J. (1988). Incorporating Women into Monitoring and Evaluation in Farming Systems Research and Extension. In *Gender Issues in Farming Systems Research and Extension*. Boulder, CO: Westview Press.

Pretty, J. and **Chambers, R.** (1992). Turning the New Leaf: New Professionalism, Institutions and Policies for Agriculture. Paper for Beyond Farmer First Conference. London: International Institute for Environment and Development.

Safilios-Rothschild, C. (1985). *The Policy Implications of the Roles of Women in Agriculture in Zambia*. New York, NY: The Population Council.

Spens, T. (1986). Studies on Agricultural Extension Involving Women: A Framework for the Analysis of Gender Issues in Agricultural Extension Programs. UNIFEM paper #3. New York, NY: United Nations.

Walker, S. (1990). Innovative Programming for Women in Agricultural Extension: The Case Study of MIDENO Cameroon. Department Working Paper #403. Washington, DC: World Bank Population and Human Resources.

Linking Scientist and Farmer: Insights from a Nepal Experience

Meredith Fowlie

This chapter presents a fresh point of view regarding the values of participatory development. Meredith shares her observations about the partnership between farmers and scientists in Nepal. Over a six month period she lived with a Nepali family and worked with a team of plant breeders who were searching for rice varieties more appropriate to farming in the harsh hill conditions of Nepal.

As an undergraduate student of agriculture studying for six months in Nepal, I find myself on an April evening in a modest kitchen with clay walls and dirt floor. Tired from a day of farming the steep terraced fields of rice and wheat, I seat myself on the floor with the others, ready for dinner. Looking up to accept a plate heaped with steaming rice that is offered to me, I am momentarily struck by the apparent incongruity of my surroundings and perceptions. Growing up in urban Canada, my understanding of life in the 'Third World' had, for the most part, been shaped by television charity campaigns and UNICEF publicity posters. Consequently, I had learned to equate images of unclothed children brushing flies from their wide eyes and mothers squatting before a hearth tending pots of gruel, with destitution and heartache.

But, sentiments of remorse and lament had no place here. I had come to know these wide-eyed children, this young mother, these girls around me. I knew the warmth in this kitchen, the fun we would have teasing the youngest boy, joking about the day's events and then leaving the kitchen to drink our spiced tea under the dusk's emerging constellations. This is not a tragic scene, these are not people to be pitied. While it is true that this life is harder than the one I had left at home, there is a strain of benevolence here that I would be hard pressed to find anywhere else.

A Fresh View of Poverty

So many of these rural communities, which are by western material-ist standards desperately impoverished, possess an intangible, dis-embodied wealth vested both in the indigenous knowledge, local social values, and nurturing patterns of living. It cannot be disputed that there are changes that could be effected, or innovations that could be introduced that could feasibly make these lives healthier, happier, and longer. There remains a pressing need to identify both the nature of these changes and how best to implement them. It is at the same time vitally important that the less tangible sources of wealth in these communities be recognized and allowed to with-stand the mad rush to usher in 'development.'

How we measure poverty affects how we perceive and character-ize development problems, and how we determine which problems are worthy of our efforts to solve them. If we choose to define pov-erty in economic terms exclusively, we will be more inclined to con-ceive of people as mere production inputs, working with capital and other material resources to generate growth in the GNP (Lineberry, 1989). To make the distinction between growth and development, and favor the latter as a goal worth pursuing, is to realize that the objective of development intervention and assistance is not to enhance productivity and/or income generating capacity as an end in itself. Rather, it is to help people gain the knowledge and the capacity to make changes in their socio-cultural, economic, and physical environments so as to improve the quality of their lives.

Thus, *progress* becomes a much more nebulous and subjective concept that defies quantitative measurement, slips between the lines of economic reports, and is affected but not enslaved by markets and profit margins. The recent emphasis on participation in development represents an effort to reorient development towards this veritable conception of progress and betterment.

The Emerging New Development Paradigm

Participatory development, heralded by many as the 'new development paradigm,' appears to have the potential to improve upon the shortcomings of conventional development approaches. Recognizing the capacity of farmers and other local stakeholders to become partners in research and technology development is at the core of this participatory approach. It has emerged in response to a perceived need to make science and development respond more directly to the needs and ideas of those most affected by 'underdevelopment.' Additionally, it aims to fill the void left by neo-liberal, bureaucratic, and market institutions which have failed to adequately deliver and distribute public goods, account for externalities, or satisfy basic needs.

I traveled to Nepal to study participatory development, and more specifically, a participatory rice breeding project in the mid-hill region. All of my previous experience with beneficiary participation in development had been in entirely different circumstances—namely local community projects in the USA and Canada, and I was especially interested to see how a participatory approach could enhance development efforts in an entirely different context. I was profoundly struck by the more intangible assets I found in the communities I encountered. I was wary of the dangers of having the conventional developmentalist approach dismantle some of the more invaluable institutions in these communities, (for example, institutions that preserved a strong sense of family and a more community oriented versus individualist mentality). It is my hope that if community members set the research and development agenda, or at least have a sanctioned place at the discussion table, less conventional ideas about development, and how to achieve it can emerge.

As a student of agriculture and development, I am well acquainted with tales of the missionary-style development of decades past, and an encroaching 'westernization' of the non-west. It is my belief that these are trends that should be reevaluated and in most cases, reversed. In order to do this effectively, fundamental changes need to be made with respect to the philosophy of development and who is defining it.

After working with development practitioners from different disciplines in both the USA and Nepal, it has become clear that 'participatory development' means different things to different people. While critically reconsidering a madcap pursuit of what is conventionally known as 'modernization' in the developing world, and making concerted efforts to seek out alternatives, international development is by no means the solitary engine fueling the movement towards more participatory development. Justifications for making development more participatory can be more essentially pragmatic, than conscientious or ideological.

Arguments for Increased Participation

I have encountered several arguments in defense of increased participation in development while working on development initiatives in both Nepal and the USA. When evaluating these arguments, it is important to remember that a broad range of distinct, though related activities fall under the somewhat ambiguous title 'participation' (Uphoff, 1992). That said, while the justifications I share with you imply varying degrees of participation in varying contexts, it is still useful to think about some important reasons why participation in development can generate increased enthusiasm and support from farmers.

- *Increased farmer participation can help to reorient development toward a more veritable conception of progress and betterment.*

When forces exogenous to a country, or even a community, are directing development, the conceptual direction of development tends to be unilinear and often economic growth-oriented. It is difficult and time consuming for researchers outside a community, to identify what is important to a community and what a community is prepared to sacrifice or change, for the sake of a given development goal or vision. After decades of breeding rice varieties with

Need an insider perspective.

increased yield being almost the exclusive breeding objective, breeders in the more marginal areas of Nepal who were experimenting with a more participatory approach to setting breeding priorities, realized that high yield was, in fact, *not* an appropriate emphasis for programs in the harsher hill conditions. When farmers were consulted, other plant traits such as resistance to cold, cooking quality, and grain color were identified as being among the most important. These priorities were subsequently incorporated into breeding programs, and farmers became more interested and willing to involve themselves with the breeding project, because scientists had listened to them, and their needs were addressed.

So the plant breeders found that increased participation of farmers in their research was critical in identifying what is important to the community. Thus, their concept of progress became more congruent with the farmers' and they reoriented their own research.

- *Farmer participation can improve the efficiency and impact of research.*

There is a substantial contribution to be made by farmers and other stakeholders who have a sophisticated knowledge of their own circumstances, and who have out of necessity had to develop specific skills and habits, to make the most efficient use of available resources. Understanding how households and communities manage their resources, and the factors that determine the trade-offs people make between maximizing short term benefits and sustaining the long term resource base, provides researchers with a sounder basis for action. Farmers (and other resource users) can help researchers better detect and characterize the often subtle complexities of interactions among local social, ecological, and institutional conditions. These are precisely the interactions which inevitably come to bear on the success or failure of newly introduced innovations, especially in resource poor communities.

In the Nepal breeding project, researchers noted significant discrepancies between their approach to experimentation and evaluation, and that of the farmer's. Under their formal research system they sought the most favorable, uniform land to utilize for trials. Farmers, however, in an effort to minimize the risks associated with trying a new variety that could potentially fail, instead chose their poorest land for the initial trial. If the variety performed better than the local one in a stressed environment, then the farmer would be willing to experiment with the variety on their better land, the following year. While such a strategy makes it difficult for researchers to statistically analyze line performances across villages or regions, given the non-uniformity of growing environments, it does reveal the true capacity of a variety to endure harsh conditions. Thus, selected lines will likely be more stable over time or changing conditions.

When participation is used as a tool to enhance the 'client orientation' of research, it is hoped that a higher adoption of the technology can be achieved (deBoef et al., 1996: 7). It seems logical that research which involves local farmers in the identification and solution of problems, will more likely result in research that is more relevant and useful for the community. There is considerable evidence which indicates that community involvement in the planning and implementation of a project, greatly increases the likelihood that the project will be maintained and managed by the community once development professionals leave. This is what *sustainable* agriculture is about, is it not?

- *Increased farmer participation improves the farmer–researcher relationship.*

Weary of past failed development efforts, many scientists are welcoming the idea of a 'cooperative' versus 'dictative' role in development. The new participation paradigm provides an opportunity for scientists to recalibrate the 'scales, measurements, and co-ordinates of perception.' Scientists are given a license to step back and reevaluate their role and potential contribution to development. As one breeder stated: In the past we were doing research on behalf of farmers, making recommendations like a doctor. We must admit that we have failed in that approach...if we involve farmers and gain more success, we can share the credit. If we fail altogether, we can share the blame (Joshi, 1996).

With a high degree of local involvement, a researcher is less likely to misdiagnose the problem and more able to screen out impractical irrelevancies early in the process.

- *Increasing farmer participation makes better use of scarce resources.*

In a more pragmatic vein, some researchers favor participatory approaches because increasing the involvement, participation, and responsibilities of those 'targeted' by development can be a means of shifting costs away from the conventional research system, making more efficient use of limited research resources. When trials are conducted in farmer's fields, more land at research centers is available for other projects; when community members are encouraged to conduct experiments and administer projects on their own, there is less work for extension workers, researchers, etc. Participation is also seen as a means of filling the void left by National Research Institutions, who are increasingly strapped for resources and are thus less inclined to provide services to more marginal, low potential areas, and because of imperfect markers, incapable of signaling the demands of resource poor farmers for research.

- *Farmer participation is a political process.*

Many see participatory development as an instrument to empower people and their access to management and information resources. Although there is much controversy over whether or not true 'empowerment' is likely to result from the administrative process of agriculture development, it seems plausible that a community could be strengthened and enhanced by the organizations or cooperative relationships in the course of a participatory development project. An individual's *real* or perceived role in development could become more viable through involvement in all stages of the development process, and thus have an empowering influence. The lack of respect and cooperation that so often plagues a farmer–researcher relationship inevitably undermines development efforts. As a result, the potential for local contribution to problem identification and solution is under-explored and researchers are prone to misunderstanding and perhaps resenting those very farmers they are presumably working to assist.

Outcomes of Participatory Research

Whether or not a more participatory approach can spawn respect and genuine cooperation between farmer and researcher remains to be seen. In theory, by treating farmers' innovative and experimental capacity as a form of inquiry in itself, research ideally would become a process of mutual learning (de Boef et al., 1996). Instead of a unidirectional transfer of knowledge 'downward,' insights and ideas are exchanged laterally and bothways, implying cooperation and mutual respect between farmer and researcher.

In the final analysis, it is hoped that participatory development can address issues of equity and maldistribution of the benefits of development. It has often been said that *the* overriding problem is not so much a shortage of resources, but rather who has access or rights to which resources. The pursuit of every development goal brings with it both costs and benefits. If the intended beneficiary for a given project is an entire community, any social stratification within that community will likely assure that some groups will benefit, while others will incur costs. Since poorer members of a community are often less likely to have their voices heard, it is often poor farmers who suffer the consequences of development in Less Developed Countries (LDC) rural development initiatives. Participatory development broadens the competency requirements of a researcher to include facilitation skills—adeptness in alliance-making, using language more effectively, making gender analyses, organizing groups, catalyzing dialogue, and resolving conflicts between individuals in groups. Thus, they can ensure that everyone's needs are considered and accommodated in the best way possible (Vernooy, 1996).

Participatory development is gaining increased support, from the smallest local NGO to the World Bank and the FAO. Today, several decades after participation first gained acceptance as a viable and favorable approach to rural development, we continue to struggle with fundamental questions:

- How to enlist this participation,
- Who and when to enlist and to what degree,
- How to mainstream these methods, and
- How to extrapolate from available case studies.

As with any new mode of research, participatory development remains exploratory in many respects even though volumes of articulate policy delineations and justifications have evolved. Although methodologies are quickly evolving and gaining momentum, the pivotal question remains, 'How *do* we do it?'

I think that people who are actively interested in issues of rural development are eager to share and compare experiences. As a student, I have been asked what I have gained from time spent studying the strengths and limitations of participatory agriculture development in Nepal. While in Nepal, I had no institutional mandates to adhere to, no project blueprints to follow, no specific issues to address: I was there to bring ideas *out* of people, not *to* them. Even though the attitudes and ideas expressed herein may be vitiated because of being perceived as the naiveté or inexperience of youth, it is my hope that my observations, insights, and conceptions are of value to development practitioners who are in a position to facilitate participatory communication. Facilitating linkages between farmers and agricultural scientists is an extremely important accomplishment, enabling capacity building and empowerment.

Experiencing the Invisible Communication Barriers

My first months in Nepal were spent living at the nation's university in a women's student hostel, where I worked on my Nepali language skills and attended classes which I hoped would better orient me to this new place. I had been at the school barely a week when a young student there (who ultimately became a good friend) approached me with a question. He sought me out because he had heard that I was trained as a plant breeder. He was interested in talking to me about a theory he had been contemplating while studying plant evolution in his biology class. He was thinking about the mechanisms by which plants adapt to changes in their environment and how they have the capacity to adjust when they are planted in foreign environments. He had been playing around with this idea in his own rice fields. When he took a stunted, low yielding plant from his poor land and planted it in better soil, he noted that after a few generations, the descendants of that plant were healthy and strong. If he took one of these stalwart descendants and returned it to its humble origins, it was able to produce healthier offspring only for a few generations; ultimately, later progeny would start to resemble the sickly, stubby plants that surrounded them.

'Its all in the genes, yes?', asked Baboram, giggling at the use of the word 'gene' as he gestured towards his own 'jeans.' 'Yes, pretty much,' I replied, laughing, 'but, as you were noticing with your great rice experiment,' (Baboram started to laugh wholeheartedly, clearly indicating that he did not think his paddy exercise merited the title 'experiment,') 'what's important is how the genes "interact with the environment".' My comment proved to be a good segue to more thoroughly discuss Baboram's theory. He became very excited and said that this indeed was exactly what he had noticed about his rice plants.

Baboram was an exceptional individual. I had been told that his family had worked tremendously hard to be able to send him to school, and that his academic achievements were highly commendable. He was an 'untouchable' and was the first from his village to ever attend college. Initially, I did not appreciate the significance of his low caste ranking since I had been told when I arrived in Nepal that the caste system had been abolished by the current king and was just a relic of the past. It did not take long, however, to realize that the caste system continues to permeate every facet of Nepali society, albeit subtly. As I got to know him better, it became clear that Baboram continued to carry with him heavy feelings of shame and inadequacy as a consequence of his caste.

He commented sheepishly that when he went home to his village, he often felt like a rice plant that had been transplanted into finer, richer soil. Taking the metaphor one step further, he postulated that this same phenomena could explain why Americans were 'more intelligent' than Nepalis. It was his understanding that Nepal was very old and tired, while America was very new. When Nepalis went over to America, their genes seemed to improve as they adapted to their new surroundings, so that even Nepalis can 'think like Americans' eventually, although upon returning to Nepal, they quickly 'regress' back to where they started.

I did not know how to respond. At a loss as to how I could convincingly illustrate that his theory was entirely unfounded, and that our respective intellectual capacities could not be quantitatively distinguished, I made an attempt at rehearsing a 'nurture versus nature' argument, or pointing out that evolution could be viewed as dynamic versus progressive and linear, but I found myself almost reinforcing his point in my attempt to disprove it. Because Baboram was so poor, and because our respective knowledge bases were so different, I found myself resorting to the 'just believe me when I say…' in an effort to have Baboram adopt my point of view, and to believe and understand that Nepalis are no less intelligent than Americans in any sense of the word, only different with different resources, opportunities, and limitations. In essence, I was contradicting myself by asking him to believe that I was right and he was wrong 'because I said' that any one person cannot be deemed to be more intelligent strictly by virtue of birth.

This would not be the last time I would try and talk my Nepali counterparts out of the notion that the Nepali intellect was biologically inferior to a western mind. One morning I was reading with my Nepali women friends who were studying anthropology at the university. My Nepalese was slowly improving, and I was always eager to practice my new skill of making sounds out of the strange characters on the page. Looking over Mandeira's shoulder, I slowly sounded out words printed under a steeply sloping linear graph in her anthropology textbook. Ever so often I would come across English words in parentheses such as 'Caucasian' or 'Negroid,' so I became curious as to what this graph was illustrating. 'It demonstrates the relationship between race and cranium capacity,' explained Mandeira, 'you are up here at the top and I am down there at the bottom,' she added, only half joking. Once again, I was consumed with the urgent need to disprove the implication of this textbook convincingly and absolutely. But, in doing so, I was virtually confirming the principle I was claiming to contradict.

'You have to realize this is entirely unfounded,' I stammered. But with no texts or graphs of my own to combat an ingrained belief in her own inferiority, I suspect that my arguments sounded hollow and patronizing.

The two aforementioned incidents illustrate a serious intercultural communication problem that can undermine both farmer–researcher and intercultural researcher–researcher relationships to varying degrees. The 'disempowerment' or 'disenfranchisement' of beneficiaries/participants, is no small hurdle in participatory development. Even if an extension infrastructure is in place, and all researchers, administrators, and scientists are in favor of a participatory approach, with ears open and pencils poised, farmers or local stakeholders may still feel that they are in a subordinate or subservient position to the project agents. Facilitating quality community participation will be unbelievably difficult, if not impossible.

On more than one occasion, I found that my credibility was pre-established because of my Canadian passport and American diploma. This is a daunting position to be in, and not one that is conducive to the type of communication needed for building partnerships and linkages between foreign scientists, local scientists, and local farmers. It seems ironic that after spending years at school, working to equip myself with skills and knowledge that would help me to acquire content credibility and grounds for having my voice heard, I would find my own 'origins' a barrier to communicating. One of the most frustrating elements of working in Nepal was to have to continually convince people that they were overestimating my credentials, i.e. passport and diploma, as indicative of my capacity to understand and ameliorate their circumstances. Senior breeders would ask my opinion on line selections, administrators would inquire as to how their programs should be restructured, farmers would ask what I thought of their field. I was, after all, a student seeking to learn from them.

Finally, I decided the only way to convince my counterparts of the realities, and perhaps limitations, of my abilities would be to work alongside them in the fields. I spent a number of days preparing seed beds, sowing seed, etc. as I learned about how difficult it really is to farm the steep terraced rice and wheat fields. My companions observed, with great amusement I might add, just how little I could do. I had to be taught everything from how to hold a farm implement, to what to do with it and why. It made both of us painfully aware of the limited application of the knowledge I had to offer, and demonstrated to them that I could learn a lot more from them than they thought in the beginning. While five days of hoeing is by no means sufficient time to understand a farmer's perspective, reversing the roles, so to speak, if only for a short time was an effective means of altering the dynamic of my relationship with the farmers and researchers. We reached a mutual understanding and respect for each other's strengths and knowledge.

In retrospect, I think my student disposition was invaluable in terms of facilitating working relationships with the people I met. I had the luxury of following no one's agenda but my own. I was not there to promote or affect or change anything. But, I was also painfully aware of my own ignorance. Being a student, I felt comfortable admitting it, even drawing attention to it in the interest of creating a dynamic that facilitated *mutual learning*.

My Dialogue with the Scientists

I had the privilege of working with some of Nepal's most talented and committed scientists in the course of my research on participatory plant breeding. They went out of their way to include me in different facets of the project and to talk at length about the philosophy of the approach, the problems they had encountered, the successes they had enjoyed.

One afternoon, upon returning to the research station after a day of informal farmer group interviews in fields and tea shops around the area, I began talking with two of the researchers of whom I had grown especially fond. A socio-economist and a plant breeder, both had traveled to the UK to complete their studies. Both were unique in their commitment to the more marginal mid-hills of Nepal where the potential for large 'breakthroughs' in yield or income generation capacity were unlikely. But the real need for smaller, location specific innovations in production technology or resource conservation practices was great.

That day we had spent many hours speaking with small groups of farmers about what varieties they were growing and what problems they were experiencing in the field. But we also heard who was getting married next week, who was ill in the village, and how the business at the local guesthouse was faring. Since they regularly made farmer field visits, my companions had established a warm rapport with the farmers of the village. Once I was identified as a visiting student interested in learning more about farmer participation in agriculture research, we were welcomed as old friends in every house we visited.

As we reflected on the day's events that afternoon, I remarked on how diverse the farmers' preferences really were. Every farmer's field differed with respect to steepness and aspect of slope, climate, soil type, access to water, disease stress, etc. When conducting farmer field trials to test new varieties, it was not unusual to find that a variety that had flourished in one field was unable to yield successfully in a field no more than 100 meters away. Economic circumstances varied, as did social customs, and personal preferences. With the smallest of areas containing so many different farming systems, it is difficult to carry out on-station research that directly addresses the needs of large numbers of the areas' farmers. The researchers at the station expressed great frustration with the current research climate that served only to exacerbate their difficulties.

A genuine commitment to farmers' needs reflects a radical redefinition of scientific accomplishment. Inherent in participatory development, at least in the context of crop variety improvement, is the conviction that scientific achievement should be marked in terms of real applicability and utility—numbers of acres planted and number of farmers adopting those varieties they helped to develop. This contradicts the more conventional measure of scientific achievement marked by scientific papers published or genetic restraints transcended under laboratory conditions. In a scientific milieu that continues to look for success in petri dishes and chi-square tests, realizing that your time is better spent in a farmer's field and then acting accordingly, is not always feasible. The researchers with whom I was working considered themselves fortunate to be working at an institution that formally recognized the importance of off-station research and which had worked to establish extension infrastructure and human support staff to make participatory development more feasible. However, they admitted that emphasis continues to weigh heavy on published papers and protocol. Thus, because of conventional expectations, researchers were repeatedly frustrated by their inability to resolve the social distance between farmer and researcher.

This issue of how scientists in developing nations grapple with a science and scientific institutions that were shaped by an environment other than their own, is a complicated one. It seems there are many forces acting to dispose LDC scientists to the unconditional acceptance of western scientific practices and rationality. Patents, textbooks, journals, and incentive structures reinforce the message that western scientific principles are synonymous with objective rationality, employing western methods leads to progress, and emulating western academic institutions amounts to education. Having been excluded in the past from world science, Third World scientists feel a sense of urgency in terms of joining in and sharing its fruits versus critically assessing what it is founded upon and what it has to offer.

The researchers with whom I was working had made personal commitments to making research more participatory and were endeavoring to change the nature of their relationship with farmers and with science to support this conviction. They are aware of the limitations of conventional scientific research methodology that is reductionist in nature and often assumes a degree of control and circumstantial homogeneity that cannot be practically obtained in experimentation in the mid-hills of Nepal. Upon reconciling themselves to the inconsistencies between the station and farmers' field conditions that routinely rendered on-station technology generation wholly impractical, the scientists began to consider new approaches that took local limitations and location specific needs into consideration. Now, they are committed in principle to placing less emphasis on formal protocols of scientific methods and more on farmer testing and evaluation. Whether or not they will be able to do this in practice seems to depend to a great extent on the system of rewards, incentives, and opportunities they face.

Enlisting genuine farmer participation has the potential to change the face of agricultural science and research. It implies working at a farmer's pace. It means a loss of clarity, a loss of control, a loss of 'professionalism' in the traditional sense. Science becomes much more nebulous and vague when a scientist capitulates a clean orderly laboratory for a farmer's field. Foregoing quantitative, systematic variables for an untidy array of hard-to-manipulate farmer criteria, and relinquishing the license to have absolute control over the research by allowing farmers to participate, even dominate the experimentation process, is risky. The scientist must be prepared to part with ownership of innovations and projects at an early stage, thereby forsaking the road toward *the* answer in favor of innumerable paths that might or might not lead to less dramatic 'eurekas.' If research administrators and directors do not initiate these changes by altering incentive structures and institutionalized professional rewards, individual researchers can hardly be expected to go out on their own when they depend on their professional reputation and credentials for their livelihood and that of their families.

When I asked the researchers how one would begin to make fundamental changes in scientific protocol or research incentives, no one had an answer. 'The problem here,' remarked a wellspoken Nepali socio-economist, 'begins with how we are educated.' He went on to explain that Nepali students are conditioned to adhere to protocol at all costs. Critical thinking is under-emphasized to the point of being discouraged. Questions asked in a Nepali classroom are for clarification only. He ended by saying: The first thing I do every day is to recite religious mantras in Hindi, a language that is not my own. Although I barely know the meaning of the words I repeat so seriously every day, this does not matter. It is the act of repeating them that assures me that I have done a good thing, even if on a tired day I do it without thinking.

All of the Nepali researchers who had gone abroad to study remarked that they had found that the approach to learning and knowledge procurement in general was markedly different. 'You are taught in Nepal to swallow science whole,' one explained. When one has been conditioned to believe that no aspect of the science we inherit is up for debate, how likely is it that one would feel justified in modifying how science is practiced or interpreted? If trained Nepali scientists feel sufficiently disenfranchised such that their own intuition is insufficient ground to reconstruct the methods and conceptions of science, how could the ideas and perspectives of illiterate farmers ever be expected to incite such changes?

Striking a Balance

R. Chamber's 1993 book, *Challenging the Professions*, was intended to help development practitioners come to terms with what was termed the 'new development paradigm.' In it, he advocates 'learning to unlearn,' 'reverse(ing) the values, roles and power relations of normal professionalism,' and turning science 'on its head.' Although Chambers' conceptualization of the ideological and practical manifestations of this new approach/revolution is both exciting and encouraging, one must be wary of investing too much confidence in the capacity of farmers and indigenous knowledge to solve the problems currently plaguing LDC agriculture. Indeed, the expectation that research can be reoriented to deliver innovations appropriate to the needs of both individual farmers and a larger system through participation alone is unrealistic. Past non-successes of development, especially in more marginal, risk-prone rural environments might seem to indicate that researchers do not know best, but this does not by default imply that farmers have all the answers. While there is reason to believe that development can be made more equitable, sustainable, and effective via considerable behavioral changes on the part of researchers and farmers both, perhaps even a complete role reversal in some respects, both parties have valuable contributions to make.

Perhaps the most invaluable capacity a scientist can bring to the development process is her/his ability and freedom to innovate. He/she keeps in mind that farmers have a wealth of knowledge regarding their local circumstances that is valuable. Scientists have been exposed to a wealth of knowledge about innovative potentials and principles within their discipline, that farmers have not. Indeed, a scientist's ability to conduct research falls outside of the practical realm of farmers. They have access to a wide range of technical options, innovative possibilities, and refined experimental methods, and the insight to provide the theoretically appropriate innovations for the local environment. This makes their involvement in development mandatory, and their partnership with farmers vital.

In short, a scientist's real contribution in participatory development is not to know what is best for farmers, but in being familiar with what the known options are. Instead of focusing on fine tuning a limited number of products and verifying them on selected sites, a scientist would aim to develop a number of options that could feasibly ameliorate farmers' problems. Instead of final recommendations, a research station can provide a basket of suggested prototypes and allow farmers to identify the real constraints of the theoretical solutions suggested by researchers or identify additional options. This approach requires that researchers get a firm grasp on what clients need and want from the outset, and that scientists are prepared to part with technologies earlier (Ashby, 1990). It also implies that both the farmer and the scientist feel comfortable using science as a tool.

Participatory development is unique in its capacity to address some of the less tangible issues that previous development approaches have tended to overlook. The key ingredient that makes this possible is flexibility.

The course and timing of community efforts to organize and the appropriateness of a particular technology at a particular time are not predictable and therefore not amenable to a master plan approach.

If participatory development partnerships between scientists and farmers are going to work, researchers must be wary of becoming preoccupied with the 'method' and oblivious to the outcomes. As

Costanza (1991: 23) warns: We must…avoid being a person with a hammer to whom everything looks like a nail. Rather we should consider the task, evaluate existing tools, abilities to handle the job and design new ones if the existing tools are ineffective.

The inability of some indigenous knowledge systems to accommodate changing circumstances begs the introduction of ideas and innovations from the outside, such as those offered throughout this book. But, remember that a development facilitator's role is highly 'context dependent,' requiring a sensitive awareness but without clear objectives or a blueprint of one's own. Intuitively, it seems that without a genuine feeling of partnership—a step beyond mutual respect—any communication which can be facilitated between farmers and scientists will be little more than a cordial and tokenistic act of diplomacy.

I do acknowledge that my own bias is toward the more political, democratization justifications for participatory development, rather than the more pragmatic, utilitarian rationale. The challenge is to forge partnerships that produce sustainable progress, not only toward more appropriate agricultural practices but also toward greater capacity of the community to continue to grow, transform, and renew.

References and Select Bibliography

Ashby, J.A. (1990). *Evaluating Technology with Farmers: A Handbook*. Cali, Colombia: CIAT.

Chambers, R. (1993). *Challenging the Professions: Frontiers for Rural Development*. London: Intermediate Technology Publications.

Costanza, R. (1991). *Ecological Economics: The Science and Management of Sustainability*. New York, NY: Columbia University Press.

deBoef, W.S., Louwaars, N.P. and Almekinders, C.J.M. (1996). Methodology Issues in Strengthening Farmers' Research and Technology Development. Wageningen Netherlands: DLO Centre for Plant Breeding and Reproduction Research.

Joshi, K.D. (1996). Addressing Diversity through Farmer Participatory Testing and Dissemination Approach, a Case Study. Nepal: LARC Paper

Lineberry, W.P. (1989). *Assessing Participatory Development*. Boulder, CO: Westview Press.

Uphoff, N. (1992). *Learning from Gal Oya: Possibilities for Participatory Development and Post-Newtonian Social Science*. Ithaca, NY: Cornell University Press.

Vernooy, R. (1996). *Do you know the python? Moving Forward on the Participatory Research Methodology Development Path*. Ottawa: IDRC.

11

Participatory Use of Economic Indicators

Josh Galper

This chapter presents a rarely expressed position about developing and using statistics for participatory community organization and decision-making. Josh suggests that learning to use statistics can be an empowering force for community members. He shows the advantage of understanding and using statistics for communicating the needs of the community. Josh provides a practical reference for practitioners of participatory community work to engage in the collection and publication of statistics. Written with the assumption that for many people, numbers are not a beloved subject, specific examples are given of community development statistic gathering efforts and methods of presentation, and some guidelines to assist the participatory community development facilitator begin the statistic development process.

People commonly rely on statistical data for understanding the needs of their community and making important decisions. It is also common to find people confused and intimidated by the way 'experts' use statistics. It isn't unusual to find people who can potentially contribute a lot to community development, 'turned off' and 'tuned-out' because of an innate fear of numbers and the way they are used. The idea that statistics can be the tool for empowering community residents is somewhat revolutionary.

While the popular notion that statistics is the realm of academics, economists, and pollsters is pervasive, a new generation of community developers are changing views and community action, by helping indigenous leaders become 'stats' literate. This is happening through participatory community activity that can result in public policy advocacy or in a data base for improving community services and institutions. But, if this empowering/literacy development process is to come about, facilitators must find community members who are willing to become a partner in generating useful statistics through a shared process of participation. How does the community development practitioner facilitate this process of learning and action?

Statistics and Participatory Community Activity

Statistics is popularly conceived of as part of the realm of academics, economists, and pollsters. At the same time the idea that community participation in research consists of 'qualitatively-based' activities such as art, video, or the recording of oral histories has dominated the thinking of the development set. Commonly, quantitative researchers discredit qualitative methods in theory building and practice.

Together, the combination of participatory community action and employing the descriptive power of statistics can be an avenue for empowering community members who aspire to develop tools for public policy advocacy. As partners in such development activities as Participatory Rural Appraisals (PAR), community members can have a stronger (more equal) voice with a research team, if their own understanding of research process and methods is greater. And, it is entirely possible to develop these understandings.

Why is Understanding Statistics Important?

Developing statistics builds self-confidence in a group's ability to define themselves and their communities to both internal and external viewers. Internally, the process of self-definition encourages recognition of internal competency and self-respect. Regular repetition of the statistic over the time of the collection gives the community reference points to track its progress in an area. Externally, as a recognized source of information the group with the statistic becomes a resource for journalists and others interested in information. As statistics have an unusual place in most decision-making processes, the collection of statistics can enter participants into a level of public discussion which is normally the exclusive realm of the power holders.

As a process, participatory development of statistics bears many similarities to other participatory processes. The collection of statistics *is discovering information*, or research, so the first question is deciding what information is important. A *method* is necessary to uncover the desired information. A process is then undertaken in order to carry out the discovery of information. *Analysis* is required to sort through the information collected. *Presentation* is the final stage.

The use of statistics has not been widely used by participatory community workers because somehow they have gotten the idea that numbers, an inappropriate subject matter for a community, are beyond their grasp. Rarely do they see that developing a capacity to use statistics can be empowering. In fact, statistics are ideal for participatory community work; they can be gathered to suit specific local needs and a substantial number of participants can be involved in the gathering process. There are no *rules* about what a statistic is, aside from what numbers can do to make a problem intuitively clear. But, there are rules for how to collect statistics so as to insure their accuracy and bring reliable results from using them.

UNICEF efforts to develop participatory community statistic gathering activity found that there is no lack of capable people in any economic or social class who can handle the task. Probably the most important prerequisite for involving people is their level of self-confidence, which can be strengthened through their participation. The final result of a participatory project should be self-actualization and self-affirmation of community residents and the empowerment of the community to organize, analyze, and publicize local issues. When the community itself enters into a conversation about their control over future community issues, then expanding internal group confidence and technical skills define the reason for capacity building.

What are Statistics?

Statistical data are facts which can be defined in *qualitative* or *quantitative* terms. This information can be collected, analyzed, interpreted, and presented. Statistical methods can be either descriptive or inferential. Statistical descriptions assist our understanding of a current or historical phenomenon. This may be information on how many women bear their children in hospitals, how many potholes there are in a mile of highway, or how many people use public transportation on a daily basis. From these data we make inferences which assist us in drawing conclusions about a wider population. Using data gathered from a small sample, such as, which candidate is expected to win an election, we can project to a larger area, for example, we can speculate that the candidate would win an entire state. Statistics, like video production or collecting oral histories, exist to tell a story, publicize a fact, compare a local situation to a larger one, or compare a local situation at one time to the same situation at another time.

Statistics are built by asking a question about a particular subject and applying that question to a sample of a population, geographical area or physical location. Door-to-door surveys (also called household or standard of living surveys) for example, are effective in measuring a living condition among a group of people working or living in the same location. Street surveys are popular in determining location characteristics such as the number of businesses in a neighborhood. Information collected from fire departments or civic organizations provides other statistics on local socio-economic conditions. Whatever the objective, the first step in developing a statistic is the *collection of a consistent and comparable set of facts* from a broad sample of people. The number of responses to a question and the type of response made, is the statistic, i.e., how many 'yeses' or 'nos.'

Statistics do not have to be an answer to a 'yes' or 'no' question. But, in fact 'yes/no' information often produces the strongest statistics because it may indicate what percentage of people support one option over another, or believe that one problem in a community warrants more immediate attention than another. This information can be graphed, charted, and publicized as easily as the number of potholes on a road. For example, in a decision regarding an old factory, let us assume:

- 43 percent of a survey's respondents believe that turning the unused factory into a playground is the best solution.
- 23 percent believe that a purchaser should be found for the land.
- 17 percent feel that nothing should be done.
- 17 percent did not have an opinion.

This information would provide useful information for a participatory community development group who wanted to redevelop the abandoned industrial site, for journalists interested in community input for a story, or for politicians who valued community input into their decision-making processes.

Statistics are different from the products of qualitative research. Statistics are not the 'telling of stories with emotion' as you can do with more in-depth information. But, statistics should in no way replace the oral recounting of histories nor the expression of emotion a group may have about a living situation. Rather, statistics complement qualitative data and support or retell the story in a more appropriate format for people outside the community and help to make comparisons with other stories of the same type. A community project that uses statistics should be aware that the results will differ from those from qualitative work. Declaring that 32 percent of households in a locality are without running water is *a fact*. Discussing the problems associated with a lack of running water is a *story*. The two both have a place in creating a community's awareness and telling their story to others.

Statistics collected repeatedly over a period of time in the same locality are called a *time series*. This information becomes valuable in charting changes in a community and making comparisons. Often, time series are used to chart the effects of an intervention over time, for example, a public agency's spending on infrastructure in a region and clean, repaired sidewalks. Some statistics may not have a clear correlation with an intervention program, or may in fact show a negative relationship. In this case either an intervention had no effect, had an effect for a short time then wore off, or had an effect but other factors were more pressing on the situation. While cause and effect relationships are difficult to prove, the collection of a statistic over time opens the avenue for considering comparisons.

The Uses of Statistics

Two traditional uses of statistics are *advocacy* and *planning.* Statistics can be used to develop resources for communities to enter into decision-making processes with valuable information. They can also involve a community in discovering or proving certain realities about the place in which they live. While not an exact science, statistics are useful as approximations of a reality when the reality cannot be fully known.

Statistics are a powerful tool for advocacy in public and private decision-making. While the inordinate leverage statistics seem to have in this arena may or may not be appropriate, the fact should be recognized and treated accordingly. If I prove with a statistic, that 65 percent of the houses in a neighborhood have insufficient trash collection, that is likely to be heard in City Hall. City Hall may do their own survey and may identify the figure as only 55 percent. Some of this difference will depend on the definition of insufficiency used by each group. However, the initial statistic will be the start of a discussion and would likely encourage City Hall to take positive action to prove or deny the findings. City Hall may have previously estimated statistics for city-wide planning purposes, and may find that their estimates were incorrect, leading to an improvement in local trash collection. Statistics are listened to at times when the telling of a story is insufficient to stir public and political opinion.

Statistics affect individuals for the same reasons that they affect institutions like a City Hall. When a community discovers that its residents are three times more likely to be illiterate than other city residents, local activists may be inspired to initiate literacy programs. Presenting statistics in terms of risk is more likely to be intuitively understood and to provoke reaction, than is a statistic alone. Aside from showing expected or unexpected results, statistics serve as a research tool that can greatly assist communities in planning for their needs.

Statistics can be used to compare the situation of one group to another group. Recently I learned that a leader of a Brazilian favela community organization had substantial data on his community. These data have been compared to the last census to show the position of the residents of the favela in relation to that of other city residents in terms of wages, health standards, education, and the like. The important argument for the favela leader is his confirmation of the location of his group's statistics in relation to the statistics of the residents of the surrounding environment. Publicizing these differences often provokes a response which leads to raising a substandard statistic up to a local or regional average.

Statistics in most cases are a means of showing a fact in an easily understandable format. This format lends itself to publicity, which most agencies involved in social or economic development rely on in some form. Statistics are short, to the point, and can be repeated in a number of contexts. They can be compared, as noted in the case of the favela, with other statistics to show comparisons in written form or in graphs. Posters can be made publicizing the statistic as a measure of organization and advocacy. Generally a viewer can absorb statistical information from graphs more readily than from a table of numbers or a paragraph of text (see Figures 11.1 and 11.2).

Figure 11.1: Bar Chart

Income Distribution in Altec County

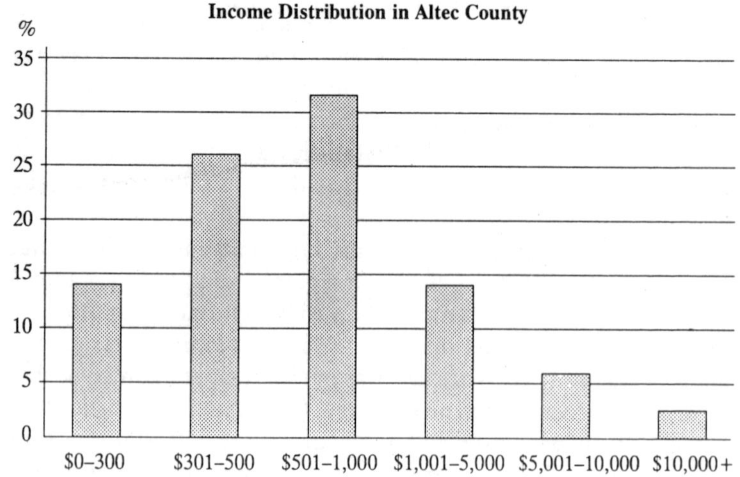

Source: Community Group Survey

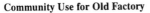

Figure 11.2: Pie Chart

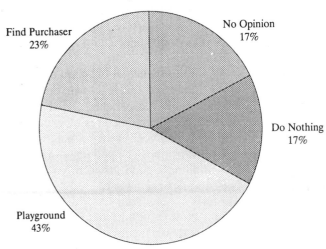

Community Use for Old Factory

Source: Community Group Survey

Guidelines for the Development of Successful Statistics

The first stage in developing a statistic is deciding what is important. A good hint is to focus when people say, 'everybody knows it's true but nobody does anything about it.' In an area where the focus is on how people live, statistics should provide support for defining qualitatively known conditions. Feedback throughout the entire process should be regular and should allow correction for unexpected conditions or potential errors. Development of a strong systematic method for data gathering is vital for arriving at strong conclusions and having confidence in your results. An indicator is only accepted as valid if the listener has faith in the presenter, and the method the presenter used to collect the data. Your method can be personal; many methods are developed with particular situations in mind. If a previous method lends itself to inappropriate results in your context, plan an alternative. While useful for comparing different communities, a previous method may inaccurately reflect a condition in your community.

A nonprofit concern in Sao Paulo, Brazil recently developed an extensive list of how to recognize a good government and techniques for organizing the information. While some items may be appropriate for use in other cities, other items may need some adjustment. When it is not necessary to compare the same item between different localities, individual factors should determine what is meaningful. In many states in the USA, where part-time employment is growing at the expense of full-time employment, a useful statistic is not the number of jobs in a town, but the number of full-time and part-time employed persons. Depending on how this information is viewed, conflicting pictures of a local economy emerge. There is an old story that goes like this: A statistician and a politician are having a conversation. The politician says 'I've got to show my public that I'm doing a good job. Can you tell me how many people have gotten work since I was elected three years ago?' The statistician thinks for a minute, then says, 'Sure, how about 18 percent? Come back tomorrow and I'll have it ready.'

The moral of the story is that statistics are arbitrary and can be manipulated. By using one set of numbers, one set of results will be produced; another set of numbers can change the results drastically. By deciding early on a methodology of your own design or following a previous work, you can assure authentic, reliable and believable results.

Statistics must be collected in a consistent manner to be reliable. While a standardized questionnaire may be used, asking the same questions of every person who enters a train station on a given day, the format for collecting the information varies. Whatever the method chosen should be made known along with the results, to make the finding more credible to the reader. It isn't always necessary to conduct a survey because statistics may already be available. For example, statistics on crime may be available at a police station, or birth and death information can be obtained from local hospitals. Community members may be the best source of help for knowing where to find statistical information, and playing an active part in gathering the data.

The authenticity of your work is vital for the development and use of your statistic. The simpler a statistic, the more forceful its impact. If anyone has doubts they can readily reproduce your study with your methodology, and verify your conclusions if your study is easily understood. In the story about the politician and the statistician, the politician may run into problems because the authenticity of his data may be in question. The method used to calculate the statistics may rely on obscure or out of date information, or the method may be so complicated as to be unable to be reproduced. These difficulties decrease confidence in your information.

Assumptions Made by the Researcher

Assumptions are an integral part in the collection of statistics, and you should be honest about the assumptions you hold before entering what is to be viewed as a potentially impartial work. In many cases, your assumptions will be different from the assumptions of your community cooperators. Insofar as possible, their perspectives are to be taken into account. They may not agree with the assumptions you made in order to collect the data, but by explaining and discussing your reasons with them and presenting the results as impartially as possible, confidence in the reliability of your basic results will build. The most contested statistics are based on assumptions held by limited segments of the population, or by a biased researcher.

When collecting data in a setting where it will not be possible to interview the entire population, a random selection is important to eliminate biases based around location, ethnicity, or income group. The more random a selection, the more likely it is that your results will represent the actual condition of the entire population. It is rarely likely that by selecting a random population you will identify without a doubt the actual condition of a total population, but you will probably come close. Random selections are also important to improve outside confidence in results, avoiding the criticism of bias—you didn't just ask your friends for opinions.

A random selection is also known as a sample. After answering a question for a large enough sample to be considered representative of the population at large, a statistic is arrived at which, we assume, represents the total population. In the case of candidates for an election, the question is, which candidate will get what percent of the votes. The sample is a group of randomly selected people who will vote in the election. If the sample is large enough the predicted results will be identical to the actual results. If the sample is too small or respondents all have a known bias (all registered with some political party, for example, in a survey on presidential candidate preferences), the survey results may not accurately represent the actual condition.

Presenting Findings of Research

The presentation of information needs to be professional. It may be that inviting a journalist to publish the information is a good strategy, as is printing up fliers and distributing them to a target audience. Bright colors are often used to emphasize parts of a graphic so as to draw attention to a particular fact. Pictures of familiar items with captioned statistics tell a story while publicizing your fact in a comfortable setting. Figures 11.1, 11.2 and 11.3 present some regularly used ways to present statistics. Note the important elements of each graph: a title for the graph, well-labeled numbers or percentages, a title for each item, and a source for the information.

Indicators that Practitioners of Community Development Can Collect and Use

A wide variety of statistics are currently in use by local, state, national, and international agencies to categorize and define issues which confront them. The following list gives some ideas of statistics that are easy to collect and publicize at the community level. For any statistic that a community group wishes to collect, research should be done on the methods previously used to collect information on the same subject.

> *Economy:* Unemployment, measured either by the number of people of working age unemployed, or the number of people looking for work who are unemployed (the two results will likely vary substantially); spending by municipal authorities in a given area by sector and by division of expenses (administration, repayment of debt, research, etc.); average income; cost of basic expenses (food, housing, clothing, transportation) as a percentage of average income.

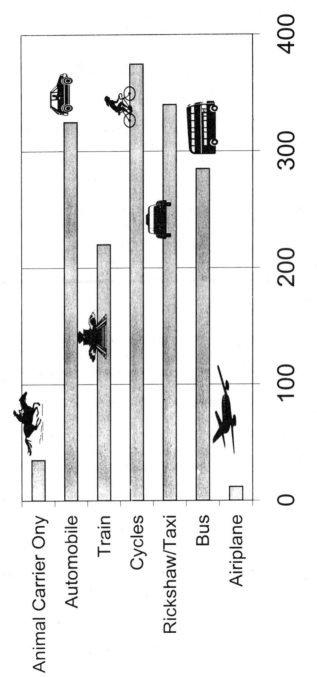

Available Transportation in 375 Villages

Education: Percent of children in school (number of children in school divided by total number of children); number of teachers per child; number of children per school; average level of education reached in an area.

Environment: Days per month or year when pollution makes walking down a particular street difficult to breathe; percent of profits of local or state firms from natural resources.

Housing and Infrastructure: Housing conditions, such as houses with recent painting, houses with running water and sewage, materials used in the construction of houses; street conditions, such as potholes, lighting, benches, and parks.

Health: Vaccinations; average number of illnesses and their severity among a group of children; number of cases of a particular disease over a period of time, and principal causes of death.

Further Resources

A number of well-designed books offer practical advice for community groups to understand and define issues and to organize the collection of statistics for the purposes described in this chapter. Since independent extension agencies and community development corporations publish most of these books, the best way to access this information is by engaging in some local research and contacting agencies directly. Good places to start are local community development corporations and municipal offices of community development. National associations such as the Urban Institute and the National Congress of Community Economic Development Organizations in Washington, DC, and international organizations such as UNICEF also have materials.

12

Facilitating Grassroots Participation in Development: New Training Models and Techniques

Chike Anyaegbunam, Paolo Mefalopulos and Titus Moetsabi

It is now popularly accepted and advocated, that the role of a rural development facilitator is to help people at the grassroots unleash the power of their innate creativity, cultural values, and knowledge in order to harness their potential. They will then have the capacity to make linkages to outside inputs that are needed to improve their livelihood. Chike, Titus, and Paolo share an innovative communication research approach known as Participatory Rural Communication Appraisal (PRCA) which they are exploring for use in the training of rural development facilitators. As an experiential training methodology, they find that it is capable of transforming lecturers and educators into true grassroots catalysts and at the same time enable local people to become better communicators. Their points of view are not necessarily that of their sponsoring agency, FAO.

It is indeed timely to share the new training methodology which is now in place to assist economic and social progress in the Southern

African region. This project was initiated and executed by the United Nations Food and Agriculture Organization (FAO) and funded by the Government of Italy. Jointly implemented by the SADC Centre of Communication for Development, the charge and challenge of the project is to build the capacity of governments, NGOs, rural development programs, and international organizations to communicate more effectively with rural communities. The intent is to better plan development projects in partnership with local communities, raising people's awareness of participatory development approaches, gaining their participation, and improving their skills.

The research and training methodology is intense and multifaceted, but most importantly, it includes in-built field practice providing development field-workers with facilitation and communication skills as well as appropriate attitudes and behavior to work more effectively with grassroots people. The rural population and the poor who need to become active in development so as to improve their livelihood, are most often difficult to communicate with. They are usually illiterate, in that they cannot read or write. Deep-rooted cultural norms, traditions, experiences, and values, which are different from those of the development facilitators, have shaped their ideas, knowledge, and practices. These differences make it difficult to engage their participation in the planning and implementation of development efforts.

The *Participatory Rural Communication Appraisal (PRCA)* training and research approach focuses squarely on this difficulty, giving field workers the methods and skills for opening dialogue with the people, involving them in a process which leads to mutual understandings and courses of action. Thus, the rural people are gaining communication skills that enable them to articulate their opinions and perceptions, identify and prioritize their problems and needs, and most importantly, in collaboration with field-staff, develop and implement development action plans with supporting communication strategies to improve their livelihood in a sustainable manner.

The Philosophical Framework and Objectives of PRCA

The communication perspective of PRCA is that of an interactive process characterized by the exchange of ideas, information, points of view, and experiences between persons and groups. In PRCA, communication is a two-way transactional process. The 'source/receiver' concept recognizes that both communicating parties are a 'source' with information and ideas to transmit. Passiveness is non-existent in this process because it requires an individual or a group to enter into active dialogue and 'mental cooperation' with another individual or group, until they come to a common awareness and understanding. The two participants in the communication transaction jointly arrive at a course of action. In the context of development work, this view of communication assumes that communicating partners are equal. The uniqueness of the PRCA approach is that it takes the position that throughout the development process one must not only focus on communication effectiveness, but also frame the process as one driven by a goal of research, inquiry, and reflection.

PRCA, unlike traditional communication research, not only reveals alternative ways of designing messages for the grassroots but also uncovers strategies and materials to enable people to create their own messages. They are enabled to voice their own perceptions of community needs, use local knowledge, open opportunities, define problems, and seek their own solutions, confronting related communication issues as they arise. Through the dialogue engendered with PRCA, both the traditional and modern communication processes in the community are discovered and mapped.

Facing Perceptual Differences

Since perceptions play a key role in communication, the need for PRCA hinges on the necessity to ensure that the facilitators and the community do not have varying perceptions of the issues or problems that they are trying to resolve. The different backgrounds of the rural people and the facilitators often influence the meanings they attach to symbols and the realities around them. As a result, the things each party says and does, and the way they interpret each other, are a reflection of their varied experiences, needs, and expectations. When these differences are neither recognized nor conscious effort made to bridge the gaps, well-intentioned efforts may result in disaster for the community.

The problem with unearthing rural people's perceptions and local knowledge lies in the fact that most of these communities have developed ways of hiding their true feelings and information from outsiders, especially when such outsiders cannot interact with the people within the people's frame of reference. Ascroft (1978) calls this ability of rural people to treat outsiders nicely without revealing themselves, *the conspiracy of courtesy.*

To overcome this, PRCA uses visual methods and community facilitation techniques for generating, analyzing, and presenting data, thus breaking through the conspiracy and removing the need for literacy on the part of the people. It is only through this process that it can be ensured that development efforts are firmly rooted in the realities of the grassroots, responsive to their perceived needs, abilities, and local knowledge.

Objectives of the Effort

It is well to note here two important objectives of this comprehensive communication for development effort. The first important objective is to assist governments to incorporate communication for development into national policies and development programs and establish the basis for sustainable *national communication for development services.* The intent is to strengthen a regional training capacity to improve communication for development skills of intermediate-level professionals so that they can improve the effectiveness of the rural development programs in which they wish to work. In addition, they want to create a group of communication for development professionals in the region through preparing curriculum and offering a regional post-graduate *communication for development professional diploma.*

The second objective is the basis of the new training program with major expected outputs: the establishment of a Regional *Communication for Development Skills Development* program introduced into an existing facility. This program was created and named the *Action Programme for Communication Skills Development* (AP), which has a goal to train about 150 development field-staff working with rural communities. Another output is the production of training packages on communication for development.

The project was engineered and developed by a number of consultants, including Professor Joseph Ascroft. They worked for over
one year in a preliminary/preparatory phase to ensure the need and
feasibility of such a project. Originally located in The Department
of Adult Education, University of Zimbabwe, it shifted to operate
under the auspices of the Southern African Development Community in 1996. In order to increase its visibility and sustainability, it
became the SADC Centre of Communication for Development
(SADC-CCD).

The PRCA Method

PRCA is a careful mix of elements from social investigation traditions such as participatory approaches like Participatory Rural
Appraisal (PRA), objective oriented project planning, visualization
in participatory planning, quantitative and qualitative research, as
well as ethnographic methods. It also incorporates ideas and techniques from the logical framework approach (LFA), advertising,
and market research. PRCA is normally conducted with the community by a multi-disciplinary team of facilitators. This is essential
because the problems and needs that emerge during discussions
with the grassroots are often multi-sectoral in nature and call for
diversified competencies among members of the facilitation team.

Because problems of the community often do cut across different
development sectors, causes cannot be determined by focusing on a
single sector. For instance, a PRCA, which addressed decreasing
soil fertility in a community, found out that one of the causes of land
exhaustion was over-cultivation. This, according to the villagers,
was partly due to an influx of population into the community. A
study that started with land use problems as the focus, gradually,
through probing by the facilitators, turned to issues of family planning. Because of the cross-sectoral influences, it is important to
seek representation from neighboring sectors during the PRCA.

PRCA provides data on rural people's perceptions, their interests, preferences, needs, and aspirations. Traditional and modern
communication networks and information requirements can be
identified and used, for planning new development projects, or re-
formulating existing ones. But PRCA is not just an appraisal. It is

also a training and empowerment process for the community. After participating in a PRCA, people are empowered and capable of identifying and analyzing their own problems, needs, and capabilities. On their own, they seek additional skills, knowledge, and outside assistance when they encounter problems beyond their existing capabilities and resources. At this stage, people also become more aware of the various external political and socio-economic factors that obstruct the achievement of their goals and often use their newly acquired skills of self-mobilization to tackle these obstacles.

It is useful if the PRCA process takes place at the same time as the development effort is being conceptualized with the community. PRCA at this stage is said to be exploratory and aims to empower the people to articulate their ideas or concerns, and voice their opinions about their situation. However, the facilitators can design and use PRCA at any point of the project cycle to formulate a communication program that seeks to initiate or improve dialogue. The outcome is that project aims and activities are more relevant to the people's needs, problems, and capabilities.

PRCA can also be a diagnostic tool since it can be effectively used for monitoring and evaluation. 'Topical' PRCA is used to investigate specific topics, issues, questions or challenges arising during the implementation of a project. In this case PRCA is useful to design communication programs which aim to solve specific problems or to improve dialogue among all stakeholders as they determine how well objectives of a project are achieved.

The PRCA Implementation Process

While it is not feasible to cover all the details of this method, we will endeavor to provide enough description to give you a 'feel' of the SADC-CCD program and the comprehensive method which has been put in place. If you have an interest in the intricate aspects of the methodology, we will be pleased to hear from you via direct contact and questions.

PRCA is part of the larger communication programme planning process that begins when SADC-CCD identifies and enrolls projects in the Action Programme Workshops. The projects, with advice from SADC-CCD, select workshop participants and designate field implementation sites.

Phases of the Communication for Development Process

The process of Communication for Development has six distinct phases with several steps in each phase. The SADC-CCD training workshops prepare participants to implement the phases and steps of the process in the field. These phases are:

- Participatory Rural Communication Appraisal and Baseline Study,
- Communication Strategy Design,
- Participatory Message and Discussion Topic Design,
- Communication Methods and Materials Development,
- Implementation, and
- Monitoring and Evaluation: Post Implementation PRCA and Baseline Study.

The Process of Training

Building the communication capacity of professional and field level development staff is a major objective. It is well to look at the Orientation and Training plan for these staff in more detail. First, the training is firmly based in practice as well as theory. It is participatory and experiential. It lasts ten weeks beginning and ending with two instructional workshops held in Harare, Zimbabwe. Each instructional workshop lasts three weeks. During the four weeks in-between participants return to their respective project field sites to conduct PRCA.

The Action Programme for Communication Skills Development originated from the needs assessment done at the preliminary phase of the regional project and during the early part of the implementation phase in 1994–95. This was the first step in preparation for a community participation effort. It puts in place the ten-week workshop, which includes experiential learning in the classroom, simulations in the rural communities located near the workshop site, and learning by doing by participants at project sites, under the supervision of one of the SADC-CCD staff.

The workshop is divided into three parts. In the first three weeks the participants become acquainted with the innovative communication research method known as PRCA (Participatory Rural Communication Appraisal). The learning process emphasizes skill development as well as the inculcation of the attitudes necessary to conduct a proper PRCA. The latter is often the most difficult task to accomplish. The experiential learning approach is achieved by taking full advantage of the expertise present in the group, doing many group sessions, and hands-on simulations.

The second part of the workshop, lasting four weeks, is concerned with carrying out the field research as designed during the workshop. During this phase the SADC-CCD staff backstops each group of participants. In the third part of the workshop, lasting three weeks, the field findings collected during the research are used to design a participatory communication strategy focused on specific issues. After training, the participants are prepared to return to their own project sites and, with the community, finalize and carry out the relevant communication activities planned with the results of the PRCA. The facilitators are given technical backstopping by staff of the SACD-CCD.

Planning PRCA with the Grassroots People

A team of 'facilitators' must do their homework before entering a community and be familiar with any existing information about the people and their development needs. But more important than that, they should not go into the community making assumptions and judgments about the people and their situation. They must be ready to be surprised by the new realities they will encounter in the community. They also need to be prepared to understand their new 'discoveries' from the people's perspective. This information helps the facilitators carry out an initial assessment of the situation, define a research framework, identify a preliminary research purpose, outline objectives, and prepare a discussion guide for the appraisal.

The process of acquiring this essential information is known as *situation analysis*. It utilizes consultations and interviews with decision and policy makers in government and development agencies as well as subject-matter specialists. The review of secondary data is also a part of this preparation. The information collected from situation analysis helps the facilitators, in the case of ongoing projects, draw a problem tree which helps in the definition of a preliminary PRCA purpose. The PRCA purpose must help to outline the general direction of the study but should not state what should be done in order to achieve the outcomes. At this stage, this is still a preliminary statement of purpose because refinement is likely to be necessary once the facilitators enter specific communities. It is only when the people's unique goals and agenda have been integrated in the statement of purpose that it becomes a shared vision, worthy of guiding the appraisal.

Selection of PRCA Sites

The information gathered from the situation analysis provides the facilitators with an indication of the general geographic areas where the development issue is of major concern, or the areas covered by an ongoing project. The communities to participate in the PRCA are then selected from these areas. It is helpful if district and provincial level officials who may have in-depth knowledge of the people are involved in selecting communities to participate in the PRCA.

Before embarking on the PRCA in a specific community, the facilitators engage in consultations and interviews with people who are knowledgeable about the community. They find out about the communities' interests and agenda. They will also have gathered data on the socio-economic, political, cultural, and environmental situation of the selected communities. They then gather information about where the people live, their means of livelihood, history, culture, and perceptions of the major issues that concern their livelihood. But in the course of the PRCA, a different picture may surface from the people. Generally, PRCA exercises flow from developing the profile of the community to identifying and analyzing the people's needs, opportunities, problems, solutions, and communication-related issues. This is often closely linked to an analysis of the community's strengths, weaknesses or threats as perceived by them.

Despite pre-research information sent to the community through various channels, there could be a high degree of suspicion of the PRCA team. This was the case in one Zambian community at the beginning of the exercise. The fact that the team lived in the village with the people for the entire research period did not mitigate this initial anxiety. As far as the community was concerned, the humility, attention, and readiness to dialogue exhibited by the team was unprecedented and therefore meant that there was an ulterior motive on the part of the team. The community was of the opinion that the team was a survey party sent in by some agency interested in acquiring their land and relocating the community.

Reasons for this apprehension were not difficult to find. First, most of the discussions between the team and the community revolved around the people's crop fields, their uses, and problems encountered. Second, the people were used to teams coming to teach them without listening to their problems or to shove pre-formulated projects at them without consulting the community. The community therefore saw the team's humility and readiness to dialogue as something suspicious. However, the team persisted in their efforts to win the confidence of the community through consultation with the influential persons in the community and social interactions with the people after hours.

The Importance of Building Trust

PRCA facilitators certainly need to stay in the community as long as the people do not see it as an inconvenience. All arrangements with the communities ideally are completed at least two weeks before the team enters the community. The community is encouraged to form a committee that organizes, supervises, and keeps a record of the appraisal. In this way, the community takes ownership of the appraisal and has an opportunity to keep and own its results.

Building trust and establishing rapport with people in the community is critical to team acceptance. Prior to starting the PRCA, it is advisable to pay a courtesy call on the people's leaders. In some communities it is regarded as a sign of good faith on the part of the visitor to present the chief or headman with a token gift. You need a guide appointed by the headman to act as your escort around the village until the community gradually gets used to your presence. Participate in as many community activities as possible—farming, funerals, weddings, and other rituals.

Explain the purpose and process of the mission as early as possible to the people and link the PRCA to future benefits for the community. Find out the customs of the people as they relate to visitors and strive to abide by them. Ensure that your body language does not contradict what you are saying. Your body language or nonverbal communication speaks very loudly about your opinion of the people. As an example, you can unknowingly tell the people that they smell bad by moving away from them whenever they come close to you or by covering your nose. In the same vein, by refusing to accept their water or food without good reason, you also might be telling them that they are not clean enough for you.

Identify and build up alliances with the truly respected members of the community. If these persons agree to act as your advisers and link with the rest of the community, your trust building effort will be fruitful in a short time. Make sure that you interact with all sections of the community including the poor, the old, and the sick. Observe the behavior and dress codes of the men and women in the community and adjust yours as much as possible so that you don't stand out. Show respect to the people, especially, the elders. It is important to learn the proper greetings for the various categories of people in the community. So, for a trusting relationship to be established, members of the PRCA team must conduct themselves in a culturally acceptable manner.

Facilitating Grassroots PRCA Sessions

PRCA cannot succeed if the facilitators do not possess requisite attributes—respect for the culture of the people, the ability to listen and learn from grassroots people, alertness, inquisitiveness, and humility. Without these attributes, the facilitator cannot create an atmosphere conducive to dialogue. In other words, without them, the facilitator cannot encourage the equitable exchange of ideas, knowledge, and experiences among the rural people themselves, and between the people and outsiders.

A PRCA can last from about three to twenty-one days, depending on the issues under discussion. It is a good idea to begin PRCA sessions with warm-up techniques to break down the barriers of inhibition and shyness on both sides. These techniques made up of

participatory group activities such as games, or songs, are specifically designed to put both the people and the PRCA team in a cooperative frame of mind so that open discussions can take place. The
local people are encouraged to come up with their own warm-up
activities.

Although the team may have consulted representatives of the
community before beginning the appraisal, it is still necessary for
the team to clarify the philosophy of the appraisal with the people
themselves and agree on its objectives and agenda at this juncture.
This will ensure that the PRCA activities are relevant to the realities
of the participants. A good team tries to understand the community's point of view and perceptions no matter how different they
may be from theirs. The facilitators must not push the community
into discussing the team's agenda but should be alert enough to spot
any potential entry points that might lead to the purpose of the
PRCA.

The job of the facilitators is to start the PRCA exercise. When
they see that people are comfortable with the activities they should
withdraw and become participant observers. Even when the team
has relinquished control of the PRCA, it still has a major role to
play in order to ensure that no one section or person in the community dominates the exercise. A good PRCA team encourages exchange of experiences, information, and knowledge among the people themselves, between the team and the people, and between
the people and outside institutions and organizations without any
groups intimidating the others. The facilitators can accomplish this
by helping to make invisible people and concealed knowledge become visible.

Normally, in every group, there are persons who tend to dominate the proceedings because of their status or role in the community or their personality. There are also people whose presence in a
group stifles the free flow of information. This category of persons
should be 'taken for a walk' to make it possible for the other members of the group to express themselves. Sometimes these dominant
figures have specialized information. In this case, individual in-
depth interviews can be held with them to discover their knowledge
as well as keep them separated from the group. Quite often, conflict
can also occur between different community groups as a result of
public expression. If this occurs, the facilitators should make an

effort to turn the conflict into a constructive discussion of the issue without making any side look defeated.

Whenever possible, facilitators try to capture the PRCA in photographs, audio, and video recordings. Community members are excited when they see their own photographs or watch themselves on video. If possible, facilitators should go into the field with a video playback unit and show their raw footage of the day's shooting to the people in the evenings. Audio-visual documentation of the community provides a very important reference for graphic artists and is a source of authentic sound effects for radio producers during the production of prototype communication materials. Audio-visuals also provide an added credence to presentations of the PRCA findings to government or donor agency officials. Copies of all audio-visual materials are available to the community for their own use.

On a daily basis, the PRCA team needs to ask itself: 'How are we doing?' in order to ensure that the research questions on the proposal are being answered and that they ascertain that information about the people's communication systems are being gathered. Depending on the schedule for the appraisal, the meetings at which this question is raised can either be held each evening after the day's work or in the morning before the next PRCA activity with the community. The purpose of these meetings is to enable the PRCA team to reflect on the information that has been collected for the day, compare it with information collected earlier in order to ensure that the research questions on the proposal are being answered. During the daily reflections, the team can decide whether some issues already discussed have been exhausted or whether they should be discussed further. These daily meetings are also mini planning sessions where the activities for the next day are reviewed and any necessary adjustments made. The community's appraisal committee should also attend these meetings.

Discovering Information with PRCA Tools and Techniques

PRCA enables the facilitators and the people to arrive at a mutually acceptable interpretation of the community's problems, needs, and solutions as well as its socio-economic and physical characteristics. This is necessary because quite often, the way outsiders see the community or the descriptions given about them in books—their norms, values, actions, and aspirations—might not correspond to the way the people see themselves. Knowledge of the people's perceptions of their situation provide the background and context for understanding the other categories of information that will be revealed by the PRCA, including those issues concerning communication.

For instance, during a PRCA in a Zambian village, the team of facilitators continually referred to the people as farmers. Toward the end of the appraisal, when the people were feeling comfortable with the team, the people revealed that they did not perceive themselves as farmers. The people at this juncture gave the team their own definition of a farmer: a person with a title deed to his land. Since the people tilled their land under the traditional land tenure system, in which all ownership is invested in the chief, they did not see themselves as farmers. The implication was that most recommendations that had been presented to these people as 'farmers' were not implemented in the village because they didn't believe they were meant for them.

Even within the community, various groups might have different perceptions of problems and needs as well as the environmental and socio-economic situation of the community. It is therefore essential that different groups in the community be interacted with separately during the PRCA in order to discover their own perceptions of the conditions in the community. This separate interaction becomes even more important in communities where some groups, such as women, are traditionally not allowed to voice their opinions in the presence of other groups, such as men. Reports from one of the field workers would support this notion when indicating that '...the group split into two groups according to sex. The women in the group had discussions with female researchers while male researchers worked with the male group. During the sessions, deliberate effort was made to draw contributions from every member of the community.'

In a similar exercise in Namibia, separating the community by gender was also discovered to be advantageous to the women. According to Elena, 'during the PRCA we've discovered that female farmers can air opinions on issues we did not know about or we thought were too sensitive for the extension workers to bring up during meetings.' She also pointed out that female farmers raised and discussed issues concerning the imbalance in the gender division of labor in the communities. 'The women discussed other sensitive issues such as the question of male drunkenness during the farming season,' she said.

Thus, a typical PRCA with facilitation from the team enables the different groups in the community themselves to develop a profile of the community, define, and prioritize its problems and needs as well as discovers its communication networks, systems, and requirements.

Looking at Communication Systems

The PRCA yields extensive information regarding the socio-economic and environmental conditions of a community. But the uniqueness of this method is that it looks closely at the communication systems and issues. The PRCA identifies traditional and modern information and communication networks and systems, within a community as well as between a community and other communities, external organizations, and institutions. The nature of the information transmitted through each network and potential uses are also identified. The attributes of the specific networks and systems preferred by the community can be determined using participatory tools. It is necessary to map the networks and systems because they are the potential channels for communicating with the community in mass, group or interpersonal modes.

The PRCA also reveals the people's needs, opportunities, problems, and likely solutions (NOPS) as perceived by various groups in the community. These are the most essential building blocks of an effective communication program. With PRCA, facilitators and the people can identify, analyze, and prioritize the community NOPS as they relate to specific groups. As each of the PRCA tools is used, the community identifies and discusses issues regarding the NOPS inherent in information collected. Perceptions play a major role on how needs and problems are defined. PRCA makes it possible for the people and the development worker to arrive at a common understanding of the community NOPS.

Priority Interaction Groups

All communities are made up of different groups: men, women, the literate, the illiterate, etc. PRCA helps to identify these groups and provides a more in-depth understanding of their perceptions, NOPS, knowledge, attitudes, beliefs, and practices. During PRCA, the divisions within the community in relation to the NOPS become more obvious. This helps to divide the people into more meaningful groups, define their characteristics, and design communication strategies that are relevant to them. Information collected about the NOPS and the socio-economic and environmental situation of the community provide the basis for identifying the groups who are most seriously affected by the current status of the community or variability in the people's circumstances.

Normally in other types of communication program planning, these groups are known as 'target audiences' and in public relations as 'publics.' However, since the approach advocated is participatory, the term 'interaction group' is used to replace the old definition of people as merely receivers of information. The term 'interaction group' presupposes that the people involved in a PRCA and the entire communication program are not passive receivers but people whose knowledge and opinions are valued and whose perceptions are seriously sought after. Interaction groups are seen as sources of information, and initiators of action as well as decision-makers. Interaction groups can be individuals, associations, agencies, institutions or cooperatives in and outside the community whose activities, needs, problems affect the people in a positive or negative manner.

Insights from Reports

An excerpt from a Tanzania report illustrates the importance of discovering the different groups in a community and their responsibilities. The report noted that:

> Traditionally it has been believed that Masai men are the ones who take care of cattle and other livestock. Masai women have been seen as playing a very peripheral role in livestock care and usage. The PRCA among the Masai of Longido District of Tanzania revealed the contrary. Through development of 'activity profiles' by gender, it was discovered that in actuality, women spend more time with the livestock than men do. The Masai themselves guided the PRCA meetings. Instead of asking them to come to specific venues, as often happens when outsiders come into this

society, the PRCA team followed the people to their work places. These were later discovered to be their conventional meeting venues. This led to a segmentation of the group initially by gender and later, within the gender groups, by age. The PRCA team observed that when livestock is taken out of the Boma (kraal), where women really dominate in its care, it is taken care of by different age groups depending on the age of the animals. Participation in discussion of the animals was dependent on this aspect. In other words, any discussion of calves and their problems was left to young children, whereas discussion of older animals was being done by the Morans (the youth). Elders participated more actively in discussions pertaining to ownership and movement of the animals.

It was observed that these groups actually moved in and out of the meeting dependent on what age or type of animal being discussed. For instance, if the discussion was on calves, it was observed that the Morans left the meeting to do other chores in the vicinity while the young children remained to talk about the calves. Once discussion reverted to the older animals, the Morans returned and dominated the discussion. Although the elders were not moving in and out of the meetings, it was observed that they did not participate when the young children or the Morans were at the centre of the discussion. During these discussions, most elders seem to dose off as if they were not interested in what was being discussed. However, whenever the discussion concerned them, they got up and rejoined the meeting.

While it was easier to notice the way age played a critical role in participation of men in discussions, it was not so clearly defined amongst the females. Since most girls are married early in life, it seems most discussions amongst Masai women were being dominated by younger women than the elderly ones even as the later were always present during meetings (Kamlongera, 1997: 9).

Communication Issues

PRCA is used to define the communication issues as they relate to the key interaction groups. By seeking answers to the questions from the key interaction groups, a better picture of the groups' communication needs begins to appear. These are some of the questions that must be answered:

- Is the group aware of the problems and solutions?
- How does the group perceive and define the problems, solutions, and needs?
- What is the level of the groups' interest and attitude towards the problem and solution?
- What are the groups' beliefs, knowledge, skills, and practices in relation to the problems and solutions?
- Why do people make decisions to act in certain ways and on what basis?

Lack of commitment and motivation to tackle a problem can be a communication problem. The people in the community might not see the problem as a priority and in some cases, peer pressure or community norms might discourage people from recognizing the situation as problematic.

The mental position or attitude people have about a problem will often determine how they behave toward it. Some people in the group might decide not to use a technique for solving some problem despite the fact that they have knowledge of it because they do not have a positive attitude towards that technique. It is therefore important to find out people's attitude towards issues under discussion. With such information, a communication strategy can be developed to change a negative attitude in order to solve a problem.

Lack of interest or a negative attitude towards an issue is often a result of the inability of the group to try out alternatives in a non-threatening situation. When there are no opportunities for the trial of new technologies for instance, the people will not be able to judge such technologies in order to decide whether to use them or not.

Communities often develop a negative attitude towards an issue as a result of the manner in which the facilitators treat the people. Many facilitators do not have respect for the people for whom they work. They see the people as inferior and ignorant and the people often sense this. A communication barrier can be created between the two parties when this happens.

The lack of appropriate policy support from government or development agencies can demoralize groups. When issues of concern to the people are neglected at the policy level, there is a tendency for people to also neglect such issues unless communication approaches are used to mobilize the community to action.

Insufficient information, skills, and knowledge to deal with a problem is a common communication problem in many communities. Cultural beliefs and practices can also become barriers to tackling problems even when the knowledge and other requirements for a solution are in place. PRCA will reveal the beliefs of the community in relation to the issues under discussion. Although some of these beliefs might appear as nothing more than superstition, making positive reference to them in the communication materials may determine the success or failure of the communication program.

Lack of skills and knowledge can also manifest itself if the development agency is producing instructional materials that are difficult for the people to understand or that do not appear relevant to the people. To ensure relevance of communication materials, it is essential to identify and utilize *local knowledge* as an entry point for the new practices. Local knowledge of the community are those techniques and practices which are essentially subsistence-oriented, distinct to a particular social group and culture and have been developed and handed down from generation to generation. These are usually built up on centuries of experience and adaptation. Local knowledge is expressed in local languages. They may have been influenced by innovations emerging from within the community, from other systems, but they essentially originated locally. Such knowledge might provide insight into how the people normally solved their problems and provided for their needs.

On the other hand, *adopted knowledge* is those techniques, processes, and practices that were originally introduced into the community from outside. It is essential to assess how much of this knowledge the community actually has. Increasing such knowledge might become an objective of the communication strategy if the level is found to be low, in which case the people will need to identify the additional information, knowledge, skills, and resources they need in order to solve the problem.

Final Important Points

The methodology we have briefly shared with you, is one that for us has confirmed that mutual trust and respect between the facilitators and the rural people is the major key to releasing the power of grassroots creativity for their quest of improving their livelihood. Our experience has shown that to produce facilitators who can generate these results in the field, classroom and theoretical training are not enough. These must be complemented with vigorously supervised practical work in the field. This is essential because without the fieldwork, the facilitator cannot experience the powers of these attributes in unlocking the wealth of knowledge and experience lurking under the seeming naïve facade presented to the outsider by the rural person.

Experience from the field shows that there are various benefits for the different actors in a PRCA. The process gives the grassroots people the skills to articulate their opinions, to identify and prioritize their problems and needs, and most importantly, to seek out ways and means of solving their problems and providing for their needs with or without outside intervention. PRCA is a way of sharpening the decision making process in the community and empowering them to face up to any outsiders who might want to impose their wishes on them.

For the facilitators, the process reveals that the grassroots people are not as ignorant as they are often made out to be. Given the right attitude, skills, and environment, the facilitators quickly learn that there is knowledge at the grassroots, albeit of a different form and nature from what they are accustomed to. The facilitators can then harness this community knowledge in any joint effort to improve the people's livelihood. An extensionist in Namibia informed us:

> We are now dealing with farmer's needs and not with our perceptions of what they need. By the third day of the PRCA, everybody was surprised not only by the amount of information collected, i.e. maps, graphics, notes, but also by the new kind of opportunities and constraints expressed by the farmers, now that they were encouraged to speak for themselves through the PRCA methods.

For the development agency, results of PRCA provide the basis for funding development programs that respond to the way the people define their own problems and their own ways of dealing with them. Such programs are more likely to succeed and, in a sustainable manner, assist in the improvement of livelihood at the grassroots.

Finally for the rural communication specialist, the findings of PRCA ensure that subsequent communication programs spring from the people's perception of their needs and problems. Such programs utilize communication materials and activities that reflect the people's culture and are rendered in idioms the people use for expressing themselves. Community identified opinion leaders, role models and influential sources of advice play a major role in such communication programs.

The innovative facilitator training program has been well received by the workshop participants, their managers, policy makers, and rural communities in the region. Most of the development projects that participated in the workshop have provided funds for the implementation phase of the program in their selected field sites. Other projects have already expanded the application of the approaches learnt at the workshops to other project sites. Some of the facilitators trained at the workshops have now become consultants to other projects in their countries. Members of the communities in which this approach has been tested say that it is the first time they have actually been listened to and truly consulted. They say that prior to PRCA, development agents had always come into their villages to teach them new ideas without trying to find out what the people know and whether the new ideas are feasible or not.

A final word, this methodology could not have seen the light of day without the involvement, support, and encouraging comments from the grassroots people. The three of us would like to thank them most heartily. We also acknowledge the immense contributions of the other staff members of the SADC Centre of Communication for Development, Centre consultants and the many facilitators who have participated in the Centre's training and field implementation programs. It has truly been a participatory experience all around.

References and Select Bibliography

Ascroft, J. (1978). A Conspiracy of Silence. In *International Development and Reconstruction/Focus*, 1978 (3): 8–11.

Kamlongera, C. (1997). Trip Report. Tanzania Rinderpest Campaign Field PRCA in Longido District.

Rogers, E. and **Kincaid, D.L.** (1981). *Communication Networks*. New York, NY: Free Press.

Ruben, B.D. (1988). *Communication and Human Behavior* (2nd Edn.). New York, NY: Macmillan.

13

The Discovery Principle: A Participatory Approach to Training

Renuka Bery

In this chapter Renuka shares the training approaches which she believes enhances people's ability to become self-determined. When people discover the power of participation and action within a safe environment, they feel more secure in taking risks in other areas of their lives. She describes techniques used to successfully facilitate participation. This is not intended to be a guide but rather ideas which can serve as an entry point for facilitators to discover what works, as their needs and those of the group change in the process of transformation from participation to action.

Giving people tools to think critically, to make informed decisions, and to take action is testament to the belief that people can become participative. This capacity to think and act independently dramatically increases a person's potential to take control of his/her own life and become a leader in the community or profession and when these skills are secured and nurtured, all one needs is a strong voice, deep conviction for the issues, and self-confidence. This is key to transforming participation into action.

Many of the examples I give come from my recent affiliation with *Communication for Change (CFC)*, a not-for-profit video training organization based in New York City. CFC's mission is to strengthen individual and community voices to influence social and economic issues important in their lives by introducing participatory communication strategies, i.e., processes which allow people to speak for and about themselves and their issues. These community members would otherwise have limited access to communication technologies and control of tools that are usually in the hands of outsiders who mediate information and representation.

Participatory communication enables individuals, organizations, and communities to *learn to use* media, rather than *be used by* media in this case. It is an exchange among individuals that values each person's perspectives and voice. In the case of video, community members produce tapes to meet their own needs. But the process continues long after a tape is completed. Playback sessions, at which members of the community gather to watch and discuss tapes, are critical to participatory video. Facilitators engage viewers in discussions about the tapes they have just seen. Through these exchanges, participants can relate what they have seen and heard to their own experiences and lives.

The Environment for Participation

Participation is founded on principles of action. It is an act of sharing dialogue and collaboration among individuals. Facilitators often motivate people to act by convincing them that they have valuable knowledge and experience to contribute to the process of changing their community. When individuals find that their opinions and ideas are valued, they gain the courage to continue taking part in events that affect their lives. In order to participate fully in the issues that impact on one's life and community, a person must be engaged and open to entering a new phase of 'discovery.' By discovering answers for themselves, they will act and learn through trial and error, how to implement the changes necessary for transforming their society.

Participation has a variety of forms, each with a different meaning. As a term, it has been used in many fora to mean *inclusion*.

Recently, the term has been used indiscriminately, turning it into a trend that has lessened its impact. So, as practitioners of participatory methods, we must clearly define our interpretations and carefully outline the necessary steps for achieving a participatory environment.

One key to creating a participatory environment is that the facilitators have mutual respect for each person's uniqueness—knowledge, experiences, and culture. When a new idea is introduced into an organization and developed, several participants are involved and that raises some important questions:

- Who owns the idea?
- How does it get integrated into a program or an organization?
- Who is involved?

Recipes do not work since every situation depends on the task and players involved. The facilitator or the group must establish guidelines, yet the environment must be flexible enough to adapt them to the needs of the wider community. My concept of a participatory environment is the creation of a safe space in which each person's role may or may not be equal but where their ideas are heard, explored, and valued equally. This requires active, supportive listening, without stereotyping or biased thinking. In addition, an open, questioning mind with freedom to make independent judgments is necessary.

Training Philosophy and Style

My teaching philosophy is founded on an ancient Chinese proverb: 'I hear, and I forget. I see, and I remember. I do, and I understand.' Whether working with village women, adolescents or educated professionals, I emphasize that there are many ways to perform a task or think through an idea. I believe that learning by doing—experimenting, making mistakes, solving problems, thinking critically, reflecting—is the most lasting, fun, and engaging way to learn. It is a process, which enables individual minds to work independently with a free flow of ideas. This training style builds confidence, generates excitement, deepens understanding for all participants and at the same time explores new territory. Participants and training facilitators are co-learners in a workshop or training situation—each with a unique set of experiences and skills to contribute.

As a trainer, I rarely give out much information or a precise agenda at the outset, although my work might be easier or more efficient if I did. At the beginning I usually provide the basics—an explanation or demonstration—from which the participants can experiment, ask questions, explain to others, and explore different ways they would like to work together. This can be frustrating to participants who would rather see the exact syllabus and a copy of the curriculum so they can prepare in advance or know exactly what will take place in the sessions. Usually, if I do provide a curriculum, I present it at the end as resource material. By then, the participants have gained enough confidence to accept the challenge of uncovering solutions for themselves. I have observed that a facilitator as an 'answer provider' discourages participants from exploring their own options or ways to do things. When participants make discoveries, they have triumphed. It is these powerful moments of accomplishment, ownership, and motivation, which enable them to act independently.

Each person has a different way of thinking and learning. Some people thrive on abstraction, others prefer images, and some need words. The material, content, and training methods, however, must be appropriate to the levels of skills, knowledge, and understanding of all participants. Using different methods celebrates different strengths. Once, as an ice-breaking exercise, I asked everyone to depict an abstract concept, like honesty. Instantly, everyone was on an equal footing: some were artists, a few found wonderful metaphors, some were humorous, and everyone succeeded. Improvization, too, is a teaching method that celebrates the creativity and participation of individuals and furthers the action agenda.

Another time, while working with at-risk youth in a children's theater, the teenagers created their own stories where they could incorporate important issues or crises they were facing in their own lives. Thus, through someone else's reality, they could explore their own. One shy and withdrawn young man examined his insecurities and social awkwardness by inflating them in his stage character and was highly successful. By taking this risk and exploring himself, he understood the importance of his contributions and was then able to voice his personal opinions freely and with confidence. This example illustrates the transformation experienced through participation. This young man learned to trust and value himself.

Using a 'learn it–teach it' approach can be valuable because teaching others is an excellent technique to reinforce knowledge. The facilitator explains something to one person who in turn tries it and explains it to the next person. The person must understand the procedure or process in order to explain it clearly. By describing a problem or by articulating a question, the answer often becomes evident to the questioner. A group of Nigerian teenagers learning video production and editing responded well to this training method because it was an opportunity for role-reversal—that is, they became the teachers. It worked also because their peers kept them honest. Since everyone had seen the demonstration, when the teen trainer made a mistake, peers pointed it out rather than the facilitator. Although this method takes a lot of time and patience, by watching and listening, the facilitator can ensure that the correct information is transmitted, but at the same time allow room for innovation.

Varying the environment and tasks keeps the participants active and alert. While conducting participatory video training, we alternate hands-on activities that require movement or outside action, with activities that are more intellectual such as watching and discussing tapes. Altering group size is also valuable. Moving from a large group discussion to small group tasks or discussions changes the tenor of the activity and ensures that all participants are fully engaged in the exercise rather than passive observers.

Facilitator Participant Relationships

The gulf between grassroots training participants and facilitators is often wide, especially when the two groups come from vastly different cultural and socio-economic backgrounds. Facilitators can do much to narrow the gap by redefining implied relationships and roles. In traditional patriarchal or colonial learning situations, the facilitator/teacher arrives to 'bestow knowledge on the uninformed.' Such a one-way transfer of information encourages a hierarchical relationship between teacher and students. Equalizing the relationship from the beginning should be the first goal in participatory training settings. To this end, physical space is important in mitigating the differences in roles. When facilitators and participants sit at the same level—either in chairs or on the floor, whichever is preferred—no one dominates by virtue of their position. Moreover, sitting in a circle enables everyone to acknowledge and speak to each other and allows anyone to assume a leadership position at any time.

In international training situations, the outside expert is often given preferential treatment such as special food, special plates, and separate dining facilities. The participants are usually surprised and honored when we, the facilitators, insist on sharing the same food and meals with them. Eating together and fraternizing equalizes the social status between facilitators and participants. This sharing approach makes the trainers more accessible and participants are not afraid to ask questions or advice from them.

Who is the Expert? Establishing Trust and Respect

In many grassroots contexts trainers from outside the community are often elevated to 'guru' status as possessors of great knowledge and wisdom. To be revered as master teacher may feel great, but the facilitator's first challenge is to dispel these myths of greatness and instead, grant everyone expert status. Every person, whether facilitator or trainee, brings unique experiences, expertise, and perspectives to the group—some with knowledge of the culture and community and others with specific skills to contribute. In a participatory training environment, both trainers and participants are a resource. But each person must have an active desire to participate, listen, share knowledge, and experience, solve problems, take risks, and grow.

In my experience, the sense of openness and trust increases when the facilitator makes an effort to learn the local language and customs. A concerted and public effort to learn the language and understand more about the culture through songs, dance, food, and conversation transforms interpersonal relationships. Stumbling over words and pronunciations or entertaining the group by imitating dances and songs demonstrates that by being curious, open, and taking risks, one can learn and be accepted. Thus, the learning environment extends beyond the classroom and participants realize that education is not necessarily limited to formal structures. It can be broader and a rich, varied, and exciting experience. In one situation, the least adept video participant was encouraged to teach me, the trainer, to sing and dance village songs after a training session. Thus, she became the instructor and gained status in the group. This role shift, outside the formal training session, increased her motivation and level of confidence for the remainder of the training.

Participatory learning environments allow people to experiment to see whether and how their knowledge works in different situations. Recognizing and valuing people's indigenous knowledge must be reinforced continually. It is not enough to allow people to express themselves and their experiences; everyone must learn to listen to each other. By hearing other worldviews, one learns to challenge preconceived ideas and the existing status quo. In one participatory communication training with rural and urban women in India, the women believed that the participatory environment had helped them expand their thinking and would be helpful in their work. Dhrutiben, a more educated woman, described how she had spoken with people she had never before considered talking with, such as a dhobian (laundry woman). Dhrutiben was surprised to learn that the dhobian had opinions and a social analysis. She had never considered asking a lower class woman about her opinions of dowry or the status of women in society. Interaction in these training sessions not only equalizes relationships for the moment, but also can trigger significant behavioral changes.

Questions and Practice: The Role of Facilitator

A facilitator's job is to stimulate the creative juices and put fears to rest. Asking questions does this by encouraging people to think for themselves and compelling them to get excited about thinking more broadly. Sometimes leading questions are appropriate; however, open-ended questions add depth and analysis to the discussion while building the respondent's confidence. In addition, the facilitator's skill and style influences those she is teaching to also open discussions. A thorough facilitator will probe the responses by asking more incisive questions such as 'Why do you think that?' or 'If you could do this differently, how would you do it?' Thus, she would achieve the desired level of depth while keeping the topic in focus.

Some trainees have commented that at first they thought we all talked together too much in the training, but by the end they realized that they had learned how to lead a discussion themselves. It is not uncommon for a participatory training style to generate this sort of response. Once participants grow accustomed to a non-didactic, participatory teaching approach, their confidence and views become stronger and critical thinking evolves. Mayaben said, 'I never knew that by asking one question it could lead to another and another.' In the beginning, the bold members will speak first. But soon, the quiet ones will also want to contribute, and if needed, the facilitator can intervene and ask them to speak out. The group also learns that if one person cannot answer, they can without embarrassment, ask someone else to help them out. This supportive atmosphere reinforces the learning process rather than inhibits it by establishing competitive relationships, which inhibit sharing of ideas.

People also learn by watching others perform the same task. Women from rural and slum areas in India, working in groups of four, were asked to interview a stranger on the street. When the group returned and listened to the interviews, they discussed their merits and ways to improve the interview. During the discussion, Varlaxmiben, who had interviewed a man on the street, said: 'This exercise was so difficult for me because I have never spoken with a man who was not related to me.' She recognized that her interviewing skills needed improvement but overcoming the challenge of speaking with a strange man filled her with pride and confidence. Her colleagues in the training acknowledged her accomplishment and felt they could do it too. Madhuben remarked: 'After listening and conducting so many practice interviews, I understood better how to control the situation. If there are arguments in the village, especially with the men, I won't be so nervous because it will be just like an interview.' These stories illustrate the value in stretching perceptions of what is possible. When trying things never before imagined, people experience a great sense of power. When they succeed in extending the boundaries of their mental or physical capabilities, they begin to envision new ways to challenge themselves, which, in turn, enables them to address issues and seek changes in their lives and their societies.

Critical Appreciation

In a training session where everyone is learning, it is important not to be overly judgmental. Harsh criticism actively prevents people from continuing to experiment and think creatively. If people come to fear making mistakes, they will stop participating in the discovery process. Because everyone has a unique set of goals and critical sensibility, what works for one person may not work for another. Learning to trust one's own opinion is a far greater accomplishment than deferring to a teacher's point of view.

Communication for Change coined a term called 'critical appreciation' to discuss and assess participants' progress in video production. Critical appreciation stresses positive reinforcement as the learning tool. Students learn that there are no right or wrong answers. They develop analytical and critical skills through positive feedback, discussion, explanation, and demonstration. Everyone, especially women and people with little previous formal education, needs positive reinforcement to build and nurture self-confidence.

The most valuable critical appreciation sessions are with small groups. Starting with positive comments, asking the members of the group what they liked about each other's work recognizes individual accomplishment and encourages team spirit and group solidarity. By framing a discussion of the positive elements of the video programs they watch, such as the aspects they liked about the content and technical quality, and why and what they learned from the tape, they begin to realize how many different perspectives can exist. Only when the group has exhausted the positive aspects of a task can they describe the things they might have done differently and why. Here too, the positive is emphasized by encouraging individuals to explore other methods of doing something—in this case, making a video program.

Sometimes tactful, direct criticism is necessary and useful, but only if it does not stifle creative thinking or the desire to take risks. Expressing critical appreciation is like all other skills: *it takes practice*. But it is especially difficult to cultivate in an environment that embraces perfection or believes that blunt criticism can motivate people to improve. However, when critical appreciation techniques are used to examine everyone's work, people begin to develop independent judgment and supportive expression that leads to an analytical perspective.

Nurturing and Evaluating Participation

One hopes that the goals for participation start with training and expand exponentially through the organization and into the larger community. For example, while a training might consist of direct involvement with twenty people, through this training they are encouraged to include others in their thinking and creating processes. As more people participate in dialogue, generate ideas and engage in new discoveries, they too start thinking about other ways to effect change in their communities. Muriam, a Bangladeshi village woman, went home and organized all the women in her savings group (*samiti*) to help with her video tape on nutrition which she produced and showed in her village. The experience of bringing her new skills to her community was important for Muriam. Showing the program in her community was at once humbling, empowering, and intensely motivating. The villagers were impressed and suggested other programs she could make next. By including her *samiti* in the planning and implementation process, she created a more coherent program and entered the community with a backbone of support because many people were involved. Her future programs will benefit from the collective thoughts and voices of her peers.

Maintaining a continuous level of participation within the program is challenging because it takes more time to elicit ideas from many different segments of society or an organization. Inspired by initial participatory video trainings which included working in the participants' own communities, one Bangladeshi organization developed its own principles of participatory video with input from the grassroots members to the organization's leaders. This commitment to redefining goals of participation reflected this video unit's evolution into an independent, unique entity. Recently the participatory video unit adopted a new participatory training style in which current members acted as resource persons/trainers. Everyone was afraid of the challenge, but each person worked hard, and in the process, learned a great deal. Bilal examined the mistakes he made as a resource person by watching the tapes his group made. Tuli was surprised and proud that her group respected her knowledge even though she was a group member. Renu admired Aziz's cleverness in maximizing her time on the equipment by pretending to be sick. Polly was relieved to have Asman in her group because she knew and trusted him. Accepting the challenges of inclusion which takes time and energy is testament to the commitment an organization places on practicing and sharing participatory approaches.

Recently I visited a project where one woman had transformed dramatically from a passive disinterested member to an active participant bubbling with enthusiasm and ideas. What happened to cause this change? A health worker, Sufia had often witnessed the problems of unsafe birth practices in surrounding villages. She spoke with the program coordinator and developed an idea for a video production about safe childbirth. She made the tape, showed it to the women in her community, and led discussions about giving birth safely. Sufia's neighbors praised and thanked her. Her peers encouraged her. She felt her ideas and knowledge were valued and valuable. Her sense of accomplishment was visible; her enthusiasm and energy were infectious and motivated her colleagues as well. This success story belongs, in large part, to the coordinator's skill in promoting a participatory environment.

Challenges to participation crop up at every turn and must be swiftly analyzed and addressed. They may be as transparent as gaining permission from one's family to attend meetings. As one Indian woman explains, 'My father-in-law wanted me to do the housework and pluck flowers in the field, but I insisted on learning video' (Video SEWA). Or, when working with the economically disadvantaged, financial compensation for lost income can be crucial to a person's ability to participate.

In assessing participation, I generally look at who is involved in generating ideas, how those ideas are developed and implemented, and who makes the decisions. Often, management structures indicate who has the control within a program or organization and how much exchange is possible. In one Bangladeshi women's organization, the coordinator of the participatory video team decentralized the locus of control by instituting a policy to increase the participation and leadership capacity of the grassroots women members. One woman is elected to a three-month term as president of the participatory video team. She is responsible for seeing that the activities are implemented and for overseeing problems within the group. The president appoints a leader to run the monthly participatory video meeting. In addition, two team leaders are elected each month; these leaders assign their colleagues tasks, and oversee them during production and playback activities, and are responsible for the video equipment. The women have become more confident and able to negotiate solutions to problems.

I also look at the environment. Has the facilitator successfully created a safe space in which everyone can ask questions, follow different paths, and embark on new discoveries? Can people make mistakes and learn from them without thinking they have failed? Is there enough time to explore ideas? Are the participants engaged in the process? Does the process include members of the larger community? Using participatory approaches requires commitment, dedication, and lots of time. Selecting participants who can always be present and focused makes the training most valuable. Discovering the many paths one can take to reach a solution is powerful, but each person must be present and engaged in the process. The rewards are great because the participants learn to trust their own thoughts and opinions. They learn to strengthen their ability to articulate issues and solutions and finally they begin to generate their own ideas and collaborate with others to implement them.

Innovation: From Participation to Action

But how does the transformation from participation to action take place? People are willing to take risks and to challenge the prevailing power structures when they see that their needs and those of their community are being addressed. They feel the need to have a voice in shaping their lives. When people see that they can gain access to local officials, they will approach them. When women understand the strength in organizing, they can exert pressure to stop social injustices. When a community is exposed to new information and broader thinking, more people will become involved in seeking change. People take pride in bringing positive changes to their communities. The following examples illustrate the ways in which some of the groups I have trained have begun to discover ways to transform participation into action.

Tuli Begum, a village woman, uses video to challenge the status quo. A local official stopped her at a village fair and asked why she had a video camera. Tuli explained that she makes tapes for her community to communicate their problems to others. The official told her that video production is not women's work and that she should be at home. Tuli said she was proud of her video work because she helps others and has gained access to many people in the community, especially decision-makers, like the official himself; had she not had a video camera, he would not have spoken with her. Tuli has discovered that using a video camera gives her access to people and places. She and her colleagues have learned that being associated with video gives them a new status in their communities.

In Bangladesh, village women have started using video to document abuses against women in their society. Using these tapes in village and formal courts as evidence and testimony has sent powerful messages into the community. Sahemuda Bulu, a village organizer says: 'Video disturbs the balance of power. I use it as a threat because a man knows I will be back with my camcorder if he hurts his wife.' She has used video in many situations to gain compensation for abused women and to prevent men from abandoning their wives. This women's organization has begun to share their experiences with other organizations working on legal aid and social justice issues. Other groups with video cameras are experimenting with ways to expose human rights abuses, to mediate for the poor and to enforce laws.

Hassina Begum is an enthusiastic, tenacious, and proud video team member from rural Bangladesh. Recently her organization has used video successfully to gain compensation for women who have been abandoned or violated by their husbands. When Hassina saw Kaberu Nesa, a woman in a neighboring village who had been severely beaten, she decided to document the story on video and to help the unconscious woman. Although Hassina is not a legal aid worker, she has been an active video team member and has produced and screened tapes in communities that have shown women their rights in legal situations. Video has been an important element in gaining justice in these situations. When she heard about this woman in distress, Hassina assessed the situation and made a decision to tape her story. This ability to think independently, to make connections, to make decisions, and to act on them is new. It was this exposure to new ideas, introduced through the participatory video program that enabled Hassina to take action. As more people learn to extend the range of possibility and to make connections, they will influence others to do the same.

Adolescent peer health educators in Nigeria conceived, developed, and implemented an AIDS training module for working youth who had little education and no exposure to pregnancy prevention, sexually transmitted diseases, and AIDS. Exposed to many different kinds of training and experiences, these teenagers discovered the importance of transferring health and safe sex information to their peers. What is more, they identified a group beyond their scope and willingly took risks to reach them. Using their participatory videos and facilitation skills, the teens reached over 300 youth with information and ideas to which they had never before been exposed. In their own analysis as peer educators they learned: 'We have to move out of the community, because it will not come to us. When we do our best people always appreciate it. No one is useless in a group. We can help shape people's lives for the better, if we only try.' Adolescents are in the process of maturation from children to adults. Thus they are often eager to take new risks, meet challenges, and ignore limitations because they are already in a constant phase of exploration and discovery. They welcome the opportunity to participate. The youth are future leaders—those who can carry the messages of community involvement and participation that leads, in turn, to action and change.

Insights

As a facilitator in a participatory environment, one's immediate goal is to provide the requisite information in a stimulating and challenging manner so the participants engage in, and take ownership of the learning process. It is most exciting to see how people who have been exposed to participatory principles take action using their newly discovered capacities to think independently and to make connections. Having transcended perceived boundaries, people begin to see and explore the infinite possibilities for implementing change in their lives and communities. Participatory methods assist people to explore reality and experiment with approaches that can transform their lives. The populations with whom I have worked are all marginalized—women, youth, the poor—but they are learning to question authority and the establishment, to trust their own voices and ideas, as well as to respect different opinions.

Critical thinking and reflection can and should be introduced into all environments—our homes, our schools, our work places, and our governments. As advocates of participation, we must be careful to practice it in our own lives as vigorously as we promote it in the lives of others. Social transformation remains on the horizon because it involves shifting the existing centers of power. Taking risks, making discoveries, learning from mistakes, and introducing the unknown is neither easy nor comfortable. But change is necessary to keep ourselves, our communities, and our world vital and alive. We need to introduce participatory approaches in all training environments to foster independent thinking and, I hope, to generate a cadre of leaders who have the strength and the vision to follow their convictions and take real risks without abusing power or compromising themselves and their communities. Everyone can become involved and active in this quest by sharing experiences and engaging in extended dialogue, honest reflection, careful deliberation, and action. A few committed individuals cannot accomplish lasting social change—we must all join in together.

References and Select Bibliography

Bery, R. (1985). All the World's a Stage: Learning through Improvisation and Commedia Dell'arte. Unpublished thesis. Middletown, CT: Wesleyan University.

———. (1995). Media Ethics: No Magic Solutions. In Rachel Slocum, Laurie Wichhart, Dianne Rocheleau, and Barbara Thomas–Slayter (Eds.), *Power, Process and Participation*, pp. 41–50. London: IT Publications.

Devine, B. (1994). Training for Social Activism. *Community Media Review, 17* (2).

Fuglesang, A. (1982). *About Understanding: Ideas and Observations on Cross-Cultural Communication*. Uppsala, Sweden: Dag Hammarskjold Foundation.

Higgins, J.W. (1993). Visions of Empowerment, Media Literacy and Demystification. *Community Television Review, 16* (3).

Hooks, B. (1994). *Teaching to Transgress*. New York, NY: Routledge.

Kline, N. (1993). *Women and Power*. London: BBC Books.

Moore, W. (1961). *The Roots of Excellence*. Burlington, VT: The Lane Press.

Protz, M. (1989). *Seeing and Showing Ourselves: A Guide to Using Small Format Videotape as a Participatory Tool for Development*. New Delhi: Centre for Development of Instructional Technology.

Rao, A. (Ed.). (1991). *Women's Studies International: Nairobi and Beyond*. New York, NY: The Feminist Press.

Riano, P. (Ed.). (1994). *Women in Grassroots Communication: Furthering Social Change*. Thousand Oaks, CA: Sage Publications.

Stuart, S. and **Renuka, B.** (1989). Powerful Grassroots Women Communicators. In *Video SEWA: A People's Alternative*.

Werner, D. and **Bower, B.** (1988). *Helping Health Workers Learn*. Palo Alto, CA: The Hesperian Foundation.

14

Planning Community Radio as Participatory Development

John L. Hochheimer

Who gets to speak, who gets to hear, and who gets to mediate, are issues crucial in conceptualizing and planning democratic media systems. John points out that deciding where radio stations and transmitters are built and who gets to own them, is at the heart of democratization. And, the struggles to keep the airways open to the voice of the people are fierce ones. Protecting the freedoms which access to radio broadcasting represents, will without doubt be one of the greatest challenges of the next century.

Facilitating New Media Systems

For those who have been politically or economically disenfranchised from the formal systems of power and those who have traditionally been socially and culturally silenced, the opportunity to have one's voice heard is an awesome challenge. It requires a restructuring of media systems within states, and a necessary rethinking of power relationships between people.

But the planning of new media systems, especially within social and political systems undergoing major transformations is a daunt-

ing task. It requires the construction of the technological infrastructure necessary to allow such media to be created, but, even more
critically, it involves the desire and abilities of many people to
assume power for themselves to speak and to act, where none had
been legitimated in the past. A growing school of scholars and practitioners has been looking into the ways in which local peoples have
been and are coming together to produce not only radio, but also
television, newspapers, and people's theater at the community level.
They see this as essential for people to reach out to others for solidarity of purpose, for information, for entertainment, and for
greater control of their own destiny (See for example, Barlow, 1988;
Dowmunt, 1994; Girard, 1992; Gunnar, 1994; Hochheimer, 1988,
1993; Jankowski et al., 1992; Karpff, 1980; Post, 1974; Schulman,
1985; Srampickal, 1994; Strauss, 1993; Thede and Ambrosi, 1991;
Widlok, 1981, 1989, 1992).

This more democratic approach to organizing community radio is
based upon a number of premises, each of which poses both ethical
and practical concerns for the producers at radio stations within
which such an approach is utilized. The ideas presented in this
chapter can perhaps be useful to facilitators who find themselves in
a position to foster democratic radio in emerging democracies. Just
as there is no universal approach to establishing democratic governance that can be applied to all situations, there is no universal
experience with democratic journalism which applies equally to differing countries, cultures, or communities at different points in history. But, the problems are fairly universal and solutions lie in people's practical experiences.

As Karol Jakubowicz (1993) points out, media can be no more
democratic than the societies within which they exist. Democratic
communication in practice implies that there is broadly-based support and participation from the communities served by the media.
Radio listeners in a participatory system are not considered an 'audience' or a 'market' as they are typically in mainstream media practice. Rather, the listeners are intimately involved as planners and
producers, as well as the receivers of programming. They are the
resources of the station, not the *targets* of their messages. Media
practitioners then become facilitators for members of the community to converse among themselves.

Creating Community-based Media

The efforts to create community-based radio stations can be seen as attempts to 'demassify the mass media,' to make it possible for people's organizations to provide alternatives to professionally-produced programs, some which have been imported from outside the local area. Drawing upon her experience working with community media in the Philippines, Florangel Rosario-Braid (1989) notes that 'demassified' media have distinct advantages over more traditional mass media for community groups:

- They are traditional in the true sense of the word and therefore have strong indigenous linkages.
- The content is not commercial and the messages have local flavor.
- The content has little, if any, colonial influence.
- They utilize appropriate indigenous materials and resources.
- They depict the people's actual reality—their ideas, wisdom, tradition, arts, and culture (Rosario-Braid, 1989: 69).

The parameters of this process can be found amidst that growing research area called *Participatory Development Communication* (PDC). Nair and White (1994) frame it within the concept of Cultural Renewal and regard it as a 'process of goal-oriented cultural and structural changes facilitated by pro-active indigenous communication transactions amongst local people within a specific cultural context (p. 138).' The process involves a combination of factors, especially those involving how people respond to time, space, themselves, their culture, and their environment. As applied to radio broadcasting, it is a process which brings people into positions of decision-making about what types of program content and styles they need, what works best for their social and cultural environment, and how programs can best be developed for them.

Dvorak Hochheimer (1994) defines the PDC process as one involving several steps, each of which are necessary components for bringing the community into the process of developing democratically-based journalism. I will elaborate five of these steps which I regard as especially critical:

- Identifying the participants
- Defining the issue or problem

- Problem-solving process/resource identification
- Goals and objectives/roles and responsibilities
- Design of action plan and community feedback

Identifying the Participants

This means determining who will be represented from the community, and who can be involved actively in the many tasks necessary to put the station on the air. As Hochheimer (1993) suggests, organizing democratic radio means identifying: Who serves whom? Is the function of the station its constituent community segments? Or, do the communities act as resources for the station to present to society as a whole? (Hochheimer, 1993: 475)

This also means identifying the various segments of the community who are willing and able to participate. Determining the participants and how they will implement the plan is important. Given the varying political interests that exist in any community, the determination of who gets to play in the game and which interests they represent, will no doubt influence outcomes.

These decisions become acute when determining who speaks for whom. Women, people of color, gays, lesbians, homeless people, for example, have traditionally been excluded from meaningful participation in constructive dialogue in the context of the USA. Women, especially, have traditionally been relegated to secondary positions and their voices rarely heard. This is even more prevalent in non-westernized cultures. They often feel hindered from speaking openly about issues of concern to them. A critical issue, then, is the development of a place within which marginalized groups can develop their own voice and sense of power from the beginning of the planning process.

Defining the Issue or Problem

Are you defining the correct problem?

This is an assessment of what the organizers of the radio station wish to do. Do they wish to supplement the existing government services and power holders or do they want to establish an independent presence in the community? Each of these would require a different strategy for developing a radio station. Supplementing existing government services might mean defining programs which the government would wish to have on the air (such as an AIDS awareness program, or a music program derived from the folk music of a particular region as was done by the Liberian Rural Communications Network). An independent presence in the community might mean to redefine what kinds of news, information, and entertainment services the community needs and find ways to provide them. This approach has been adapted with a great deal of success in Bolivia among women (Ruíz, 1994) and miners (O'Connor, 1990), in The Philippines (Lewis, 1974), in Canada (Widlok, 1981) and in the United States (Barlow, 1988; Schulman, 1985; Widlok, 1989, 1992).

Problem-solving Process/Resource Identification

Now comes a critical juncture in the process, that of identifying resources in the community which can be tapped for programming. It is essential to address the following issues:

- Who has experience working with people in the community
- Whose are the leading voices
- Which interests do they represent
- What kinds of mechanisms can be set up to integrate competing interests within the community
- How is outreach into the community organized

These are critical, since the station's primary reasons for being—the identification and coordination of a listener and creative base, require ongoing action. Resource identification can take place through schools, churches, and sports clubs, unions, and other regular meeting places within the community. Holding regular meetings in which people are invited to participate, speaking about issues that they have in mind, and providing a safe place for such discussions, are all necessary factors.

This, of course, assumes that people feel free to discuss issues of concern to them in a public place. This is often problematic, especially where there have been experiences of repression of dissent, of punishment for openly criticizing or complaining, or where a culture may dictate that women, for example, have no rights to speak publicly about issues of particular concern to them (Arriola, 1992).

This was noted in a workshop for promoters of popular communication for various neighborhoods in Lima, Peru:

> To participate in radio is not easy, even more so for women. Not only because of a lack of familiarity but because they have made us believe that our word is not valuable, that only the educated, the cultured, the men can speak. That's why many times we don't want to be leaders, because we can't speak well, nor use impressive and difficult words. And we're always afraid and prefer that others speak for us. And some people take advantage of this passive attitude and without consulting us to speak for us.... But we have to know what we want, what we seek and talk for ourselves, because in this way we can be sure that we're not being used, control what we are saying and when we should be quiet.... (AAVV, 1987: 40).

> We have to begin with what we know how to do. And we're very good at dramatizing, telling our problems with socio-dramas; we do it with such emotion that we're very convincing. ... because we know how to get ourselves listened to that way. Our children are witnesses of how we know how to dramatize and tell stories (Mata, 1994: 205–206).

The station planners need to work from within to find the means for the community to decide who should speak for them, and on what terms. An ongoing 'facilitated dialogue' needs to be initiated within the community in order to enable members to come together and identify common purposes. Community members, rather than station managers, define issues on their own terms, and determine who can be the most legitimate spokespeople for them. Who decides what voices are to be heard is an ongoing issue and must be periodically evaluated. There are other issues to be addressed:

- Who speaks for which community interest
- Which points of view are the most compelling
- What happens when ideas or technical skills are at odds
- How are community views solicited or encouraged. In other words,
- To what degree does/can stations bring the audiences into the process of making program decisions for themselves (Hochheimer, 1993: 476–77).

Just saying to people 'now you are free to say what you like' is not nearly the same as their own belief that such freedom is real, that there will be no punishment for their actions or that they have something worth saying and will be heard. This is true for media professionals as well.

Success experienced under a totalitarian regime is not measured in the same way as success experienced under a more open system. Similarly, expectations for media practitioners will differ. Working in a free market system requires, for example, understanding how to compete for work, how to bill clients, how to set up competitive pricing schedules—all unfamiliar modes of operation (Goldberg, 1997). Organizing a community station in an open market requires understanding how to assess audience size, needs, and interests. It also requires an understanding of how the station fits into the larger business community in which profits (or at least sufficient monies to pay salaries and the electric, telephone, and other bills), not government dictates, rule. We recognize that the needs of a community change over time; the people who are willing, or able, to participate change over time as well. Successful station planning identifies and assesses resources and actors in an ongoing process of adjusting to these changes.

Goals and Objectives/Roles and Responsibilities

It is expected that the media organization set goals. These will evolve over time as the station evolves. At the beginning, a goal might be to secure funding to purchase equipment while at a later point in time, the goal might be to plan for changing audience size or type. Planners should have goals for the short-, middle-, and long-term, depending upon the needs of the station's personnel and the community. Indicators for 'success' need to be pre-determined in order to assess when goals have been met, in appropriate time, and on whose terms. Success for a commercial station is usually defined in terms of profitability when the goal is framed in terms of making money for station owners. But, for community stations, where the goals are for community presence and participation, the definition of success is a different and more difficult matter. If a station emanates from a growing awareness of common needs for communication, as was the case of campesinos in Peru, and for poor people living around Sao Paulo, Brazil (Mata, 1994), then success would be judged on how well those needs were met.

At first, a community station may well consider getting the station organized, as success—finding sources of money for necessary equipment, organizing a staff, obtaining and testing equipment, initiating community outreach projects, and obtaining access to reliable sources of electric power. In the intermediate stage, success might constitute getting on the air—defining audience needs, planning station formats, making sure that sufficient numbers of radio receivers are in the community so that people can hear the station, and publicizing the station so listeners know when the station is broadcasting. In the long term, goals may possibly be to build audience participation in program planning, to find means to better connect the station to the communities the station serves, instituting events as dances, fairs, forums on current issues of interest, poetry readings, or fund-raising events. The station can also broadcast all of these events for listeners who cannot attend. The more the station is identified by community members as being an integral part of the community at large, the better the station's chances for long-term success in terms of community support (McClear, 1982).

Roles and responsibilities change as the station 'matures.' As participation increases, the likelihood that different people with different goals and agendas for the station will emerge, also increases. It would be natural for struggles for power to ensue. There may be resentment from longer-term members at attempts to redefine the goals and methods of 'our station' by newer members. As with earlier stages of the evaluation process, facilitators need to be sensitive to the interrelationships of people. When power and decision-making have become 'entrenched,' conflict resolution skills are necessary to mediate differences perhaps between newcomers and founders of the station (Hochheimer, 1993: 477–78).

Embedded within this change process is the very nature of decision-making within democratically constituted stations. If the goal is for everyone to participate actively within the station, who makes decisions? Who decides who gets to decide? What internal checks can be instituted to authorize and check upon those who are empowered to make decisions?

To decide that decision-making should take place 'democratically,' is to decide that a large portion of the station's time and

Giving a voice is part of the democratic process.

energy will be devoted to making decisions. This may well be at odds with the need to reach out to the community and to engage in constructive dialogues within and between communities to promote their interests via the station (Hochheimer, 1993: 478–82). Deciding to run the station in a more traditional hierarchical manner may improve efficiency, but this comes at the cost of widespread input from all community groups involved. Again, each case needs to be examined individually and the benefits of participation weighed against costs of community input. The participants need to make structural decisions based upon their own political/cultural dynamics and history of community action. In the final analysis, the stake of the people in the community station will determine its effectiveness and survival.

Design of Action Plan and Community Feedback

Once you have the station, what do you do with it? The approaches to action plans are as varied as are the locales and interests of the communities that exist around the world. No one approach works best; each must be addressed depending upon the goals of the stations and the needs of the identified communities. These may well differ also due to differences in culture, national identity, and the particular dynamics within a given community of interest. As Jallov (1992) contends, even among radio stations dedicated to promoting women; great differences in approach can be found in France, Holland, Great Britain, Norway, and Denmark.

For example, *Les Nanas Radioteuses* in Paris wanted to create a forum for feminist discourse through an independent women's channel. This was organized by involving women from various differing communities in all aspects of producing a once-a-week, six-hour program. Topics covered included employment, traditions in women's songs, news from the women's movement, and historical portraits. Special attention was given to specific topics: abortion, housework, childcare, legal matters, and women's solidarity.

In its formative years (1981–1987), *Vrouwenzender* (Women's Senders) in Nijmegen, Holland, concentrated more on issues within the women's movement—radical feminism, lesbianism, working class women, young girls, and women's lives and culture. Later it provided more news and informational programming of interest to women, that was being ignored by more traditional media. *Women's Airwaves* in London focused more on producing audio cassettes and training for activists in the women's movement, and less on active program production. The goal was to assist young urban girls to consider a variety of employment options and alternative lifestyles.

Radi Orakel in Oslo sees itself less as a movement radio station than one in direct competition with the other stations in the area. They chose to focus their efforts on producing professional quality programs focusing on women's issues for the general community. In time, it became the fifth most listened-to station in the region. Copenhagen's *Kvindeboelgerne* (Women's Waves) is part of a larger grassroots collective which devotes one day a week to women's programming. Its focus was intended to be primarily the realities of differing women in the region, centering mostly on the feminist movement. It is unclear how successful this approach has been (Jallov, 1992: 218–21).

Radio Donna in Rome was a highly regarded station produced by and for women in the 1970s. It broadcast two hours per day, focusing on listeners calling in to discuss issues such as wife battering, contraception, and abortion, which had been excluded from Italian State radio. In January 1979, the station was attacked and set on fire, resulting in great damage and several serious injuries (Karpff, 1980). At the least, this experience speaks of the powerful forces which can be generated by intense interest in public discussion of issues but which may threaten other large segments of the population.

Other examples seem more promising. The *Ondes des femmes* project of Radio Centre-Ville in MontrJal was organized to counter male dominance of the station, and to 'support collective action to transform society in the direction of marginalized sectors, of which women, unfortunately, all too often form a part' (Radio Centre-Ville, 1992: 56). Women from many women's groups throughout the city were invited to participate and, within two months, roughly fifty women shared in the production of more than twenty broadcasts in French, Spanish, Creole, and Chinese. Subjects discussed in the programs deal with women's rights, conjugal violence, employment, culture shock, and integration (Radio Centre-Ville, 1992: 57). Examples of other approaches include:

- using radio to promote literacy in the sahel region of Africa (Aw, 1992);

- opposition to official government media in Mexico (Valenzuela, 1992), the Philippines, El Salvador; Nicaragua (Lewis and Booth, 1990) and Haiti (Georges with Fortin, 1992); and
- national reconciliation in Cambodia (Zhou, 1994).

A Final Observation

Establishing a community radio station is not the starting point for organizing people. It is the extension of efforts to draw upon local people's felt and articulated needs to communicate among themselves and with others to establish their own sense of personal and community power. The primary issue in planning a participatory development project is the facilitation of a dialogue among the diverse components of a community, not the imposition of a solution from outside. Only people within a community can build upon their common background, shared culture, and experience with oppression. The experienced outsider as a facilitator can help them to articulate their needs and assist them in finding new ways to speak to each other. This is not to suggest that 'the wheel needs to be reinvented each time' by experienced outsiders but rather, it implies that the tool needs to be adapted to the uniqueness of each community by those who will provide the inputs which sustain the project in the community's best interest.

Democratic journalism or media development is not a matter of formal structures. Instead, it is a matter in which all interested members of a community believe they have a stake in the establishment of the station, something worth sharing with others, and the means to facilitate an ongoing program of outreach. Communication implies dialogue. The development of a truly democratic medium of communication means that all participants from the outset of the project must respect the practice of meaningful dialogue.

From this vantage point, when a community radio is identified as a community aspiration or goal, it is an intermediate step in the long path toward greater power and control at the grassroots. Planners who build upon existing local networks of social and political solidarity, or who facilitate the development and maintenance of such networks, will find that the likelihood of success of their stations is greatly enhanced, no matter how that success is defined by community members in mutual consultation. This is a critical realization about the development of truly *democratic* media in emerging democracies.

References and Select Bibliography

AAVV. (1987). *Palabra de mujer. La experiencia de ser promotora popular de comunicacion.* Cited in Mata, 1994. Lima, Peru: Calandria-Tarea.

Arriola, Tachi. (1992). The Feminist Radio Collective of Peru. In B. Girard (Ed.), *A Passion for Radio*, pp. 114–120. Montreal: Black Rose Books.

Aw, E. (1992). Pluralist Responses for Africa. In B. Girard (Ed.), *A Passion for Radio*, pp. 41–149. Montreal: Black Rose Books.

Barlow, W. (1988). Community Radio in the US: The Struggle for a Democratic Medium. *Media, Culture and Society, 10* (1): 81–105.

Dowmunt, T. (1994). *Channels of Resistance: Global Television and Local Empowerment.* London: British Film Institute.

Dvorak Hochheimer, J. (1994). Participatory Development Communication Theory. Unpublished manuscript. Department of Communication, Cornell University, Ithaca, NY.

Georges, G. and **Fortin, I.** (1992). 'A New Dawn for Freedom of Speech: Radio Soleil. In B. Girard (Ed.), *A Passion for Radio*, pp. 95–105. Montreal: Black Rose Books.

Girard, B. (1992). *A Passion for Radio.* Montreal: Black Rose Books.

Goldberg, V. (1997). Surviving Freedom after the Wall Came Down. *The New York Times*, Jan. 26, Section 2, pp. 39–40.

Gunnar, L. (Ed.). (1994). *Politics and Performance: Theater, Poetry and Song in Southern Africa.* Johannesburg, Africa: Witwatersrand University Press.

Hochheimer, J. L. (1988). Community Radio in the United States: Whom does it Serve?, *RTV: Theory and Practice*, Special Issue #3.

——— (1993). Organizing Democratic Radio: Issues in Praxis. *Media, Culture and Society*, 15: 473–486.

Jakubowicz, K. (1993). Stuck in a Groove: Why the 1960s Approach to Communication Democratization will No Longer Do. In S. Slavko and J. Wasko (Eds.), *Communication and Democracy.* pp. 33–54. Norwood, NJ: Ablex Publishing Corp.

Jallov, B. (1992). Women on the Air: Community Radio as a Tool for Feminist Messages. In Jankowski, et al. (Ed.), pp. 215–224.

Jankowski, N., Prehn, O. and **Stappers, J.** (Eds.). (1992). *The People's Voice: Local Radio and Television in Europe.* London: John Libbey and Company.

Karpff, A. (1980). Women and Radio. *Women's Studies International Quarterly*, 3: 41–54.

Lewis, P.M. (1974). *Media for the People in Cities.* Paris: UNESCO Press.
Lewis, P.M. and Booth, J. (1989). *The Invisible Medium.* London: MacMillan.
Mata, M. (1994). Being Women in the Popular Radio. In P. Riano, (Ed.) (1994), *Women in Grassroots Communication: Furthering Social Change,* pp. 192–211. Thousand Oaks, CA: Sage Publications.
McClear, R. (1982). General Manager, KCAW–FM (Raven Radio), Interview, July.
Nair, K.S. and White, S.A. (1994). *Perspectives on Development Communication.* New Delhi: Sage Publications.
———. (1994). Participatory Development Communications as Cultural Renewal. In S.A. White, K.S. Nair and J. Ascorft (Eds.), *Participatory Communication: Working for Change and Development.* New Delhi: Sage Publications.
O'Connor, A. (1990). The Miners' Radio Stations in Bolivia: A Culture of Resistance, *Journal of Communication, 40* (1): 102–10.
Post, S. (1974). *Playing in the FM Band: A Personal Account of Free Radio.* New York, NY: The Viking Press.
Radio Centre-Ville. (1992). Inventing and experimenting: Radio Centre-Ville. In B. Girard, *A Passion for Radio,* pp. 49–58. Montreal: Black Rose Books.
Riano, P. (ed.). (1994). *Women in Grassroots Communication: Furthering Social Change.* Thousand Oaks, CA: Sage Publications.
Rosario-Braid, F. (1989). Communication and the Community. *Solidarity,* 123: 66–71.
Ruíz, C. (1994). Losing Fear: Video and Radio Productions of Native Aymara Women in Bolivia. In P. Riano (Ed.) (1994). *Women in Grassroots Communication: Furthering Social Change* (pp. 161–178). Thousand Oaks, CA: Sage Publications.
Schulman, M. (1985). Neighborhood Radio as Community Communication. Unpublished doctoral dissertation, The Union Graduate School.
Srampickal, J. (1994) *Voice to the Voiceless: The Power of People's Theatre in India.* New Delhi: Manohar Publishers and Distributors.
Strauss, N. (ed.). (1993). *Radiotext (e).* New York, NY: Semiotex(t).
Thede, N. and Ambrose, A. (1991). *Video the Changing World.* Montreal: Black Rose Books.
Valenzuela, E. (1992). New Voices. In B. Girard, *A Passion for Radio,* pp. 150–155. Montreal: Black Rose Books.
Vreg, F. (1990). Dilemmas of Communication Pluralism in Social Systems. In S. Slavko Splichal, J. Hochheimer and K. Jakubowicz, (Eds.), *Democratization and the Media: An East-West Dialogue,* pp. 10–19. Trieste: Faculty of Sociology, Political Science and Journalism, University of Ljubljana, Romania.
Widlok, P. (1981). Sprachrohr fhr Minderheiten: Vancouver co-operative radio, *Medium, 11* (10): 28–32.

Widlok, P. (1989). Indianerradio in den USA: KILI–FM in South Dakota, *Rundfunk und Fernsehen, 37* (4): 511–523.

————. (1992). *Der andere H'rfunk: Community radios in den USA*. Berlin: Vista Verlag.

Zhou Mei (1994). *Radio UNTAC of Cambodia: Winning Ears, Hearts and Minds*. Bangkok: White Lotus.

15

Facilitating Participation: Accessing Internet Services for Development

Don Richardson

Through this contribution Don hopes to help development facilitators understand the potentials, limitations, and challenges of the Internet. His focus is on issues of participation, power, and control as they relate to the planning, implementation, use, and evaluation of Internet applications designed to serve development goals. As with other methods and tools used to facilitate development, Don thinks the Internet works best when development stakeholders participate fully in planning, implementation, use, and evaluation of Internet applications. The challenge we face with the Internet is how to transform this ideal of stakeholder participation into reality.

Ian Smillie in his book, *Mastering the Machine: Poverty, Aid and Technology* notes that:

From the beginning of time, technology has been a key element in the growth and development of societies. But technology is more than jets and computers; it is the combination of knowledge, techniques and concepts; it is tools and machines, farms and factories. It is organization, processes and people. *The cultural, historical and organizational context in which technology is developed and applied is the key to its success or failure* (emphasis mine) (Smillie, 1991: 3).

The Internet is not a panacea for development, but it can and does bring new information resources and can open up new communication opportunities and challenges between people and their organizations, institutions, and governments. By providing an open and uncontrolled means for interaction, dialogue, and information sharing, the Internet offers intriguing opportunities for bridging the gaps between development professionals and the stakeholders they serve. The source of the Internet's 'obsessive appeal isn't technology or information, *but people*. In fact, it is really an interpersonal medium in which information plays a supporting role' (Smolan, 1996). It can enable bottom-up articulation and information sharing on local needs and local knowledge, through providing a new and cost-effective means of communication. For example, the Internet is supporting previously unheard of processes of 'south-south' communication and knowledge sharing, and its use increases daily.

Unfortunately, in today's knowledge-based economies there are 'information-haves' and 'information-have-nots,' and there is a large gap between them. The Internet is not responsible for this gap. But, unless we can make the tools of the Internet and other basic telecommunication services like the telephone more widely available, especially to the rural poor, the expanded use of the Internet among the 'information-haves' will widen the gap.

The processes of globalization, and the transformation of industrial and agricultural economies into economies based more and more on information and knowledge infrastructure, require us to devote considerable energy to enabling the 'information-have-nots' to gain access to information and knowledge infrastructures. Without this access, the 'information-have-nots' will be at the mercy of external forces, with little or no ability to understand, respond, or direct the forces that affect their lives. It is imperative to find ways to access the Internet to intermediary peoples' organizations and local agencies that serve the poor. Rural and urban families who are struggling to achieve prosperity through learning and knowledge no doubt would embrace use of the Internet if it were available to them.

Benefits of the Internet

The Internet's most important benefit is probably its use as an inter-personal communication tool that is the foundation of participatory communication. The term 'participatory communication' is used to describe processes of two-way dialogue and expression that encourage the sharing of feelings, desires, beliefs, and experiences. Together with problem analysis, people communicate with one another to search for solutions to their problems, and engage in bottom-up communication, which raises the awareness of decision-makers to those problems (Bessette, 1996). The basic tenet of participatory communication is that the communication *process* is more important than the production of media products or their content. Participatory communication within the field of communication for development tends to involve facilitated interventions and media used to catalyze two-way communication, dialogue, and problem-solving (Richardson, 1997).

The Internet, like its sister media, the telephone, fax, and postal system, opens up entirely new channels and options for us to stay in touch with friends, family, and peers. It enables us to communicate, instantaneously, inexpensively, reliably, and globally. Benefits to development include increased efficiency in the use of resources. It can open opportunities to reduce duplication of efforts and promote collaboration. Reduction of communication costs, global access to information and human resources used for planning, consultation, decision-making, and action can be outcomes of the use of this technology. The Internet's biggest drawbacks are dependency on largely urban-centred telecommunication infrastructures and the availability of computers that are affordable. Generally poor levels of Internet service exist in countries—both developed and developing—which have monopolistic, expensive, state-run telecommunication systems.

In spite of the Internet's drawbacks, there has been a rapid increase in the use of the Internet in developing countries (Richardson, 1997). But, none of the potential development benefits of the Internet will be fully realized by the technology alone. Its potential development benefits can be realized only when people, including development planners, development beneficiaries, private sector telecommunication providers, and other stakeholders work together to plan, implement, use, and evaluate Internet applications. Projects that fully involve intended beneficiaries in planning, design, and implementation and meet their needs at the same time, tend to focus less on telecommunication infrastructure and computers, and more on basic communication and information applications that meet people's needs. Thus, access to and use of Internet services are more likely to be sustainable.

There is a tendency among Internet advocates to see the Internet as the single most important information communication technology (ICT) on the planet. This presents a danger to development planners and stakeholders who might be seduced by the Internet's tremendous capabilities. In many cases, the Internet is simply not an appropriate tool for providing the communication and information applications that meet peoples' needs. The Internet is only one medium among thousands, and there are other electronic media such as the telephone, the fax, and the photocopier whose development potential has never been fully tapped by development communication specialists. There are traditional communication systems, folk communication processes, and simple printed media as well that have powerful communication advantages.

As a rural development and participatory communication facilitator, I see everyday how rural people benefit from the Internet. Five years ago I made a decision to devote much of my career to helping rural people and farmers 'get on-line.' Since then my work has taken me across rural areas of Canada, Chile, Egypt, Mexico, the Philippines, Senegal, South Africa, Zambia, and Zimbabwe to assist rural organizations and farmers' groups to help their members to access the power of rural telecommunication systems, telephones, and the Internet. I have seen first hand how farmers in rural Chile get better prices for their crops because they use the Internet to gain up-to-the-minute farm market information from the website of the Chicago Board of Trade. I have seen how rural development practitioners in Senegal communicate across their country by e-mail, bypassing a terribly inefficient postal service. In Canada I have seen how rural people in my own area use the Internet to sell hay and advertise free kittens to their neighbors.

I was not always an Internet enthusiast and I am all too aware of the Internet's faults. As someone who really does not like computers, I can remember arguing vehemently that e-mail is a tool for computer 'geeks.' I refused to use an e-mail system that had been installed in my university office. With pressure from my students however, I eventually relented and let my students teach me how to use e-mail and how to 'surf' the World Wide Web. After finding some very useful information and discovering that I could actually communicate with an old friend in northern Labrador, I was hooked. I quickly realized that this tool could revolutionize communication in the rural areas in which I work.

In 1993, with the help and encouragement of some enthusiastic students I set out to see if we could create a community-oriented Internet service in the county surrounding my university. At that time there were very few non-computer-geeks using the Internet. However, a few pioneers in Canada and the United States were promoting the concept of 'Freeness' or free access, community-owned and managed computer communication networks connected to the Internet. My students and I learned everything we could about the Freenet movement and embarked on a two-year community development initiative to create one of the first low cost, high access rural community networks in North America. Today, the Wellington County FreeSpace network (http://www2.freespace.net) serves twenty-one rural municipalities and one city. The lessons learned from that effort are now being applied in rural communities around the world (Richardson, 1995, 1996a, 1996b). In the process of developing FreeSpace, I also learned a great deal about the Internet, its history, its limitations, and its empowering nature.

Facilitating Participation within Internet Initiatives for Development

The nature of a participatory communication initiative via the Internet is difficult to understand until a person has an opportunity to participate in such an initiative. Organizations that do not have strong community communication and outreach orientations, are prone to scepticism and dismissal because they may fear greater contact with the public, particularly if they are also engaged in community 'turf wars' or 'empire building.' The same is true for Internet initiatives within organizations. If an organization, or the organizations within a community, are not already functioning with participatory management styles, there may be little value in introducing a

264 The Art of Facilitating Participation

communication tool that can optimize communication flow. This is an important factor for facilitators of Internet initiatives to understand. It is necessary for facilitators to spend time in the early days of an initiative in order to get a better understanding of the complex nature of community, organizational, and stakeholder politics, as well as leadership personalities and political manoeuvring.

The keenest participants in participatory communication initiatives involving the Internet are people who are predisposed to participatory communication and participatory management styles. Facilitators during the community organizing effort of the Wellington County FreeSpace network reached this conclusion. The facilitators, based at a university, prompted a vision of a community-owned and managed network that would neither be owned nor controlled by the university, but by community organizations.

The facilitators experienced frustrations with the lack of leadership, commitment, and understanding among county governments, libraries, and school board officials. So, they found themselves evaluating prospective partners based not on the extent of their profile in the community, but on the prospective partners' existing record for participatory communication, openness, and information sharing within the community. The FreeSpace facilitators began holding community information sessions to introduce the community network vision to stakeholders from all corners of the county. Very quickly they noticed that the people and organizations with the most interest and commitment were organizations that were already deeply involved in various aspects of local community development, or providing meaningful local services.

Eventually, three key leaders of community organizations came forward to publicly champion the project. The champions of the FreeSpace project were people who required only a minimal introduction to community networking, or the technology. They quickly determined that such a network would be a tremendous resource for enhancing their work and helping to solve problems in county communication, outreach, and information sharing. Their strong commitments to community development and continuous communication with their clients and members was the primary factor in engaging their support. The legitimacy that they brought to the project did what countless hours of 'preaching' to county government officials could not. Once the community network began service, their profile helped foster broad public attention, and helped bring in the hesitant community organizations (including the county government) to support the project.

Lessons Learned from FreeSpace

This experience convinced the facilitators to start keeping track of 'lessons learned' so that they could share those lessons with other Internet advocates and facilitators of community-owned and managed Internet services. These insights can spare you of at least some struggles and potential mistakes, we hope.

> *Lesson 1: Start working with community organization leaders who already see the benefits of community networking—those organizational leaders who are predisposed to collaborative, open, and participatory communication approaches to community development. Do not spend time trying to convince organizational leaders predisposed to 'turf wars,' or 'empire building and who demonstrate little regard for public participation processes.*

Community leadership, advocacy, and vision came from unexpected sources throughout the FreeSpace project. Over time, the facilitation team came to recognize this and remain open to voluntary organizational support, rather than spend time on 'preaching' efforts. A community mental health centre, for example, was not identified by the team as a possible source of project leadership, yet that organization emerged as one of the strongest and most valuable proponents of the project. Despite the lessons being learned, significant time was spent trying to achieve official support from county government officials, but they continued to remain unsupportive of the project.

It was a small grassroots rural community development organization, the North Wellington Advisory Group—an organization with a strong track record of participatory community initiatives, that took the central leadership role in the project by assuming responsibility for proposal development and fund raising. Another champion from an unexpected source appeared, when the major urban city in the county hired Canada's first female police chief. Within days of taking office she contacted the outreach team to help bring community policing and information services 'on-line' in order to help open a new avenue for police and community communication. Her public actions helped profile the FreeSpace initiative and her support opened the door for some quietly supportive city government officials to openly advocate on behalf of the community network. Her community policing homepage on the World Wide Web was one of the first of its kind in North America.

Lesson 2: Real, risk-taking community leadership is not necessarily found within elected bodies and local government bureaucracies where one might normally expect to start looking, and we should expect community champions to come from unexpected sectors of community leadership. The 'obvious' champion organizations, especially local government, may not immediately buy into a community access Internet project.

Generally, the most enthusiastic champions for the project were women, and young people. In community development circles it is often said that 'women-run communities,' and in the case of Free-Space, women tended (and continue) to provide the practical leadership necessary to accomplish necessary tasks. Many males engaged in fruitless policy and tedious technical debates while women engaged in tangible and productive tasks such as phone support, raising money, marketing, volunteer mobilization, strategic planning, and partnership building. Their efforts were often not recognized by self-important and technically knowledgeable males engaged in the more 'important' tasks of debating worst case technical scenarios, debating software and hardware choices and wrangling over complex rules and procedures for membership and participation in the network.

Young people, whose enthusiasm and dedication also often went unrecognized, were responsible for developing and creating much of the World Wide Web information and content residing on the network. Members of 4-H groups (a rural agricultural youth organization) and other youth groups demonstrated significant leadership, and efforts are currently underway to develop new mechanisms to make better use of these talented and creative young leaders.

Lesson 3: Provide many opportunities for women and young people to actively volunteer their time and energy for practical and identifi-

able tasks. Recognize and reward their efforts at every opportunity, and provide mechanisms to insure that they can participate in key management roles.

The fund raising stage brought new wrinkles to the project. The Province of Ontario had begun providing matching grants to 'network infrastructure' programs. However most of its funding at that point in time had gone to closed-access municipal, health, and social service internal network infrastructure projects. None of these networks provide access to members of the general public. A source of frustration for the facilitators was an attempt by county government, hospital, school board, and library officials to develop their own network proposal for a 'closed' network, based on the same Internet technologies that would drive the community access network. This 'closed' network would provide services only to bureaucrats and officials, and would not be open to citizens.

These same officials expressed no interest in combining their efforts with more grassroots community organizations, despite the fact that the community network would cost an equal amount *and* be able to meet *everyone's* needs. The technically ignorant excuse of 'security concerns' was publicly stated, while in private, officials would often relate that they did not want the 'organizational hassles' associated with providing a wider community service. In order to compete with local governments for the network infrastructure project funding, the newly formed FreeSpace Management Committee had to develop a cloak of bureaucratic and organizational legitimacy that would be recognized by the Provincial Funding Committee.

Creating *organizational legitimacy* for a loose coalition of grassroots community organizations entailed creating numerous volunteer committees and management structures. Unfortunately, this happened before there were many tangible things to volunteer for or manage, and it became a decision that the FreeSpace organizers would soon come to regret. It was, however, a necessary evil given the funding guidelines of the Province. The funding agency guidelines were written for long-standing public corporations, not for diverse coalitions of grassroots community champions. Inevitably, committees and management structures with no direct purpose began creating work that was not necessarily required. Months went by during which bylaws and policies were debated and rewritten, with little tangible result, lots of frustration, and a great deal of volunteer burnout.

Almost two years from the start of the initiative in 1993, a funding grant was approved and received in May, 1995, but the bureaucratic momentum of the various committees slowed down the building and implementation of the network during the next six months. More volunteer burnout and more participant frustration was the result as the community impatiently waited for the promised network.

Eventually, the rural development organization corporately responsible for the project disbanded many committees and streamlined management to a small group of advisors and paid consultants. At this point, network use and development accelerated and the benefits of the community network began to be realized.

Lesson 4: Fast and decisive network implementation yields the desired results of participatory community communication, and a small team of consultative decision-makers is far better than management by networks of committees. Open and participatory community management must be maintained, but a small team of accountable decision-makers will accelerate the organizational process during the creation of an Internet project.

Once built, a community network requires many volunteers to develop community information and communication services, as well as deliver user support, training, and community awareness initiatives. These volunteers need to work within clearly defined plans, and this does mean that everyone is responsible for having input on every policy and planning decision. Democratic mechanisms for policy and planning are best activated after the infrastructure is in place, and the Internet communication mechanisms that are the reason for starting the initiative in the first place, are more easily available.

In retrospect, the FreeSpace facilitators and the community champions recognized that they had neglected to provide themselves and community volunteers with human resource development support. Only after the network was operational were plans developed to provide leadership and project management training to the community management team, and to provide volunteer support and strengthening programs. Despite the human resource development background of many of the project facilitators and champions, it was unconsciously assumed that management effectiveness and teamwork qualities would be naturally present.

Lesson 5: Provide training in, and human resource development support for, project management, leadership, and teamwork.

Despite numerous difficulties and challenges, Wellington County FreeSpace went on-line in November 1995 and now has over 1,500 participants. With streamlined management, focus is now on fundraising, revenue generation, partnership building, and the further development of community information resources and community discussion services on the network. A research project has been initiated to examine the use made of the network by farmers and rural residents, and their usage patterns will be monitored over several years to determine the impact of the network on rural and agricultural communities. A project that began as a rural networking initiative created new alliances and partnerships between rural and urban organizations, and has significantly enhanced urban understanding of rural issues in the region.

An unexpected, but likely inevitable, consequence of creating the network was the local emergence and strengthening of commercial Internet service providers and World Wide Web developers within the urban sectors of the County. These commercial activities compete with the revenue generation avenues available to FreeSpace. FreeSpace had created strong local awareness of the Internet during a time when national and international media attention was only beginning to focus on the subject. In some senses, FreeSpace helped develop and channel consumer interest, thus developing a ready and willing local market for commercial Internet service providers. At some future point, competing Internet service provision (which tends to come with advanced home and business connectivity options, such as very high speed connections) may jeopardize the community network's sustainability, unless it is able to compete by providing expensive and technically up-to-date connectivity at little or no cost.

In the near future, low-cost community-owned and managed networks in Canada or in developing countries may have to cease Internet service provision in the urban areas which have a high concentration of commercial competitors. They may instead have to concentrate on service provision to grassroots community organizations, people who have difficulty paying high commercial services costs and rural users who are normally left out of commercial service areas. At the same time, these networks will need to focus attention on efforts to enhance general community information, and facilitate local dialogue, which are the primary objectives of a community network. This methodology has been followed quite effectively by SangoNet (South African NGO Network—http://wn.apc.org) which provides one of the most high quality NGO and development information systems in the world.

An alternative to narrowing service delivery to key stakeholders and rural areas, is to combine high quality user service with low pricing policies, efficient management *and* community development activities in order to effectively compete with emerging commercial competition. This is the case with Zamnet in Zambia which has emerged as one of the best Internet service providers in Sub-Saharan Africa (Robinson, 1996). Zamnet has made the important decision of strengthening its services through the addition of staff with strong marketing and business backgrounds. At the same time they continue to implement their policies of enabling local organizations, educational institutions, individuals, and government services to access the Internet at a low cost (personal communication with Shuler Habeenzu, director of Zamnet). This is critically important service in one of Africa's poorest and least developed nations.

One could look at the future of community-owned and managed Internet systems with pessimism, but the desired results and vision of the original Internet pioneers of the early 1990s, around the world, may still be realized. Communities will be networked together, sharing information, communicating, and gaining access to the information and communication resources of the global Internet. The commercialization of Internet service is a reality, and if community networks can stimulate peoples' participation in using the Internet to advance community and social development, there is no reason that people cannot find the same value from commercial networks. Community networks create their own problems because they do simulate the markets that enable commercial Internet service providers to emerge. This can be seen as a positive outcome of pioneering community networking initiatives that provide the initial leadership and sensitization that creates a consumer demand for service.

Lesson 6: At its core, a community network's goal is to enhance community communication, information sharing, help educate people about valuable Internet services, and encourage the application of the Internet in support of local development.

A community network does not necessarily have to be an Internet service provider. Rapidly changing contexts for commercial Internet service provision, in both the North and the South, may result in the demise of community-managed telecommunication technical infrastructure. Thus, community networks should stick to first principles, while continuing to strategically orient themselves to provide service where none exists. The developmental results of community networking initiatives may continue regardless of whether or not the community network, or a commercial service, provides the technical infrastructure, particularly in urban areas.

Other 'Lessons Learned'

Some of the other 'lessons learned' by the facilitators of the Free-Space network, have been verified by these same facilitators in other areas of Canada and in developing countries:

Lesson 7: If you desire to use the Internet within your community or organization to enhance participatory communication, start now. Do not be afraid to start small.

There is a temptation to wait for others to build the network, or to wait for money, or to wait for more sophisticated equipment. The longer you wait, the longer you will be without the benefits of an electronic network and access to the global information of the Internet. If others build the network for you, there is a very good chance that it will serve their interests and not your community's interests. If you have a computer and a phone line, you can establish a very basic e-mail community network using free software and a $100 modem. There are thousands of small community 'telecentres' in developing countries that provide local phone and fax services to citizens in urban and rural areas. Many of these 'telecentres' are beginning to provide access to e-mail and World Wide Web searching, particularly in countries like the Philippines, Malaysia, and in parts of West Africa and Southern Africa. One Internet computer in a small telecenter can provide services to countless individuals and organizations. Some telecenters do a good business simply providing telegram-style e-mail services between families, friends, and small businesses among communities within a nation or region.

> *Lesson 8: Start from the bottom-up. Large, government initiated, top-down networking efforts have a high failure rate, are unsustainable, and cost large amounts of money. In areas where expensive top-down solutions have been applied, there has been serious damage to the seeds of local community network organizations and have set back community networking initiatives by three to four years (Sam Lanfranco as cited in Ontario Africa Working Group, 1994).*

Top-down solutions fail because electronic communication involves reciprocal exchanges, dialogue, and relative freedom, not unidirectional information distribution or elitist information hoarding. Bottom-up solutions tend to be less expensive, more practical, and intrinsically relevant to the participants who helped to design and create them. According to Tindimubona and Wilson (1992), the spread of FidoNet networks in Africa has spread in a grassroots, non-hierarchical manner, and 'top-down' organizational structures have met with resistance.

> *Lesson 9: The distinction between information providers and information users has little meaning in an electronic commons (Graham, 1994). Everyone is both information provider and user in the midst of a web of human communication and sharing.*

> *What we were trying to do depended upon a human network first. There is no point in promoting the use of computer-mediated communication unless there is a strong human network that underpins that. (Richard Labelle, as cited in Ontario Africa Working Group, 1994)*

> *Lesson 10: Build an energetic steering committee. Electronic networks are about people, not technology. Start your initiative by*

building a team of enthusiastic proponents who come from diverse backgrounds. Do not stack your committee with 'techies,' or 'computer geeks.' Actively seek people who know more about communities than computers.

Lesson 11: Always try to work with people who work with community-minded organizations or community development agencies. Their experience and contacts in the community will help ensure that you will find the resources and support you need.

Good organizations with which to begin working include service clubs, health clinics, and churches, educational institutions involved with outreach and continuing education initiatives, libraries, and non-governmental organizations involved in economic development. When linked together through improved communication systems, the power of such grassroots organizations can be multiplied manifold. At the same time they can use their Internet connections to enhance inter-agency collaboration, joint service offerings, and joint planning.

Lesson 12: Use local expertise whenever possible, and provide necessary training and capacity building where the expertise does not currently exist.

By using local expertise, you help to insure that you can manage future administrative and technical difficulties, as well as equipment repairs. If you are building an African network, use African expertise. In Africa, the United Nations and the International Development Research Centre (IDRC) are supporting the Pan-African Development Information System (PADIS) based in Addis Ababa, Ethiopia. PADIS is heavily involved in networking in Africa, particularly in the training of users and system administrators (Adam and Hafkin, 1992). IDRC is also supporting a community-oriented Internet initiative in Africa, known as Acacia, after the name of the famous African shade tree used for community gatherings. In Asia, IDRC supports PAN, the Pan-Asia Network that helps to establish development-oriented Internet services in over a dozen Asian countries (IDRC, 1997). Both PADIS and PAN are helping to build the technical and service knowledge base necessary to ensure the sustainability and spread of such services.

Lesson 13: Take a business-like approach.

An electronic community network is often organized as a collectively-owned or cooperatively-owned infrastructure. Whatever the ownership model, the community network is still a business and should be run like a business. Thus, it is wise to include a handful of veteran business people on your steering committee. Their advice and knowledge are consistently valuable. However, it is wise to avoid working exclusively with business interests, or allowing business interests to dominate the community network.

Lesson 14: Take sustainability seriously.

While you will want to provide free or very low-cost access to the network, you must also find creative ways to generate revenue. Advertising, value-added services, and re-selling of network services to government bodies and large organizations are some ways to create the revenue needed to keep the network running. Low-cost or free access is the first step to creating a thriving pool of users. A thriving user base is 'essential in generating sustainability for a network' (Tindimubona and Wilson, 1992: 3).

It is also important to recognize that it is more important to address the sustainability of the improved relationships that the Internet helps establish, as opposed to sustainability of an Internet service organization. The world of Internet service is dynamic and subject to rapid technological change, and small organizations that provide Internet services sometimes have a short life span. If they are successful in encouraging users to use the Internet to enhance relationships, those relationships will far outlast any particular Internet service.

Lesson 15: Community ownership is important.

Do not build the network for your organization alone. Build it with and for your local community. Electronic communication is only valuable if everyone has the opportunity to participate. If it is accessible only to an elite group, the benefits will never be realized. If people have an ownership stake in the network (however small), they are likely to take an active interest in supporting and promoting the network. The consumer cooperative model is a model that operates successfully in many Canadian communities. We concur with Graham (1995):

> The essential element for community network development is grassroots control. Community networks are not 'infrastructure.' Community networks are caretakers of electronic public space created by the community, not providers of something FOR the community (p. 3).

Lesson 16: Participatory community management will help a network thrive.

Community members need mechanisms for influencing network management, system, and software design, as well as acceptable user policies. Democratic structures serve this purpose well. Each user should have the opportunity to become a member of the community network organization (usually upon payment of a small membership fee) and have a vote in deciding network policies and electing an executive council to oversee the network.

Lesson 17: Provide opportunities for students and young people to learn about the technology and the community development potential of the Internet.

Electronic community networks in Canada spread rapidly during the early 1990s because schools, community colleges, and universities provided Internet access to their students. Students quickly learned about the value of the Internet and, upon graduation, were often the first people to begin organizing community networks in their home communities where Internet access was generally limited to institutions. The creativity, energy, skill, and enthusiasm that young people bring to these initiatives is a tremendous resource.

Establishing university Internet services that are accessible only to senior faculty and administrators, as is the case in many developing country institutions, is a poor use of resources. Not only does this result in the acquisition of expensive 'Pentium paperweights,' but it prevents grassroots research and development. Creative and talented young people are usually responsible for designing some of the most valuable communication and development Internet applications. NetScape software, which was first developed by a group of young people under the age of 25, is an obvious example. It is common knowledge (acknowledged or not) in university settings that the majority of new and effective Internet applications for teaching and learning are designed by students.

Lesson 18: Strategic marketing brings resources.

Community network infrastructures are built with capital and equipment. A strategic marketing effort can bring many of the resources you need. Marketing new community network initiatives is difficult because people rarely commit resources to something they cannot see or touch, and an unbuilt community network is difficult to see and touch. Letters, advertisements, and verbal appeals are largely ineffective marketing techniques. The only strategy we have found effective is to bring demonstrations of realistic prototypes to where people are—right to someone's office or home, giving them a 'hands-on' experience. Large public demonstrations are useful to create interest and awareness.

In Canada and in our work in developing countries, we have experienced considerable success with demonstration of software disks that mimic community network applications. A floppy disk is placed in a computer and it delivers an interactive 'slide show' of network services. Bureaucrats, officials, politicians and community leaders can become quick converts to community networking when they see how the network will work from the personal computer on their desk. 'Seeing is believing,' and many uncommitted financial supporters have opened their wallets after seeing the benefits of a community network first hand.

Lesson 19: Aim for equitable access.

Try to extend your network services to people who would not normally participate. Create discussion fora for people of diverse ethnic, cultural or linguistic backgrounds. An interesting example of equitable access is the Montreal Free-Net. The Montreal Free-Net is the world's first bilingual (French and English) electronic community network (Graham, 1995). It is providing a positive forum for creating understanding between members of francophone and anglophone cultures, increasing the quality of learning and discovery on the network.

Lesson 20: Train volunteers to train new users.

Once a network is operational, training becomes the number one priority. A well-supported group of volunteer trainers can provide a low-cost and effective program for helping new users to configure their modems and navigate the system. Train your volunteers well, provide them with on-going support and advanced training opportunities. Training is needed at various levels: training in planning, installing, promoting, using, managing, repairing, and maintaining an electronic network (Tindimubona and Wilson, 1992: 3).

Lesson 21: Share resources, ideas and lessons learned with other community networks.

Once your network is operational, you can help other community networks by sharing your experiences. The lessons you have learned will help new networks find their feet faster.

Lesson 22: Enlist the support of 'Respectable Wired Elders.'

Within many nations, regions, and organizations, there are often Internet enthusiasts with influence or decision-making authority who, by virtue of age, wisdom, and established credibility, can lend significant support to specific development initiatives. We call these Internet champions the 'Respectable Wired Elders,' because, unlike many of their younger peers, their voices and visions can capture the imaginations of 'un-wired' politicians, funding agency bureaucrats, and private sector benefactors. They are often an untapped resource, but their support can add a fantastic boost to a project.

The Future of Community Networks

The future growth of community networks and other Internet services that support developmental objectives, can be facilitated by funding agencies such as IDRC which supports Internet extension programs. Funding levels do not have to be large or extravagant. Indeed, there is very good evidence from IDRC's work that small amounts can produce better outcomes than do large amounts when applied to Internet and development initiatives.

The establishment of community network extension services, regionally, nationally or locally, could provide programs for enabling communities to develop strong community organization strategies for establishing community networks. They can also provide a mechanism for enabling the regional and national networking movements to share resources and ideas and provide opportunities for collaborative projects. At the same time they can help focus advocacy efforts on improving telecommunication infrastructure for regions with poor phone services, particularly rural regions.

Ideally, Internet extension services will provide a seed-capital funding mechanism for helping to start community network initiatives. A funding mechanism that involves a peer review process will help insure that people from within the community networking movement, and not ill-informed bureaucrats, review funding proposals. Internet extension services could also provide public statements of support and encouragement, as well as learning opportunities for politicians and policy-makers, to provide momentum for the community networking movement.

Around the world, people are working hard to build a vibrant network of Internet services that support community development and general human, social, and economic development goals. In the process we are all learning some valuable lessons. These lessons need to be continuously shared with emerging Internet and development champions, especially those coming up in developing countries. As we strengthen communication and information sharing about means for enabling the Internet to serve developmental goals, we can also share our other ideas, knowledge, dreams, and visions, easily and seemingly within the electronic commons of the Internet.

References and Select Bibliography

Adam, L. and **Hafkin, N.** (1992). The PADISNET Project and the Future Potential for Networking in Africa. In *Electronic Networking in Africa: Advancing Science and Technology for Development*. African Academy of Sciences/American Association for the Advancement of Science, Washington, DC.

Bessette, G. (1996). Development communication in West and Central Africa: Toward a Research and Intervention Agenda. In G. Bessette and C.V. Rajasunderam (Eds.), *Participatory Communication: A West African Agenda*. Ottawa, Canada: Southbound, Penang, Malaysia and the International Development Research Centre.

Brummel, S. (1994). Information Infrastructure: Reaching Society's Goals, Report on the Information Infrastructure Task Force Committee on Applications and Technology. US Department of Commerce, Technology Administration, National Institute of Standards and Technology (http://www.yuri.org/Webable/disabled.html).

Burke, J. and Ornstein, P. (1995). *The Axemaker's Gift*. New York, NY: G.P. Putnam's Sons.

Carroll, J. and Broadhead, R. (1995). *The Canadian Internet advantage: Opportunities for Business and Other Organizations*. Scarborough, Ontario, Canada: Prentice-Hall.

Graham, G. (1994). Why Canada Needs Telecommunities. Unpublished Paper presented to Information Canada '94, Toronto, Canada.

——— (1995). A Profile of Canadian Electronic Community Networks, Communications Development Directorate, Industry Canada and Telecommunities Canada, Ottawa. World Wide Web address: (http://www.ncf.carleton.ca/freenet/rootdir/menus/free net/conference 2/profile.txt.).

IDRC. (1997). IDRC World Wide Web Site (http://www.idrc.ca.).

Negroponte, N. (1995). *Being Digital*. London: Hodder Stoughton. (http://www.unet.com/hodder/book.htm).

Ontario Africa Working Group. (1994). Transcript of Presentations and Discussions of the African Connectivity Conference, Ontario Africa Working Group, University of Guelph, Guelph, Ontario, Canada, November 29–30, 1994. Ontario Africa Working Group, University of Guelph, Guelph, Ontario, Canada. World Wide Web address: http://tdg.uoguelph.ca/˜gnesbitt/OAWG. html/oawg_index.html.

Ramírez, R. and Richardson, Don. (1997). The Global Barangay of the 21st Century: Philippine Barangays Pole-vaulting towards the Global Village of the 21st Century. Concept paper prepared by the Municipal Telephone Project Office, Department of Transportation and Communication, Government of the Philippines, Manila, Philippines.

Richardson, D. 1995. Community Electronic Networks: Sharing Lessons Learned in Canada with our African Colleagues. Presentation to the MacBride Roundtable on Communication: Africa and the Information Highway, Tunis, Tunisia. (http://tdg.uoguelph.ca/˜drichard)

———. (1996a). From the Ground Up: Lessons from using a Community Development Approach to build the Wellington County FreeSpace Community Network in Ontario, Canada. Presentation to the 6th

Annual Computers in Agriculture Conference in Cancun, Mexico. (http://tdg.uoguelph.ca/~drichard/)

Richardson, D. (1996b). *The Internet and Rural Development: Recommendations for Strategy and Activity*. Rome, Italy: Food and Agriculture Organization of The United Nations, Sustainable Development Department. (http://www.fao.org/waicent/faoinfo/sustdev/CDdirect/CDDO/contents.htm)

————. (1997). *The Internet and Rural and Agricultural Development: An Integrated Approach*. Rome, Italy: Communication for Development Publication Series, Food and Agriculture Organization of the United Nations.

Robinson, N. (1996). Bringing the Internet to Zambia. In J. Black (Ed.), *Bridge Builders: African Experiences with Information and Communication Technologies*. Washington, DC: National Academy Press.

Smillie, I. (1991). *Mastering the Machine: Poverty, Aid and Technology*. London: Intermediate Publications.

Smolan, R. (1996). *24 hours in Cyberspace: Painting on the Walls of the Digital Cave*. Toronto: Somerville House Publishers. (http://www.cyber24.com)

Tindimubona, A. and Wilson, A.A. (1992). Summary. In *Electronic Networking in Africa: Advancing Science and Technology for Development*, p. 3. African Academy of Sciences/American Association for the Advancement of Science, American Association for the Advancement of Science, Washington, DC.

Weber, T. 1996. Who Uses the Internet?, New York: *The Wall Street Journal*. December 8: R6.

Part 3

The Art of Community Building

16

Opening the Door
for People's Participation

Marilyn W. Hoskins

In this chapter Marilyn shares some of the radical changes in con-
cepts, organization, roles, and responsibilities of people who are en-
deavoring to make development programs more participatory. She
reviews the initiation of a community forestry program that uses a
participatory approach, following three phases of the program, from
initiation to the present. Finally, she reviews some of the lessons she
and her colleagues learned about participation and decentralization.
Her forthright reflections can be a source of encouragement to grass-
roots facilitators.

What *is* this all about? I am an anthropologist with a communications background, concentrating on local control and governance
and participatory methodologies within community development.
In 1977 I shifted focus to concentrate specifically on people and
their relation to tree and forest resources. I also shifted from working largely with non-governmental groups in the field to managing a
progressively participatory decentralizing program from within the
headquarters of a large international intergovernmental organization rampant with bureaucratism. Both of these shifts were a challenge and a learning experience.

Local Welfare and Trees

'When forestry projects come, we lose. Farmers and herders…we all lose areas, often our fallow land, which we use for hunting and collecting fuelwood, medicines, fodder, and food,' said a Voltaic woman in a workshop. A dozen others agreed that this was a major problem.

Peaking my Interest and Increasing Understanding

It was the most animated session of the workshop. A discussion on forestry was not even planned. All of a sudden the women participants, professionals, social workers, teachers, community leaders, and farmers, took the lead and started discussing trees. This happened in 1975 during a series of workshops in which women in Upper Volta (now Burkina Faso) looked at how they were faring in their dry to arid country in West Africa. The workshop themes were on various sectors, e.g. medicine, enterprise, law, but not forestry. This session was on agriculture. In an emotional discussion, women spoke about the importance to their families of trees, bushes, and forest products. They knew many advantages and disadvantages of trees both in providing products and in performing services (such as controlling water and wind erosion) as well as their potential competition with other land uses. They spoke of many projects which took over land which outsiders saw as 'not being efficiently used,' often because it was in the farming system a fallow cycle. The women explained how with each year of the fallow cycle, the land provided different products to local women and men, while it was rebuilding its fertility for future crops. When this land was taken over by projects, farmers and herders had their traditional land-use cycle broken. Outsiders, generally foresters, managed the land for different objectives while local families lost access.

I learned two major points, which were reinforced by five years of work as a development anthropologist in the region and later in other parts of Africa, Asia, and Latin America. First, women and men without formal training knew and cared much more about natural resources and their management than foresters and other development agents recognized. Second, trees and other perennials are essential to farming systems and livelihoods of both landed and landless people. These resources often strengthen food security in years when erratic rainfall or other disasters stress annuals. They provide the needed income during agricultural off-cycles or when periodic events such as weddings, illness, and funerals cause economic hardships.

How I Got Involved

In the 1970s, a number of organizations and development workers began to identify the local importance of trees and forest resources to their rural development strategies. This new concept of focusing on increasing opportunities for local people to themselves manage and benefit from tree resources upset a number of foresters, planners, and development workers. But, it caught the attention of many others who began to think of a new, people-oriented type of forestry.

The Swedish International Development Authority (SIDA) had discussions with FAO and funded a study group of top level foresters from around the world to explore what was being done in various countries. In 1997, with SIDA funding, FAO hired a well-known and respected forester to consider how this could be done in cooperation with the Senegalese Forestry Service. SIDA insisted that social scientists and experienced community development persons, women as well as men, be included. I was included on this first mission. The Senegalese, FAO and SIDA found the new approach useful and successful. FAO was then requested to develop a community forestry trust fund proposal for SIDA.

Forestry's Special Challenge for Participation

Local control and management is more complicated in forestry than in other sectors. The resource is often 'owned' by the government. Foresters are often trained in managing and protecting forests and keeping 'intruders, squatters, and illegal users' of the resource at bay. Community forestry, therefore, often has an extra layer of bureaucratic and legal complications to address, as

> *participatory methods require major power and locus-of-control shifts. More recently, many conservation organizations have joined the conventional foresters by supporting and reinforcing lack of local access to forest resources, both groups believing that local people cannot be trusted to manage with a long-term perspective.*

So, in 1978 the FAO/SIDA program, Forestry for Local Community Development was begun. It is still functioning in 1999 as a collaboratively managed program called Forests, Trees and People Programme Phase II (FTPP II). Additional donors and country organizations have become involved and it has grown.

In 1984 I was hired as the first social scientist to work within the FAO Forestry Department and for almost a dozen years served as the Senior Community Forestry Officer and coordinator of the trust fund program. Over this time people from different parts of the world have joined me in the evolution of understanding the concepts of local participation along with the issues which make community forestry work. We endured the pain and joy of decentralizing and experienced genuine 'participation.' We agree that 'people's participation,' is only a step, albeit a critical one for reaching community forestry goals.

Participatory Focus for Forestry from within a Large Bureaucracy

> ### *The Community Forestry Concept*
>
> *The FAO approach has defined Community Forestry as enjoyment of both short- and long-term benefits, created through self or joint management and use of trees and other perennials along with their outputs, by local people. Community forestry improves livelihoods, especially of the poor, in an equitable, environmentally sensitive, and sustainable manner. Its specific goals include local control and effective management of trees and/or forest areas by either groups; user organizations and/or individuals, through farm forestry.*

I have witnessed this new approach to community forestry with its focus on learning and on flexibility to respond to collaborative analysis and the role changes which result. At the local level, the concept and practice of participation has radically changed people's role from consultation, to local control and management.

Participation as Collaboration

In the context of the FAO program, participation is considered as collaboration or partnership between local women/men and technicians (extensionists, foresters, project staff) in designing and managing forestry activities but with the local goals, concerns, and benefits paramount. The integration of indigenous knowledge and existing practices and organizations is considered a basic starting point of all analysis for technical or organizational development. Participation seen in this way is not an end or goal, but an approach to, or a stage in reaching community forestry goals (local control and management). The current philosophy of the program is that using participatory methods is only successful when the activity is in response to local demand. Technicians must do less managing and controlling, becoming more of a source of information and options. Most generally the FAO community forestry program described here does not work directly with communities but focuses on strengthening tool and skill building and positive perceptions and policy environments within local organizations along with support structures for this to take place.

The FAO Community Forestry Trust Fund Program

In the following sections I will trace the development of this FAO program. Focused on local participation but managed by a small unit within a large international organization with funds controlled by donors and activities, it has, at various stages, been strongly influenced by different national and sector pressures. The goals, activities, participation, (including changes in participants and their roles) and the results (the good, the bad, and the ugly) for each phase are depicted. Through this detailed, though brief discussion, understanding how large bureaucracies become more participatory and less controlling, will hopefully become more vivid.

Forestry for Local Community Development (FLCD, 1978–1986)

Goals

In the beginning, the main program for FLCD was to raise the consciousness among policy-makers and high-level forestry officials that the skills and resources of forestry services could be used to improve both short- and long-term livelihoods of rural communities. It also had the explicit aim to incorporate this element in FAO and SIDA forestry projects. Although the documentation discussed the wide variety of needs rural people have for trees, some participants had more limited foci. For example, a number of the SIDA representatives had specific goals focused on fuelwood since energy had been raised to the level of a global problem and they felt an alternate source of fuel would protect the forests from local destruction. Some national foresters conceived community forestry in terms of changing only scale, making small village plantations without modifying species and goals of biomass production used in commercial plantations.

Activities

FLCD activities were mainly concerned with identifying, analyzing, and sharing relevant field experiences among policy-makers and collecting and analyzing data to help fill information gaps in order to plan appropriate community forestry activities. There was a component of ongoing analysis of opportunities and constraints for effective community forestry. Activities included workshops, study tours, focused research, and project or activity design.

Participation

A number of different groups participated in FLCD in different ways and received different benefits from that participation. These included Swedish, FAO, and host country advisors and local people.

SIDA (the donor) developed an advisory forestry group within Sweden, which gave FAO and SIDA advice. Members had the benefit of participating in and becoming consultants for workshops, study tours, and ongoing discussions. SIDA representatives not only obtained a continuous flow of information from this group but also sent representatives to an annual Expert Consultation. This ongoing analysis and exchange kept the donor aware of new ideas and reasons for change, thereby strengthening their support of change, and allowing flexibility in the program.

At FAO there was a Forest Department advisory group and an Interdepartmental Task Force to assure inclusion of ideas from a range of technical specialists, not only in forestry but in areas such as marketing, agriculture, training, women in development, livestock, or the people's participation program. Both of these groups met and actively advised on direction and activities. Members were able to tap into the funding when they identified ways in which their speciality could be useful to community forestry.

A group of host country nationals involved in forestry at the policy level, many of whom had been in the original FAO/SIDA study group, now became members of an annual Expert Consultation. This consultative group generated a great deal of information about national issues, initiated activities and policies which supported community forestry within their countries, and learned to acquire technical assistance for small studies for specific purposes.

As far as local participation was concerned, FLCD studies and integrated project/activity design teams obtained ideas from local people and local focus groups. These discussions greatly influenced forestry project design and policies to better reflect local interests.

Results

Over forty countries participated in some manner in FLCD activities and many asked for follow-up community forestry projects. A number of forest policy-makers, (including those in SIDA and FAO) started using participatory development vocabulary while dealing with issues such as gender, food security, or the role of land tenure. The activities and the number of community forestry projects managed by FAO moved from almost none to several hundred.

A number of newly designed large FAO-managed projects were based on community forestry ideas. In other words, many of the aims of FLCD were reached.

But these were disappointing as well. FAO, NGOs, and others did not have the tools and methods to carry to fruition, the goals of community forestry. Many countries lacked the policy and legal environment for local management and control and there were few models upon which to build. Many foresters lacked the commitment for local management of trees and forests, and their training institutions did not have materials with which to introduce the needed new skills. Most of the concepts and ideas had not been tested in field activities.

There were really few backlash (ugly) results at this stage. Not enough was being done at the country level to create discomfort for those who were not convinced about local management or were afraid of losing power. The Expert Consultation recommended that the FLCD be considered successful and complete. Thus, a new and more highly financed program called Forests, Trees and People Programme came into being.

Forests, Trees and People Programme Phase I (FTPP I, 1986 to 1989)

Goals

The new program goal was to bring about more in-depth field-based understanding and testing approaches that would address the issues involved in community forestry. The Expert Consultation advised that the program work with fewer countries in an action research mode within a few highly-monitored small projects, which also fed information into a network made up mainly of the staff of projects.

Activities

FAO was to submit four projects designed with a participatory process by local people, but at the last minute, the donor requested documents before funding would be released. This was extremely disappointing and seemed contradictory to the participatory process, as it bypassed the local people. But documents were written with as much flexibility as possible to allow local input to the detailed planning and implementation of activities. With the idea of institutional strengthening, the projects were designed to be implemented by host country nationals.

Four parallel FTPP partner projects were also designed by a university in Sweden (SLU) and funded separately by SIDA. Of the four projects managed from Sweden, two were run by Swedish-based NGOs and two by Swedish consulting firms. Action research on traditional knowledge and management, local rules of use, non-timber forest products, and tenure, were designed to be carried out in all projects, as found appropriate. Some discretionary funding was kept at the CFU for studies and workshops on emerging themes. A small newsletter was produced in Sweden mainly for staff of the eight projects to share experiences and to read about new issues in community forestry.

Participation

Between FLCD and FTPP there was a change in the people and groups who participated in the program and this very change caused problems. Those who were no longer participating felt deprived and in some cases, actively antagonistic. Some of the new actors were not well informed or committed to community forestry concepts.

SIDA no longer used the advisory forestry group consultants but funded a team at SLU to participate as Swedish FLCD partners. Consultants who were no longer officially participating and advising in FLCD felt that the program was no longer participatory. At the same time, SLU was mandated to integrate the lessons learned and tools developed in FTPP into firms most of which were no longer profiting from direct involvement. The firms resented this as an intrusion.

At FAO, the Forest Department advisory group and the Interdepartmental Task Force members could no longer make major changes in the activities nor have access to considerable grant funding as the majority of funds and activities were controlled directly by the project documents. Though the groups continued to meet, the meetings were largely of an informative nature and participation less enthusiastic.

A new actor within FAO was the Forestry Operations Service whose director was enthusiastic to have more projects in the portfolio. The focus had moved from policy in FLCD to implementation in FTPPI and therefore fewer policy-makers, mainly from the eight countries with project activities, remained as members of the Expert Consultation. A number of FTPP project staff also became members of the Consultation. Governments where projects were functioning had a direct role in the success of the field projects, as they held, for the first time, the majority of the program funds in the terms of signed project documents.

Projects had been designed as frameworks, as local people were supposed to be involved in completing the design. However, some preselected goals or activities were not local priorities. In most cases the local staff, and in other cases the policy-makers, did not value or have skills in the participatory approach. Backstopping missions reported that community members were not actively participating in an enthusiastic or sustainable manner. Within the Community Forestry Unit I struggled to work with much smaller discretionary funds, trying to make the projects participatory when they had not been allowed to be designed that way.

Results

After a little over a year, the new Expert Consultation group met to analyze results. On the positive side, they judged the themes on which research was being done, to be well chosen, and the documents which were being published by the program as excellent. The small network with a newsletter distributed principally between the staffs of the eight projects, was described as especially important though too small.

The Consultation found the field projects themselves disappointing. One issue was that, similar to most projects, these projects had not been designed in a participatory manner; they were not necessarily what government, staff, local people, or even the Forestry Operation Officers in FAO would have chosen. The projects were agreements with governments, usually with forestry ministries or services, and it was up to them to sign off on decisions and many activities. Governments no longer perceived that they were receiving additional funds for an exploratory activity, but felt they now had funds for forestry development. Some forestry directors were not pleased with social science inputs, or working with NGOs or others with these skills. They preferred to use the funds for their forestry staff. One government changed the location of the project, for political reasons, to an area much less appropriate for the design. Like FAO Operations Officers, the local staff found the process goals frustrating. Some feared they would be overlooked for promotion by working with these small and less visible projects. They felt that the research activities detracted from reaching visible physical targets (e.g., area of trees planted) which they and their departments valued. The staff also found that they lacked the tools and personnel to carry out the action research and participatory organization called for in the project.

Local people were involved more in some projects than others, but other interests undermined the cases that most interested local people. Some ugly backlash came from those who had previously participated with the program and who now felt they were on the sidelines. Within FAO, the program was seen by some, who had previously been advisors and received grants, as having become exclusive and unfriendly. Some host country policy-makers who were no longer involved in the Expert Consultation felt personally hurt and isolated from the process.

The Expert Consultation found that there were not adequate tools, methods, approaches, and people who could apply them, to continue with this approach. They concluded the original design was faulty, as it was impossible to develop tools through action research and at the same time apply them in a project. The project timeline of three to five years was not suited to the ongoing processes to deepen understanding, develop, and adapt tools, and strengthen institutions and local personnel in their use.

The Expert Consultation recommended that the FTPP involvement in projects be stopped as quickly as the activities could be absorbed by other ongoing projects and that the FTPP be funded in a new phase as forestry program support. They recommended that document development and publication be increased and the newsletter and network be expanded much beyond eight projects and into more regions. They urged that more donors be asked to join. The program was to concentrate on building the tools, methods, and approaches and training personnel within existing centers, already working on relevant community development activities in their own countries. The Dutch, Swiss, French, Italian, and later the Norwegians, joined SIDA as participants and funders.

Forests, Trees and People Programme Phase II (FTPP II—Present)

Though there were differences between FLCD and FTPP I, the radical departure from conventional approaches took place in FTPP II. In this phase the program systematically and progressively decentralized both planning activities and budget control and participation moved one step closer to the rural communities.

The first step in the strategy for designing FTPP II was to consult a number of policy-makers, NGO and, university staff, local networks and individuals within selected countries in Central and South America, Asia, East and West Africa, about opportunities and constraints for community forestry. Discussions were held with local institutions or organizations working on these issues and interested in becoming part of a global network. Following a consultative process, plans were made in each country and lead institutions and facilitators within those organizations were identified. To participate as lead partners, organizations had to be working with rural communities using participatory methods and be willing to support FTPP II activities with their own infrastructure and resources.

Currently, there is a two-tiered structure with focal or partner institutions (mostly NGOs and universities, but sometimes government bureaus) in which facilitators are responsible for management of the program including the budgets. Other institutions advise and help the planning and monitoring of activities nationally or regionally. Still others join with FTPP in giving or receiving training, carrying out studies, field-testing, and adapting new tools or other periodic activities.

Goals

FTPP II aims to work with host country institutions to develop and adapt tools, methods, and approaches for community forestry, strengthen local institutions and human resources to carry out more effective community forestry, and to share information both locally and globally through an FTPP network of community forestry activists. Facilitators do not carry out programs directly with local communities except as part of tool development. Instead they work with locally based groups, networks, and projects which are working at the community level.

Activities

Each year, facilitators from participating focal institutions meet with their local partners and collaborators to identify opportunities and constraints for community forestry, first at national, and then at regional levels. Then within the framework of the three-year program, and in relation to ongoing activities, they make a plan within their budget for the following year. Once a year there is a meeting of a Steering Committee which has replaced the Expert Consultation. This Committee is made up of representatives of the facilitators from each region, donors, and FAO. Facilitators present the year's activities in terms of what had been planned, what actually happened, and any differences. They then describe the planning process they have undergone and the proposed plans for the upcoming year. The Committee discusses ideas and global implications, and confirms work plans and budgets for the following year. Links are highlighted between tools, methods, and approaches developed or adapted regionally or nationally, training in the use of those tools, and sharing information with others globally.

Each year facilitators also have one or more separate global meetings to look at issues and consider how they may share information and activities. For example, facilitators from East Africa were concerned about local communities being expelled from areas that had been identified for conservation needs. They decided that it was important for the policy-makers in their region to see what was happening in India and Nepal in terms of local participation in the management of forests, planned with facilitators from those countries, and put some of their funding into study tours for policy-makers. They reported that it was a constructive use of their funds as they saw some changes in policy favoring local management and access.

Even publishing and material distribution has been decentralized. Regional centers produce Latin American and West African versions of the FTPP newsletter. The global newsletter is produced and distributed by SLU. The quarterly newsletter has a readership of over 10,000. Also, there are currently over fifty documents, films, and training materials available from Rome, and these and many more are available from the networking centers in Asia, Latin America, East Africa, and West Africa. The University in Sweden has become the European networking and document distribution focal point and the International Society of Tropical Foresters performs that function for North America and the English speaking Caribbean.

Participation

A great deal of change has taken place in FTPP II as to who participates and how. There are no longer signed documents with countries as the activities are not establishing new organizations or projects but working within existing organizations. Government officials no longer control budgets and sign off on activities. However, in some countries there are interested officials who participate in annual FTPP planning meetings and in West Africa some foresters have been released from some other duties to work as facilitators with FTPP. Most of the facilitators and the staff of collaborating institutions already have a track record in community forestry and within that group, there is a mutual learning environment.

More donors participate and their representatives have joined in the annual Steering Committee meetings. Donors have less direct influence on project planning and more discussion partners at these meetings. However, one donor quit because the country was not getting enough separate recognition and because 'experts' from their country were not managing the field activities.

At FAO, the various advisory groups have no role, since planning is done in-country. There is no activity for the Operations Officers as there are no projects. There is much less oversight role for the FAO representation at the national level, as the work plan is done by national institutions, as is the organization of training and other activities.

The Community Forestry Unit in FAO headquarters continues to have an administrative role that will hopefully diminish as key facilitator groups progressively take over these responsibilities. Funding has largely been distributed to regional institutions to be administered by facilitators, so limited discretionary funds are coming to the CFU. CFU's role is increasingly one of identifying experiences which might be useful to share, and sponsoring information exchange as well as initiating studies on new and emerging topics, which it makes available to the regions to see if any of them wish to join in. An example of one such topic was conflict management, for which CFU-managed FTPP funds covered a literature search, initial case studies, and a workshop. Thereafter all the regions put some funding in the topic and the CFU sponsored an e-mail conference with accompanying national and regional workshops and information exchange, as well as a workshop on policy related to addressing conflicts in relation to community forestry at the World Forestry Congress (Turkey, 1997).

The key participating actors in FTPP II are the regional facilitators who coordinate and manage the regional activities and budget. Networking facilitators coordinate the local documentation and newsletter publication and distribution. Cooperating and collaborating institutions, projects, and organizations plan and carry out activities. CFU helps provide stimulation, information, structures information exchanges, and supports networking.

Results

Probably the most exciting result from my perspective has been the ownership, commitment, and professionalism which the facilitators have developed. The energy and commitment devoted to FTPP by these professionals is exceptional. The level of discussion at each of the annual meetings is always more profound than at the last. Each region has gone its own way in planning and focusing on various topics so as to respond to its realities. In some areas as much as 60 percent of the budget now comes from other sources e.g. training or material development jointly funded by government or NGOs. Almost always the regional reports indicate that more was accomplished than was planned since facilitators work in a collaborative and dynamic way. A number of topics of importance for community forestry policy, planning, training, and implementation have been explored, and more in-depth understanding made available. Tools with which to work in field locations have been published and widely distributed. New tools for community groups have been developed as well as the more generic extension agent materials. One document illustrates how to develop local indicators for project success from the community perspective. A community group supported by a facilitator and adapted by a number of other communities, with support from collaborating institutions and projects, developed this method.

The bad or frustrating results of FTPP II relate largely to the difficulty monitoring, evaluating, and describing participation and its processes. Informing non-participants of the philosophy and way of FTPP work, has been time consuming partly as it is quite different from conventional projects. FTPP II is a program, not a project, with a process approach that builds on a learning process, and a deepening understanding and commitment to supporting local processes. Although this is really simple for insiders to understand, it has been difficult to put into the project-reporting mode or to explain to those who are familiar with controlled participation, and a dependency-creating way of working.

As the program has grown, new facilitators and donor representatives join, which means training about FTPP at each annual meeting. Only through fully informed and recurring participation at the Steering Committee can the mutual learning process continue and can facilitators retain the flexibility required for their work.

For me, the most frustrating thing about the process of decentralization was not the loss of control and decision-making. I find many new ideas and activities identified at the country level more exciting, relevant, and varied than would have been planned from a central office. But, the most frustrating thing was the loss of detailed information about the growing number of specific activities being carried out. Since the facilitators had the freedom to be dynamic and manage their own budgets, they started collaborating with more than just organizations (more than 200 globally).

As the positive results have greatly multiplied, the ugly reactions or backlash has increased. The program has developed broad international recognition through the network, the publications, and the work of the facilitators. At the same time, there are even more people who used to be in the loop, who are no longer controlling decisions, doing the planning, having access to budgets or obtaining visibility and recognition from the program. This accounts for some of the backlash.

At the country/regional level, success has raised expectations too high. Facilitators generally have no staff and many only work part time for FTPP. Their budgets vary per country but are limited, as they are for seed or top-off money. FAO representatives, directors of well funded and staffed projects, government bureaus, and other organizations may not understand the limitations of this program focused on tool and understanding development, local institution strengthening, and networking. Often requests come to facilitators to perform services or training, or to work as consultants to projects. These requests are often opportunities, but can also create problems of two kinds for overworked facilitators. The first, if the requests come from institutions that are not part of the planning process, may not be within the mandate of the FTPP, or within the scheduled time, or budget available. A second more difficult problem comes when requests are not actually within the philosophy of FTPP. For example, a very large and well funded regional project considered by outsiders as participatory, requested validation of tools it had developed and would not accept facilitator or community inputs modifying the tools themselves before they were tested. Facilitators were reluctant to broadly apply top-down tools they felt were poorly designed, and the project director was very angry.

Another potential problem for FTPP II is, strangely enough, decentralization of FAO and some donors. FTPP is a program and network working at national, regional, and global levels with decision-making and budgeting already decentralized way below country or regional administrative offices. FAO is considering having FTPP administered by its regional offices and some donors entirely administered and managed from their in-country offices. This change would add another layer of control to planning and budgeting, and complicate global planning and sharing.

Within the FAO the CFU has similar problems as the facilitators. It has only two full-time professionals who are supported by excellent but short-term young interns (Associate Professional Officers), consultants, and occasional volunteers. This small office has an unusually high demand for project backstopping and bridging with other groups within FAO and outside FAO as well as the FTPP. It is a case where success yields increased demand and resentment, when requests simply cannot be fulfilled.

For example, many topics such as forestry and food security on which FTPP has collected and analyzed data and produced comic books, videos, concept papers, field manuals, and case studies are of growing interest to FAO and other organizations. Requests for input on policy papers and collaborative activities are a sign of success, but the resources (especially human resources) with the unit have not grown to support this increasing demand.

Considerations and Challenges

It is difficult to think about all aspects of participation. Participation can be good or bad depending on the perceptions of the people involved. There is almost always more than one party participating in relation to natural resources use. In the quote below we realize that the Dyaks were participating less in the management of their resources while the contractors were participating more.

> 'Give us back our land! We have three acres of rattan land. The contractors have come and taken it away. How are we to send our children to school? We cannot cut one tree in the forest but contractors can cut the whole forest. Please! Give us back our land!'
>
> Intervention by a Dyak Adit leader at a Workshop on Community Forestry, Indonesia, 1997.

Community Forestry is a relatively new field and is much more complex than originally conceived. It is gaining visibility and developing during a complicated and changing time when forest resources are diminishing, national governments are increasingly vulnerable, and when other forces, including both NGOs and international markets, are gaining in strength. Frequently, powerful groups want increased access to forests, water, and land in situations where no clear policies and regulations protect those who may have managed it for generations. Even in situations where the poor are given a new resource to manage, if they improve its value, it may be taken away.

It is dangerous to use words and phrases about participation and equity without explicitly recognizing that some voices are more important, and must be given more weight than others in order to reach community forestry goals. Generally, it is agreed that greater voice should be given to those with a long history of use, who are dependent on the resource for their food security, who are vulnerable to loss of the resource and have no other options. But specific situations illustrate how complex even such weighting is. For example, new refugees may have no history in the area but may be desperately dependent on forest resources; forest workers may have little investment in the region but have no other option for employment.

As far as decentralization is concerned, there is wide agreement that the locus of control should be at the lowest possible level. But what level is this in a situation where a government may 'own' much of the resource and many actors are counting on its use? International conservationists and corporations are both putting pressure on forest use, and both may disadvantage the forest dwellers and users.

In times of rising national debt, many countries are counting on these forests and lands to help keep them afloat. Interests may include timber, mining or petroleum or agro-business and these industries may be intimately connected to government officials or their families. Different local groups such as downstream users of water, local forest workers or miners, indigenous peoples, herders of livestock, long-term or new settlers, are all intimately concerned with forest use and management.

There are conflicts over rules of use between local communities. Within communities other struggles emerge between social groups, types of users or age or gender groups. Forest resources are often difficult to monitor and yet managers must have rights to exclude others who are not part of the management plan if the returns are to be adequate, relative to costs of management. For any use-management situation there will have to be layers of actors who may not be using the resource but who must support any agreed management plan either actively or passively. There will never be one solution for all places, and all attempts to work out arrangements must be seen in the light of mutual learning and deepening of our understanding of the concept of participation.

I have described some of the steps that a program, which I helped design and manage, went through to try to reach community forestry goals. The program can be considered in part successful, mainly because it has carried out a great deal of analysis with a range of partners and has had the flexibility to apply learning and change. It no longer simply consults or plans activities for local participation, but has deepened its approach to support of local control. But there is still much to learn about both the concept of participation with equity, and about decentralization.

The greatest concern I have about participation is that there has been no disaggregation of the term. We have no patterns to help understand what kind of participation can be expected in differing resource, economic, political, historic/cultural, and social environments. We still have no tools to clearly record the processes that take place and are needed in this type of program. We surely must be ready to move on from a nose count or even a voice count or a record of number of meetings held. When are the meetings or agreements really representative of the needs and concerns of the poor, and when are they just reinforcing the more powerful group, which is part of the problem? Yet a great deal has been learned about how to work with communities and a number of tools including participatory assessment, monitoring, and evaluation have been developed and are being widely used. It is now time to take stock of their impact on the poor.

Decentralization can be considered part of the FTPP II in that the program's work plans are designed by local NGOs and other national organizations which also control the available budgets instead of being controlled in Rome or other faraway centers. However, it is time to consider the great waste that has apparently taken place as talented individuals in the outside layers of control have been peeled off and often feel that they have been discarded. It is obvious that local groups may need the support of policy-makers, members of bureaucracies which make up the donors, and other organizations which are able to form alliances and networks and in other ways support them in their quest to gain or retain access over adequate resources. We had not fully understood the negative feelings of those participants who were left behind as the process was moved a step closer to the people themselves. It is not that I feel we should not have decentralized. Quite to the contrary, I feel we should have done that sooner. However, there was a great deal of experience, knowledge, and skill in the layers that were left behind, that no longer supported the process. Perhaps there are ways to provide other roles or to make those in control own the decentralizing process.

There are three challenges I would like to share with those of you working with community forestry, or indeed with any participatory processes and the decentralization of control.

- We desperately need to know more about the term 'participatory.' It is obvious that participation will take different forms in all the different situations and part of what we do in the name of participation does not empower those with the least voice and the most need, and may have the opposite effect.

- We desperately need to have better ways to monitor, evaluate, and describe processes so that we can understand and learn from what we do, as well as clearly communicate with those with whom outputs have been the major focus.

- We desperately need to learn how to train all levels of people involved in how to contribute to the decentralizing process, including how to let go of control and building environments for local success in both short- and long-term forest resource management.

In all of this, we need to keep in mind the Voltaic women who depend on the fallow land, and the leader of the Dyak group who like their ancestors depend on rattan to feed or send their children to school. Our job is to help them secure access to and keep the resources they need for a satisfying locally chosen way of life. And for the many layers of decision-makers that relate to programs being decentralized, including ourselves, we need to help identify alternative roles and find joy in letting go.

One time I saw a statue...

... that was not particularly remarkable in its size and shape or subject. But, I remember it was a limestone statue of an egg with the head of the chick poking out a little over a foot high. I did not find this statue remarkable until I read its title. It was called, 'The

Triumph of the Egg.' Had it been called the 'Triumph of the Chick' I would never have remembered the statue. But as it was, the broken egg was the part that had triumphed. To me it seemed to symbolize the essence of participatory development. Only when the egg was broken, when it had let go of the chick, when it was no longer in control, had it succeeded. We have much to learn about the triumph of letting go.

17

Enabling Participatory Decision-making at the Grassroots

Joseph Ascroft and Ilias Hristodoulakis

You cannot help people permanently by doing for them that which they can do—or be taught to do—for themselves. Joe and Ilias remind us that this simple dictum underpins the principle of participation. But it is easier said than done. It is easier to say what participation is in principle, than what it is in practice, particularly in carrying out programs which ask to change their lifeways in often radical, though beneficial ways. They share how UNICEF's 'Child-to-Child' Participatory Strategy is putting participation into practice.

On the face of it, the principle of helping people help themselves seems straightforward enough. People designated as beneficiaries of a development initiative—in health, agriculture or industry—have a right to participate in decision-making on all aspects of the initiative. The problem is that the responsibility of enabling people to participate in such decision-making has been left up to the aid-givers and they don't know how to do so. They do not know the methodology for ensuring effective people's participation. Intended beneficiaries often number in the thousands or millions, often include a variety of ethnicities, dialects, social strata, and often as a group, are separated from their aid benefactors by cultural, linguistic, and educational gulfs that render impractical easy communication between them. For those who are expected to operationalize the participatory principle in real life, these constraints often appear as imponderables that they are ill-equipped to overcome.

Focusing on Health Needs: Historical Perspectives

In 1978 a conference took place in Alma Ata, now the capital of Kazakhistan, to consider the state of primary health care in the world. At issue was the high rate of human morbidity and mortality prevailing particularly in the urban ghettoes and rural areas of developing countries where the bulk of humankind resides. One pre-eminent conferee, United Nations Children's Fund (UNICEF), drew special attention to the 'most at risk' population segment: children, especially infants under one year. UNICEF noted that a quarter million children died weekly of diseases which could be prevented by personal hygiene, environment sanitation or inoculation. Legions died from diseases and ailments eminently responsive to medication (UNICEF, 1990).

Remedial measures such as the removal of human waste and environmental refuse, making water safe to drink and use, and recourse to antibiotics and rehydration therapies, were known to be widely practicable, readily available, and not all that difficult to comprehend and apply. Yet, the conferees concluded, health care measures of even the most fundamental kind were little known to, or practiced by vast majorities of Third World populations. Governments and the development community were thus urged to do something about it. *Health for all by 2000* emerged as the conference's leitmotif and its ultimate goal. Relieving health care ignorance on a massive scale via health education, i.e.,enlargement of health care choices, was tagged as a strategy of highest priority for achieving this goal.

Implementing the health education strategy however proved to be problematic. The often cited constraints were lack of financial, material, and human resources to activate the program. Of these, none has taxed the problem-solving capacities of facilitators within the development community as much as the human resource constraint—a scarcity of personnel trained to spread health care to the masses scattered across the globe. UNICEF followed up on Alma Alta by declaring 1979 as the Year of the Child during which the development community was enjoined to intensify the search for an answer.

Child-to-Child Participatory Strategy

The problem at hand could be framed as 'gaps' in the socialization of developing country (DC) children, i.e., gaps in the process by which people acquire the beliefs, attitudes, and customs of their culture (Stewart and Glynn, 1971:59). The earliest socialization of a child occurs at home, with family and friends serving as the primary agents. Basic fundamentals of science-based health care presumably are learned in the home and fleshed out and refined as the child moves into formal social structures beyond the family, starting with school.

However, the problem at lower economic levels in DCs is that these fundamentals are not yet part of the knowledge systems of families. Children of such families may or may not enter a school where they acquire the necessary knowledge. For most, their destiny is to grow up with 'inherited ignorance', thereby perpetuating the cycle. When children lack health care fundamentals from the family, schools are forced to play the parent role.

It was from pondering this dilemma that a remarkable and ingenuous approach to its solution emerged:

- *Why* not use children in school to reach other children not in school?
- *Why* not train them as surrogates for over extended health workers, in order to augment and multiply health knowledge and care, for children?

The advantages of such surrogacy were self-evident. Children in school were a captive audience accustomed to top-down instruction and tractably amenable to discipline and control. They were integral members of their communities, steeped in their cultures and traditions. Children were available in quantity at relatively little cost.

Thus, the conceptualiztion of a child-to-child approach was framed. Eventually this conceptualiztion evolved as the *Child-to-Child Trust* in the Institute of Child Health and Education, University of London. The Trust serves as an international registry and information clearing house for child-to-child projects. This organization provides both moral support, in the form of encouragement and advocacy, and technical backstopping, in the form of curricular and outreach ideas and advice. The Trust has accumulated a wealth of Child-to-Child books, papers, research findings, instructional aids, documentation of activities, and other materials housed in an archive which is open to anyone in the world interested in the subject

A Close Look at the Child-to-Child Model

Child-to-Child as originally conceived, was a model of simplicity. It was initially limited to children teaching other children, to older children helping teachers to play catch by teaching younger children entering school for the first time. It was then expanded first to include preschool siblings at home, schools without similar programs. Eventually, spurred by children-to-children successes, people started experimenting with channeling information through children to their parents and other adults.

This step-by-step extension outreach has come to be characterized as 'an information cascade flowing from level to level.' From health experts to school personnel, from teachers to their students, from children in school to other children, and from children in general to parents and other adults in the community, health information flows. The image of such a multilevel cascade is strongly suggestive of an event with a succession of decision-making nodes at different levels. Decisions associated with each level are successfully negotiated before progressing to the next. Since the beneficiaries of capacity-building at each level are usually different from each other, the cascade uses a variety of decision-making approaches to explore their actual and potential roles.

One is likely to encounter a range of potential decision-making nodes in a typical child-to-child project encompassing the full cascade. At each node, critical decisions are to be made; from problem-finding in the process of setting health education goals, to problem-solving in the design of goal-achieving strategies. The cascade model enables identifying those persons most likely to make decisions, as well as those most likely to be left out of decision-making.

Participatory Decision-making Options

Who is most likely to be left out of the decision-making process? Most easily identified are decision-makers who represent formal organizations. But who is to accurately represent the people and how they are to be selected, remain thorny questions for human development facilitators. This was an important consideration in the child-to-child projects, but is a challenge for any development project. Drawing from social marketing methods, subjectively selected key informants can serve as representatives, i.e., objectively selected, representative focus groups, can serve as 'qualitative' active participants; and preexisting special interest groups, previously created for a specific purpose (related to decision issues).

Currently, there is effort underway to develop a 'composite methodology' combining all three of the selection methods. It is useful to look more closely at these three.

Key Informants

These persons are selected subjectively as those who are likely to know much about the local people and their political economy, their cultural norms and values, and their traditional beliefs and customs. Often they are selected from formal organizations; advisory or chief's councils, religious groups, trade unions, farmers cooperatives, PTAs. Social activists, issue-oriented opinion leaders, community dignitaries, traditional elders or other distinguished personages are identified and selected as key informants. Unfortunately, selections at times may be biased. It is not unusual for 'topdowners' to fill seats on their project management committees just to satisfy 'participatory requirements,' with no expectation of input.

Key informants can at times bridge gaps between 'outsider' and 'insider' decision-makers. When selected from the 'elite' segment of the population or from its better educated classes, key informants should be equally at home interacting with top-level government officials (sometimes foreigners) or poor peasant elements, rural or urban. Often, their cultural norms reflect modern social systems that value the scientific method, rather than those of the masses, rooted in tradition. Key informants are essential, but keep in mind that their views do not sufficiently reflect those of Third World populations, and so cannot fully represent them.

Representative Focus Groups

Participants are selected by random research methods to answer questions in depth on behalf of segments of populations they are selected to represent. Open-ended focus group interviews seek for qualitative 'depth' in the answers allowing knowledge, attitudes, feelings, and perceptions to be probed at length. A sample's size can range into the hundreds and even thousands to represent a population adequately. Interviewed one at a time, focus groups range in size from seven to fifteen people, and respond to questions interactively. Everyone has an equal chance to participate in interaction. Focus group members 'react' and 'interact' under the guidance of a 'moderator.' This person catalyzes interaction, poses questions, prompts discussion, keeping it free-flowing and within bounds, and stimulates group rapport. The spontaneity of focus groups tends to bring subliminal, preconscious information to light, to prompt anecdotal or metaphoric explanations, or unveil relevant customs, beliefs, and mores that cannot be expressed in structured interviews. It allows for more thorough and unrestrained discussion, debate, and flow of information.

How to select the focus group can be problematic. A single focus group cannot adequately represent a population so it is necessary to create a number of focus groups to represent different geographic areas, different ethnic groups, or different social strata. If a sample survey of the population has been undertaken, another way to form representative focus groups is to randomly assign people selected from the survey in the same geographic area. Researchers have devised many approaches to selecting focus groups, taking into account the purposes of research, and limits of resources to conduct the research. Whichever way they are formed, focus groups can be useful to decision-making in many ways. For example, by combining the information gained from groups in one region or ethnic affiliation or age group, a broader, more composite picture can be gained. And when all the information from each of the groups is amalgamated together into the big picture, a well-informed planning and project design can take place.

Special Interest Groups

Created for special purposes like monitoring the environment, watching over the rights of people, ministering to special needs, or to take care of a variety of community functions, these persons bring diversity to decision-making. In the schools system, for example, an active special interest group is the Parent-Teachers Association (PTA). With the role of monitoring and sanctioning whatever happens both formally and informally within the school and between the school and its social environment, this is a body with an obvious vested interest useful to child-to-child program.

Representative Sample Surveys

Persons are selected objectively, using classic survey research methods. Questions about what the population knows or feels about specific issues (public health topics, for instance) or how they behave with regard to those issues, can be answered through surveys. If done according to statistical principles, generalizations can be made based on the data. For example, in the 1960s, 'KAP Surveys' were frequently used in DCs to measure people's knowledge (K), attitudes, (A) and practices (P) on family planning issues (Rogers, 1995: 70). Frequently they were done as baseline surveys in the formative stage of projects to measure preexisting KAP on given topics. After executing initiatives to change people's KAP, evaluation surveys were repeated in order to find out how well the initiatives worked.

Selecting representative samples of a population in Third World settings can often be a problem because sampling 'frames' are often not available in urban ghettoes or rural hinterlands. However, these problems have been addressed by researchers, and surveys do have an important impact on policy and decision-making. By identifying the extent of knowledge gaps, the presence of constraining attitudes, and the existence of old practices which need to be discarded, courses of action can be outlined. This information can be useful for planning what gaps to fill, what cooperation or resistance to anticipate, and what old behaviors to modify or new ones are needed to enhance people's capabilities. Answers are usually quantified and aggregated into an impersonal 'average' answer. 'Sampled' individuals have no control over how their answers are interpreted, nor are they aware that they are contributing to decision-making.

Participatory Rural Communication Appraisal (PRCA)

PRCA is a composite methodology designed to bring intended beneficiaries of agriculture development into active decision-making participation with officials and technical field personnel of rural development projects. The Food and Agriculture Organization of the United Nations (FAO) is currently developing and testing this methodology. PRCA methods and techniques combine the participant options just presented in a regional project based in Harare, Zimbabwe.

The methodology offers both development workers and beneficiaries the opportunity to learn rapidly and systematically about each other's norms, values, perceptions, and attitudes in the process of debating and evaluating proposed new ideas and practices. The process results in formulating goals that are mutually agreed upon and workable courses of action to achieve them. Understandably, PRCA requires project personnel to undergo intensive weeks of training to gain the necessary operational knowledge and skills to employ this methodology.

Potential Participants in Decision-making

A public health education project is essentially an exercise in problem-solving, but solving a problem first requires finding one. In the context of health care, problem-finding consists of identifying the development goal in terms of precisely what health-care knowledge and skills are needed for what purpose. Problem-solving, on the other hand, consists of formulating strategies for solving problems expeditiously. Those people responsible for problem-finding are not necessarily the same people as those responsible for problem-solving. While there may often be overlap between the two groups, the functions are sufficiently different and merit more lengthy discussion. Our discussion is framed by our experiences with the Child-to-Child program.

Participants in Problem-finding

In identifying child-to-child decision-makers, both actual and potential, we started by forming two groups: those traditional decision-makers who under the old top-down paradigm took the responsibility of deciding on behalf of intended beneficiaries; and those nontraditional decision-makers who, under the participatory model, need to be built into the process. Included in this latter group are the intended beneficiaries, and others identified as essential to the process. There was no shortage of problems:

- *What* is the desired state of public health knowledge and skills in a given population?
- *How* short of this state are the people?
- *What* enlargement of capabilities is needed for them to make up the shortfall?

Finding public health problems generally involves answering questions such as these. First, let us take a look at these two identified groups:

Traditional decision-makers who are specialists with the diagnostic skills necessary to find public health problems, are typically found in government Ministries of Health (MOH), or on the rosters of such ODA givers as UNICEF, the World Health Organization (WHO) or on the US Agency for International Development (USAID). They are also found in international NGOs such as the Red Cross, Redd Barna, the Aga Khan Foundation, or in a grassroots NGO or within local government.

MOH personnel usually take leadership in health initiatives or collaborate with other organizations. They are free to identify problems at any level of society including those with nationwide ramifications that affect a limited geographic region or segment of the population or localized in a community at the grassroots. The problems can be transitory, such as the outbreak of an infectious disease calling for an immediate remedy, or long-term, such as finding gaps in public health knowledge and skills, requiring permanent institution-building.

Official Development Assistance (ODA) givers and NGOs however play somewhat different roles from each other when it comes to decision-making. International agreements preclude ODA givers from initiating or running projects of their own, independent of government control. They can suggest initiatives, respond to assistance requests, or even participate in decision-making, but only as counterpart advisors to government. Even though it may not always seem so, de facto realities notwithsta..ding, it remains the government's prerogative to make all official development decisions. NGOs, on the other hand, whether international or local, have a freer hand, depending on a country's rules and regulations, to formulate and pursue goals either on their own, or hand-in-hand with local authorities, with international NGOs or even with the government itself.

Just what is likely to be included in a body of public health knowledge and skills identified by experts in the field? Drawing on the data bases of the Child-to-Child Trust, the following is a summary of topics that provides some idea of what comprises the body:

- *Environmental sanitation*, e.g., latrines, garbage disposal, safe water, habitat cleaning.
- *Personal hygiene*, e.g., bathing, washing clothes, tooth and eye care;
- *Infectious disease control*, e.g., immunization, respiratory transmissions, diarrheal therapies;
- *Sex education*, e.g., safe sex (STDs, HIV/AIDS), family planning, contraception;
- *Safe life styles*, e.g., first aid, antismoking, antinarcotics, or *Caring for others*, e.g., the physically or mentally disabled.

Non-traditional Decision-makers can play two roles in problem-finding. One is delineating the body of public health knowledge and skills that today's well-rounded citizen needs to have in his or her repertoire. The other is finding out what in that body of knowledge is already known to them, and of what is known, how much of it is complete and free of error or distortion (in other words, the K of KAP). Finding all this out is not possible without their participation.

Participants in Problem-solving

In theory, the number of ways to achieve a given goal is limited only by the imagination and inventive skills of those charged with designing a strategy to reach it. In actuality, feasible strategies are limited by available resources. A public health campaign could ideally consist of flooding a targeted population with teams of health workers armed with the state-of-the-art audiovisual aids, and backed by mass media messages. But the reality often is that field workers are too thinly spread to do any good, and mass media either does not exist or cannot be accessed to address the issues. The child-to-child surrogacy can be an effort to overcome such constraints. In this event, there are a series of questions to be answered corresponding to each level of the child-to-child cascade described earlier.

At the Teacher-to-Student Level—What public health knowledge and skills are to be taught in the schools? How is this information to be incorporated into the schools' pedagogic system; as required subjects integrated into the regular curriculum, as elective extracurricular topics, or both?

At the Student-to-Other Children Level—What fundamentals should be taught to which other children—younger ones in same school, siblings at home, peers not in school, or students in other schools? In what way is content to be handled—teacher-controlled and supervised, or child-directed catch-as-catch-can?

At the Children-to-Adults Level—What fundamentals are to be extended to the community at large—to parents and family, to adults in general? And in what way—adult-controlled and supervised, or child as a freewheeler? How does one mitigate adult misgivings of children as information sources? Over and above these concerns are the issues of project monitoring and evaluation. How is oversight of the various cascade levels maintained to ensure they remain on a goal-achieving course and how will goal-achievement be measured?

Level I: Teacher-to-Student

Opting for child-to-child surrogacy is only one decision-making input to strategy design. Others include planning the strategy step by step and ensuring that it is compatible with cultural norms. In the top-down paradigm, all this tends to be unilaterally made by traditional decision-makers. In the participatory mode, inputs from those who will execute the strategy as well as those who will benefit from it, become necessary.

Traditional Decision-makers—If the health problem is identified by MOH at the top as requiring a nationwide solution (in response for instance to the Alma Alta Declaration), having recourse to school-based child-to-child surrogacy introduces the Ministry of Education (MOE) into decision-making equations. New subjects may need to be added to regular curriculum of schools, or new matter to subjects already being taught, or new topics to the extracurricular program. These activities, the ramifications of which could well include modifying teacher-training and instituting special in-service courses, require skilled syllabus and curriculum designers. As often happens in DCs, the MOE may not have all the expertise on hand and may need to seek assistance from ODA givers of its own—the United Nations Educational, Scientific, and Cultural Organization (UNESCO) or the education unit of USAID or from NGOs, particularly the Child-to-Child Trust in London with its extensive data archives and specialized knowledge of strategy.

If the problem does not require a national perspective (a province, district, or community), and involves one or just a few schools, the movers are likely to be NGOs, either international, such as India's involvement with the Aga Khan Foundation, or a local one as in the case of Kenya's Volunteer Development Services. They could also be local community activists (politicians, development advocates) or 'do-gooders' (spouses of UN and diplomatic officials). If the need is to manage a temporary crisis (controlling a cholera outbreak, containing an epidemic), problem-solving is likely to be initiated by field-based MOH personnel in liaison with school personnel, it being the rare exception for health workers to opt for child surrogacy outside the school system.

Non-traditional Decision-makers—It is an irony of development that key actors of a strategy, teachers as its executors and children as its recipients, are often the ones least likely to participate in decision-making. Yet it is teachers who will need to design instructional aids and materials and create activities to assist learning, and it is students who will need to prepare themselves for their future role as surrogates. In a nationwide problem-solving exercise, focus groups drawn from each group could prove most salutary.

However, there is yet another usually neglected constituency to be involved: parents of school children and the population at large. Just is it was necessary to have their passive inputs into problem-finding so as to refine the goal to be achieved, it is necessary for them to contribute to strategy refinement. This means measuring prevailing attitudes toward any aspects of the identified body of knowledge and finding out if there are any preexisting old health practices needing to be supplanted; in other words, adding the A and P to the K already discussed, to create a full KAP study.

The idea is to pinpoint in advance, potential attitudinal constraints and contradictory practices that may otherwise frustrate goal-achievement under the dictum that, to be forewarned is to be forearmed. For instance, attitudes in many societies may not look kindly on the inclusion of sex education or family planning material in schools' curricula. In others, the way they treat diarrhea consists of withholding all liquids from the patient for the duration of the illness, which is directly opposed to the purpose of oral rehydration therapy. Parents can be brought into the decision-making matrix by way of focus groups or, where available, by activating PTAs.

Level II: Student-to-Other Children

Just how far along the cascade to go, whether to target younger children in the same school or to reach out to siblings and peers not in school, or in other schools, will of course depend on resources available for the purpose. The MOE, for instance, is more likely to provide resources for the development of formal subjects for inclusion in the curricula of schools but may balk at participating in non-formal extra-mural outreach programs. For this reason, especially in the case of nationwide programs, many projects terminate at the teacher-to-student level. Though falling short of the optimal potential of the strategy, completing Level I is by itself no small feat. At least it gives strong promise that the children who benefited from it will grow up to be better informed socialization agents than were their parents. Critical decisions to take at this level in addition to which children to reach out to, are what health topics to cover (or avoid) and where to include them, how deeply to delve into topics selected, and what materials, games, and activities to use as instructional aids.

Traditional Decision-makers—In the case of nationwide problem-solving, the formal organization with the greatest stake in child-to-child outreach beyond the school gate is the MOH. What goes on outside the school is seldom seen as essential to the needs and responsibilities of the MOE. However, it is not unusual for ODA givers and international NGOs to be prime movers and funders of outreach activities. In more limited ventures, so far as the MOH is concerned, decision-making is more likely to be initiated by field level personnel than by their top-level bosses. It is however more likely that the initiative in such ventures is taken by international or homegrown NGOs, often in collaboration with UNICEF because of its special mandate for children.

Non-traditional Decision-makers—It is not unusual for those committed to health education to involve only school personnel in decision-making, thus overlooking those most essential to the process, the surrogate-to-be students. If students are to be the main outreach agents and to be that on a voluntary basis, they are entitled to decision-making inputs on such issues as how to go about contacting client children, how to motivate them to pay attention, and what teaching aids and strategies to use. Parents also constitute another often neglected significant group. After all, it is their children who will be going about the neighborhood spreading the word about health care, and parents, especially in traditional societies, are answerable for the action of their children. They are thus also entitled to participate in deciding what, if anything, their children do and say in the context of child-to-child.

In the nationwide situation, focus groups comprising children on the one hand and parents on the other, could be formed in order to help the MOH plan and implement outreach programs representing all sectors of the nation. But, there are promising alternatives involving student clubs and PTAs that would work equally well in the nationwide as well as in the more limited situations. Some schools that have gone beyond Level I have seen fit to organize extracurricular Health Clubs with student office-bearers. These clubs can, with the assistance of faculty, plan and mount outreach programs that can range from being adult-supervised and con- trolled to where students are pretty much on their own, free to accost other children wherever and whenever they find them.

The PTAs provide an opportunity for health workers to secure parental and school cooperation in planning and executing child-to-child outreach programs. Parents particularly can legitimize the activities of their children by 'going to bat' on their behalf to gain community acceptance of the child-to-child exercise. PTAs may also have a special role in cajoling or motivating teachers to participate in outreach activities. In promoting health education via child-to-child, health workers are merely doing their jobs. Teachers however are often pressed into extra-mural service without the prospect of remuneration.

Level III: Children-to-Parents and/or Communities at Large

Some projects proceed systematically from one level of the cascade to the next, completing each level before moving on. Still others skip Level II altogether and go straight to Level III on the under- standing that extending outreach to the community at large includes extending it to all children as well. It is also possible that some may do Level III in tandem with Level II. There are however just as many projects that terminate at Level II because it is as far as they wanted to go from the start, or because they may have exhausted resources and/or resolve to carry on.

Traditional Decision-makers—Where a nationwide solution is de- cided upon, it remains likely that HOH (often prompted, assisted, encouraged, and even funded by its ODA, UNDP, UNICEF, WHO and NGO cohorts) will spearhead the decision to take the step of reaching out to other children in need of health education. How- ever, with the emphasis now shifting to the non-formal educational sector, the MOE is most likely to fade into the background or even out of the picture.

If the problem is localized to a less than national perspective, the likelihood increases for top-level MOH officials to fade into the background. This leaves problem-solving up to its field level front-line personnel, to international NGOs such as the Aga Khan Foundation, or to homegrown NGOs of various stripes, or a combination of them to initiate Level III outreach decision-making. Very often, MOH front-liners will go it alone as part of their everyday ongoing duties. However, it is not unusual to see MOH efforts strongly supported with funding and expertise provided by such ODA givers as WHO and UNICEF acting with the permission of the central government. NGOs may also share the burden of planning, funding, and execution, or work independently, perhaps to fill the void left by MOH in a community or region.

Non-traditional Decision-makers—Using children as extension surrogates to educate their elders is not compatible with the traditions of most Third World communities. The custom in such traditional societies is rather for the adults to teach children, to prepare them for adulthood by teaching them how to raise crops, animals, and children, how to cook food, build houses, and treat the ill. It is for children to do the bidding of their elders, to defer to them at all times. So, to suddenly reverse roles and expect elders to sit at the feet of their children and learn from them, defies tradition. And, to do this without their willingness, is to court disaster of the highest order from which there is no easy retreat. Thus, the elders are to be involved in deciding the form and manner of child-to-adult surrogacy from the very outset, even if it often means cutting out health information which might be deemed unsuitable for children to pass on to adults. Legitimizing the child-to-adult approach and working out acceptable modalities is necessary. Often, the outcome of such participation is to design a version of child-to-adult that is uniquely compatible with local norms that allow children to disseminate information without overstepping the line of difference. For instance, acting out their messages for instance in plays, concerts, puppet shows or in booths at village fairs and fêtes, under the guidance of adults rather than moving out on their own, confronting adults in their homes or in the streets, is likely to be more effective.

Final Words: Borrowing from Social Marketing

The methods and techniques for effectuating the principle of participation—sample surveys, key informants, focus groups, and still others such as case studies, field experiments, and participants observation—are by no means new. These methods have been around for long and have been the stock in trade of commercial marketers through much of the present century. They have routinely used them to get even the poorest of the poor living in the slummiest ghettoes or the deepest hinterlands, to adopt, with seeming ease, a variety of commercial products, ranging from the utterly trivial to the absolute essentials for everyday life.

The development community has recognized the potential utility of adapting these methods and techniques in operationalizing the Child-to-Child approach. But HDRs in their zeal to promote the new goal of human development and its corollary, participatory decision-making, have not yet acknowledged and used marketing methods which are appropriate to their goals. It is as though those responsible for diffusing innovations in the Third World have divided themselves into two communities: the commercial community with its devotion to the 'make profit' motive and the development community with its commitment to the 'do good' motive. But the development community seemingly dismisses methods that can so effectively serve the needs of commercialism. Yet, if every person in the world who regularly drinks Coca-Cola, would also use a condom or diaphragm, the population explosion and a host of sexually transmitted diseases would likely be under better control.

In the 1980s an effort was made to breach the divide, with marketing entrepreneurs such as Richard Manoff crossing over into the development community, bringing with them adaptations of the commercial world under the rubric of 'social marketing.' His book, *Social Marketing: A New Imperative for Public Health* (1985), helped introduce the term to the development community to imbue it with a patina of acceptability. But the development community still clings to the largely top-down, but comfortingly familiar methods of extension developed to diffuse agriculture innovations.

Social marketing is not a new concept. It has been around for the better part of the century. Borrowing from its resource of methods is a good idea for facilitators of participation. Philip Kotler's *Social Marketing: Strategies for Changing Public Behavior* (1989) is a good reference. This book points to additional sources, including those useful for gaining competence in such methods as constructing sample surveys, conducting field experiments, and organizing in-depth focus groups. But there are a couple of caveats to observe by those seeking to incorporate the participatory methods of social market-ing into the operation of their projects. Social marketing in all its ramifications is not a quick study. One cannot acquire its knowledge and skills overnight simply by reading a how-to book or attending a familiarization workshop. And the methods of mounting surveys and setting up focus groups even in small communities are not cheap. They cost a lot in terms of money, effort, and time and the cost-benefit of doing them are not readily understood and appreci-ated by lay people.

In sharing basics from the Child-to-Child participatory approach, we hope we have aroused interest in the potentials it holds. Partici-patory decision-making is costly and time consuming and unfortu-nately, in times of tight budgets, may not be perceived as a high pri-ority. But, the essential truth is that projects are doomed if the principle of participation is ignored, and money will continue to be wasted when projects fail to catalyze people's participation. Acting as a catalyst and facilitator to activate such programs is a complex, but achievable, role. We are challenged to practice what we preach: *'Learn by doing!'*

References and Select Bibliography

Kotler, Philip (1989). *Social Marketing: Strategies for Changing Public Behavior.* New York, NY: Free Press.

Manoff, Richard K. (1985). *Social Marketing: A New Imperative for Public Health.* New York, NY: Praeger.

Rogers, Everett M. (1962). *Diffusion of Innovations.* New York: Free Press.

Rogers, Everett M. and **Svenning, Lynne** (1969). *Modernization among Peasants.* New York, NY: Holt, Rinehart and Winston.

Stewart, Elbert W. and **Glynn, James A.** (1971). *Introduction to Sociology.* New York, NY: McGraw-Hill.

UNDP (1990–96). *Human Development Reports.* New York, NY: Oxford University Press.

UNICEF (1990). *State of the World's Children.* New York, NY: Oxford University Press.

18

Confronting Conflict through Collaborative Action

Anne Marie Johnston

To assure the rights of individuals and minorities to participate, collaborative models need to replace ineffective paternalistic and confrontational approaches. This is Anne's perspective regarding the development process. She points to consensus-building and search-conferencing, examples of emerging viable alternatives. She notes that by using collaborative processes, community members can constructively explore their differences and through dialogue, search for solutions that go beyond the limited vision of individuals.

Today communities face increasingly complex issues. Socio-cultural diversity and a wide range of interests challenge ways of solving community problems that may have been successful in the past. Collaboration facilitates sharing of essential information among stakeholder groups and the affected public. Through the collaborative sharing process, fair representation, equitable choices, agreed upon consultation methods, and styles of discourse are ensured and thus enable achievable closure and solution of problems which impact an entire community. A cooperative process itself can enhance a community's capacity to deal with current and future issues. Networks of mutual respect and trust tend to generate new norms of reciprocity. When properly facilitated, collaboration provides a forum for understanding disagreements, if not a resolution of them. One such example occurred in Bridgeport, Connecticut. A recent study indicated substantial unemployment in a state economy claiming to be thriving and having a shortage of workers. A non-profit organization brought together community representatives to discuss and respond to the findings of this study. An outside facilitator assisted in selecting and organizing representative negotiation teams and their participation strategies, as well as facilitating team sessions to address the issues. Four stakeholder groups representing the city, the business community, the state, and the general public participated. Each team worked individually, then cooperatively, to identify problems and barriers. They then mapped out alternatives through consensual agreement, for a strategic action plan for training and employing 500 welfare recipients to alleviate the unemployment problem. This plan specified the roles each interest group would play in the implementation of the strategic plan and problem-solving in relation to it (Carpenter and Kennedy 1988). Thus, a community united its diversity and collectively solved an identified problem.

Consensus-based Collaboration

Collaborative group problem-solving is a method used for several decades by facilitators. Most of their approaches have been consensus-based. In 1984, Phil Marcus guided task forces organized to handle environmental disputes, by defining a problem as a first step and using a technique that emphasized reaching mutual agreement. Then, as a facilitator, he assisted the task forces as they developed joint solutions that took into account fundamental stakeholder interests. He used brainstorming, interest identification, issue clarification, and reflective discussion to bring about consensual agreements. He carefully ensured that nothing was reported as an individual's idea and that disagreement was a group responsibility. In the course of task force deliberation each issue area was identified, along with existing conflicts, possible actions that might be taken toward resolution, and potential impacts of an agreement. After comparing demands on resources needed for each issue in the light of an agreed-upon time frame, task forces chose to initially focus on one issue where they felt they could have greatest impact and potential for consensus.

These are small examples, but are helpful to view consensus-building resolution processes as they have evolved over time. Carpenter and Kennedy (1988) outlined characteristics of these processes. They noted that:

- Participation is inclusive.
- Participants are responsible for the success of the process and continue to offer suggestions to make the process more workable.
- Participants are responsible for keeping their constituents informed.
- Participants mutually agree on a constructive definition of the problem.
- Participants educate each other about their perceptions of the history, context, concerns, and views as they address the problem.
- Participants collectively identify a range of options.
- Participants reach decisions through consensus, modifying options until they can agree on an acceptable one.
- Participants decide on a plan to implement options.
- Participants monitor the implementation of the solutions(s).

No doubt there are appropriate and inappropriate occasions for using the consensus-building process. One can assume that the process will work when it is appropriate, but when might it be inappropriate? These are some times:

- When quick solutions are required as in the case of a community emergency,
- When legal clarification is necessary before a consensus process can be initiated,
- When relevant information will not be available for a long period of time,
- When there is a mandated deadline and not enough time to achieve consensus,
- When the conflict focuses on polarizing value differences, and
- When one or more stakeholders is unwilling to participate because they feel they have enough power to implement a solution on their own and are indifferent to other concerns of participants.

Situations which are most amenable to a consensus-building process, are ones that deal with complex problems that affect many
people. When no one individual, group, agency, or organization has
complete jurisdiction over solutions to the problem, and the issues
are seen as negotiable by all cooperating participants, then people
tend to be willing to become involved.

Carpenter and Kennedy (1988) suggest alternative ways to structure a consensus-building collaborative problem-solving process.
The most common structure is that of a committee with task groups
or subcommittees. The committee may have ten to sixty stakeholder
representatives who are concerned about a problem or conflict. Size
is arbitrary—large enough to be representative, but small enough to
be decisive. The larger committee establishes procedures, identifies, and prioritizes issues, collects information, formulates options,
and either proposes recommendations or reaches an agreement.
Then task groups with broader participation and additional resources focus on specific topics, provide additional information,
and suggest alternative resolutions. Normally these groups organize
around topics but may also at times represent geographic areas, or
both.

Search-based Collaboration

Another more extensively used structure is the 'search conference,'
a method first developed in Australia in the 1970s. This model is
one of the most effective approaches to arrive quickly at plans of
action and at the same time achieve the commitment necessary
to follow through with implementation. A systematic approach is
structured to assist a group in identifying commonalties and discovering differences. This is preliminary to establishing collective interests and mapping goals. Participatory experiences of sharing ideas
and reflecting on directions become a powerful motivating factor
for establishing courses of action.

Setting up a search conference involves establishment of an
event-planning task force that represents 'willing' interest groups.
The individuals in this task force are responsible for generating a
willingness to participate in the upcoming search conference among
their constituencies. This task force will also pose an initial 'search

question,' which may be clarified by the larger search conference group at a later date. For example, in 1994, the Seneca Nation of Indians met in Ellicottville, New York, to discuss a search question defined by representatives: *'What do we have to do today to assure our survival as a Seneca people and to improve our quality of life for the future?'* The group included people with varying roles, experiences, and perspectives, virtually all those who considered themselves part of the nation. Publicity included individual brochures, press releases, and public presentations to encourage participation. Native American rituals were incorporated into the search process. The search conference format enabled many diverse voices to be heard at the offset.

Facilitators explained the guiding principles, for the process that the participants would experience:

- The search is a beginning and the recommendations and plans that result require commitment to action.
- All participants are equally important and everyone is there representing their own personal views.
- Agreement is not necessarily the goal of the search, but rather to develop understanding of all views. The goal is collaboration for future planning not necessarily consensus.
- Ground rules reflect openness, creativity, learning potential, and a future orientation.

Reviewing significant events of a shared history was their starting point for envisioning future strategies for participants with the Seneca Nation of Indians Search Conference (Rich, 1994).

The content of future planning stems from the search conference itself. Understandably, results are unpredictable and non-linear due to the complexity of group interactions. The process for participants of learning how to plan shares equal importance with specific conference outcomes. Outcomes are frequently modified as planning becomes more detailed and more resources are made available to carry out the plans. Search conferences have proven particularly successful within cultures accustomed to using consensus processes, as was the case in the Native American community.

In order to make the negotiation process as manageable as possible, it is desirable to establish specific goals which can provide the framework for selecting and/or bounding the issues to be discussed.

The goals set would be determined by the nature of the conflict itself. In some cases, a goal might be simply to reach settlement on a single issue. Broad public policy 'debates' would require several more specific outcome goals to be set. Multiple problems would require selection and prioritizing of salient issues to be addressed within the allocated time for the conference.

Some facilitators would distinguish between a focus on interests rather than positions. Fisher et al.. (1991) note that interests are not always perfectly aligned with positions, which are often perceived as pro or con. If issues under discussion match interests at stake, then modification of issues may enable participants' interests to be sufficiently satisfied and an agreement reached. Others cite situations where focusing exclusively on interests may be unwise, e.g., when stakeholders have deep and conflicting ideological differences and when agreements only on smaller issues may be achievable. Facilitators will determine when there is need to work within a narrower set of interests rather than a complete array of underlying interests.

The Facilitation Role

The facilitator's role and style can be pivotal to the success or failure of collaboration, search, and resolution processes. Frequently, a facilitator must provide leadership and resources to ease and educate participants unfamiliar with procedural aspects of conflict resolution. Gaining the trust of all stakeholders is essential. The facilitator must be perceived as competent, confident, conscientious, and most of all, as an unbiased communicator. The labels of 'facilitator' and 'mediator' are often used interchangeably to describe the person who employs group process techniques to assist in collaborative problem-solving among disputants or problem-solvers. Facilitators/mediators are generally outside third parties but occasionally an inside participant facilitator is used. Ideally, one of each can provide optimum facilitation, where the outsider is primarily used as a process consultant.

Facilitator roles vary according to individual values and professional norms. Some prefer active involvement in proposing solutions and formulating an agreement while others strictly reserve their skills for process facilitation. Participant facilitation may be beneficial in ensuring participant control of process design and implementation as well as fostering empowerment. However, distrust may be problematic with participants questioning issues of fairness and detachment, and may in turn have the effect of diminishing stakeholder willingness and cooperation.

It is crucial that the facilitator be responsible to the entire group and not to individuals or factions. Remaining neutral without substantive comment on issues or expressing opinions is as essential as refraining from making a substantive decision for the group. If for any reason facilitators must break with this tradition, they must clarify that they are removing themselves momentarily from the facilitator role. Other behaviors to be avoided by the facilitator include criticizing participants or debating their positions, making a procedural decision for the group without asking for their preferences, pressuring them into a decision and talking excessively.

Facilitators need a repertoire of facilitation techniques such as:

- Setting an agenda;
- Focusing discussion and reflection;
- Listening effectively, clarifying, and summarizing;
- Dealing with intense emotion;
- Enforcing ground rules;
- Maintaining a supportive climate;
- Exploring and accepting ideas;
- Checking procedures and perceptions;
- Testing for and restating agreements; and
- Most importantly, keeping a positive, optimistic perspective

Facilitators may want to employ active listening techniques such as paraphrasing and perception-checking responses, e.g.,'*You said you understand, but you look confused. Are you?*' Facilitators will find it necessary to monitor both the verbal and emotional level of discussion. The verbal level may be characterized by socially acceptable remarks and used to satisfy emotional needs. Emotional outbursts should be respected and acknowledged by facilitators and not repressed. On the other hand, ground rules should be enforced discouraging emotionally abusive personal attacks and diffusing the attacks when they do occur.

The facilitator will be confronted with a wide range of behavior in the conflict resolution process. Carpenter (1996) suggests the following when dealing with difficult people:

- Name what is happening;
- Describe how the situation is affecting you;
- Ask the person/others in the group for suggestions on how to proceed;
- Offer your own process suggestions and check them out;
- Refocus on interests;
- Allow people to save face;
- Keep in touch—talk with the person in private or ask a friend to check it out;
- Expect them to be reasonable; and
- Use ground rules.

A number of strategies for reaching agreements such as synthesis, compromise, dropping an issue, linking, and trading off and agreeing to disagree are readily facilitated by a skilled intervener. The group will express a direction toward a specific strategy or may utilize several before an outcome is reached. Consensus has been reached when participating stakeholders recognize they have achieved the best decision for all involved. Not every stakeholder will like the solution equally well nor will they necessarily be equally committed. As Fisher et al. (1991) recommend, not only should stakeholders protect themselves against a bad agreement, they should make the most of their assets in order to achieve the best agreement. This can be accomplished by having each stakeholder group:

- Invent a list of actions to be conceivably taken if no agreement is reached;
- Improve some of the more promising ideas and convert them into practical alternatives; and
- Select the one most beneficial alternative solution.

Facilitators can play a meaningful role of bringing unhappy stakeholders back to the table should they become angry or slighted. They may be able to bring them back with an improved perspective after consulting with them privately or employing 'shuttle diplomacy' until interpersonal relations have mended. Serving as an objective third party or mediator to convey messages between stakeholders who are not willing to negotiate face-to-face, often provides a face-saving mechanism as well.

Commonalities in Collaborative Conflict Resolution

There are some commonalities to conflict resolution processes that use a consensus-building approach. The first of these is the *pre-negotiation* which entails getting questions of representation settled, drafting protocols, setting the agenda, and joint fact-finding. The second phase is *actual negotiations* which call for inventing options for mutual gain, packaging agreements, producing a written agreement, binding the parties to their commitments, and ratifying agreements. *Post-negotiation* is characterized by linking informal agreements to formal decision-making, monitoring and creating a context for *re-negotiation* if needed. (Susskind and Cruikshank, 1987).

Pre-negotiation

Critical to this process is the handling of the pre-negotiations. Stakeholders need to be serious about preparing for the process before they sit down with other stakeholders for discussions. Manring et al. (1990) suggest that participants' questions pertain to the following:

- Their concerns and objectives with potential issues to be discussed;
- What specifically they hope to accomplish by participating in the process;
- How they will employ checks and balances in ensuring they do not lose sight of their interests given potential process momentum;
- Who they are not representing as well as who they are representing;
- What communication channels will be used to maintain contact with their constituency throughout the process; and

- Their alternatives and how these might be improved to strengthen their position (Manring et al., 1990: 77).

Susskind and Cruikshank (1987) would argue that the primary concern in the pre-negotiation stage should be coalition-building, i.e., attempting to organize the greatest possible number of groups and individuals with shared interests, with only the smallest number of legitimate spokespersons actually coming to the bargaining table. A united front, they claim, will provide additional power once a BATNA, or 'best alternative to a negotiated agreement,' has been identified. An interdependent relationship is essential to consensus-building. Power relations need sufficient balance. They are also cognizant of realistic deadlines and the need to reframe the dispute in terms that are workable rather than terms that reflect 'sacrosanct values.' Nothing could be more detrimental than conflicting messages emerging from members of a coalition.

Facilitators may recognize imbalances in power relationships if stakeholders use complementary communication, in which one party consistently manipulates with language or non-verbal behaviors reflecting a 'one-up' position, forcing another party into a 'one-down position.' For example, if a stakeholder community group is concerned about potential toxic wastes to be emitted from an industrial plant under construction. The company's BATNA may be to ignore the group's concerns or to keep them talking until they complete construction of the facility.

Central to shaping the consensus-building process is a solid foundation of structural procedures often referred to as 'ground rules.' A clear presentation of the preliminary rules and procedures ensures good faith bargaining and builds trust. In some situations, these are pre-established, in others, participants determine ground rules unanimously, and reserve the right to alter the process rules as the process progresses and participants deem necessary. In several cases reported by Crowfoot and Wondolleck (1990), it was this factor of participant control over the process which proved most influential in causing stakeholders to continue despite meeting-length and difficulty. Examples of the types of procedural decisions to be pre-negotiated are:

- Establishing what procedure will be used to reach a final decision;

- What time frame to expect; and
- How stakeholders will deal with the media, e.g., open or closed meetings, the issuing of press statements, and the use of sub-committees or working groups.

Another area to be clarified prior to negotiation is the role of each stakeholder representative, as participants need to know the limits of their decision-making authority and the frequency with which they must consult their constituencies. Often this authority will vary among interest groups, but it has significant implications for time-lines dictated by organizational constraints.

Although reluctant participants may be persuaded to come to the negotiation table, there will be occasions when stakeholders will decline to participate at all. It is a challenge for the facilitator to ensure that the non-participating stakeholder's interests be repre-sented by other participants or to develop an alternative to face-to-face negotiations.

Negotiation

Negotiation furthers the collaborative process in that the history and context of the problem are reviewed from a perspective and common issues are identified as well as interest groups. The consensus-building group needs to agree both on data collected and options presented either on individual issues or a comprehensive proposal. A draft document normally is reviewed and negotiated until a final agreement is reached. There are several approaches a facilitator may draw upon for achieving a final consent agreement. A few of the most common are:

- Negotiating a general framework of agreements in principle and then working out the specifics;
- Negotiating each issue, incrementally constructing a set of accumulated agreements; and
- Inviting each interest group to prepare a comprehensive proposal to be discussed and integrated.

In the final negotiation, participants may decide to abandon the process if it does not protect their interests, or reject parts of it and accept others. The final agreement is case specific and determined by factors such as method of decision arrival, e.g., majority rule or unanimous consensus. A written text is essential for minimizing differences in interpretation and providing the necessary documentation for future reference and monitoring details of the agreement. If legal and financial responsibilities are involved, official protocols may dictate who signs the final settlement. Another possibility is a list of recommendations or a final agreement signed by designated authorities representing each stakeholder group.

When resources become overtaxed, including the stakeholders themselves, plans for implementation monitoring may be neglected. It is often necessary for the group to include stipulations for monitoring within the final text of the consent agreement. Since implementation usually takes longer than anticipated, having a monitoring plan to fall back on, can serve as a mechanism to move the process forward more quickly. Monitoring can take many forms: observing and lobbying, delegating oversight to a third party, or perhaps designating a task force for this specific function.

Post-negotiation

If a plan for a monitoring procedure has been included in the final agreement, a decision as to how problems with implementation will be handled will need to be negotiated. A process for renegotiating agreements in response to changes and new developments needs also to be established. Details of the agreement's implementation may not have been sufficient, for instance, a decision as to what will happen if responsibilities are not fulfilled may not have been included in the final document (Carpenter, 1996).

Final Considerations

A thorough understanding of group dynamics is critical preparation for facilitators, not to mention considerable experience in separating relationship/process issues from substantive issues such as terms and conditions of agreement. A positive working relationship, e.g. attitude of acceptance, degree of mutual understanding, use of persuasion, balance of power, emotion, reason, and communication ease are critical elements for achieving sustainable outcomes. Facilitators need a level of maturity that will not permit them to succumb to pressure tactics. They can readily raise behavioral concerns without judgment and propose fair procedural principles consistently maintaining a forward-looking perspective. If their capacity is limited then they need to co-facilitate with a more experienced facilitator until sufficient experience is acquired (Fisher et al., 1991).

The sensitive facilitator is mindful of the inhibiting effects of rigidity. Consensus-building by nature adapts to the community cultural and situational context. Conflict resolution processes that are constructed by the community more likely will reflect community cultural differences and are more likely to be effective. But how do we measure success? Some facilitators claim they feel they have been effective if results are tangible and substantial, systemic not merely reactive, and sustainable. Others feel that even if a final agreement is not·reached for numerous reasons, the process itself is an empowering one characterized by joint fact-finding, all-inclusiveness, and multiple relationships. A more informed and enlightened community, one that has reached new heights of understanding, can only be a richer one. These are the personal satisfactions of the facilitator. But most generally, they are the ones silently enjoyed and not necessarily publicly acknowledged.

References and Select Bibliography

Baruch-Bush, R. and **Folger, J.** (1994). *The Promise of Mediation: Responding to Conflict through Empowerment and Recognition.* San Francisco, CA: Jossey–Bass.

Beer, J.E. (1986). *Peacemaking in your Neighborhood.* Philadelphia, PA: New Society Publishers.

Carpenter, S. (1996). *Multi-party Collaborative Problem Solving.* Ithaca, NY: Cornell University Center for the Environment.

Carpenter, S. and **Kennedy, W.** (1988). *Managing Public Disputes.* San Francisco, CA: Jossey–Bass.

Chrislip, D. and **Larson, C.** (1994). *Collaborative Leadership.* San Francisco, CA: Jossey–Bass.

Fisher, R., Ury, W. and **Patton, B.** (1991). *Getting to Yes.* (2nd Edn.). New York, NY: Penguin Books.

Flower, J. (1995). Collaboration: The New Leadership. *Healthcare Forum Journal*, November/December: 66–71.

Gray, B. (1989). *Collaborating: Finding Common Ground for Multiparty Problems*. San Francisco, CA: Jossey–Bass.

Manring, N., Nelson, K.C. and Wondolleck, J.M. (1990). Structuring an Effective Environmental Dispute Settlement Process. In James E. Crowfoot and J.M. Wondolleck (Eds.), *Environmental Disputes: Community Involvement in Conflict Resolution*. Washington, DC: Island Press.

Rich, B. (1994). *Search '94 Conference Report*. Seneca Nation of Indians; Ellicottville, NY, June 7–9.

Crowfoot, J.E. and Wondolleck, J.M. (1990). Environmental Hazards and the Public. *Journal of Social Issues*, 48 (4): 1–20.

19

So What's All the Limping About?

Shirley A. White

Recognizing that people are the most important of the world's natural resources, the development debate must center on the goal of providing a broader range of choices for the world's future generations. The major challenge is to give new meaning to the concept of 'sustainability' for development. When focus is on people, that translates into the need for exploring more fully, ways to facilitate the resources needed for human development without further depreciating the finite natural resources in the process.

It isn't difficult to see that there are a number of individuals and agencies struggling to come to grips with the concept of *sustainability* and the realities of *walking the talk of participation*. They are 'limping' along the bumpy, sometimes rocky, pathways of development for many good reasons. Whenever one is intervening in the lives of people and their *way of life*, it is serious business fraught with uncertainties. But, there is a difference between 'limping' and walking slowly and cautiously, in order to avoid a fall.

But, Why Are We Limping?

I would say that almost everyone begins their journey of development motivated by commitment—the desire to make a contribution, the satisfaction of seeing others grow and develop, and become critically aware. The confidence that communities must be given an opportunity to create their own social, political, and economic change further energizes one to head down the helping path. However, it isn't long before the path becomes slippery and one's sneakers become grungy! At that point the limping begins. *Why???* My point of view:

> *As a facilitator, immediately confronted with the realities of on-site activity, it is extremely easy to lose perspective. You become overwhelmed by the charge to use participatory approaches and soon revert to an 'expert' status for protection. You quickly lose the courage of your convictions. Because of feelings of fear or inadequacy, it becomes easier to retreat to an authority position and dictate the terms and the process, using the people simply to validate plans which you have devised externally. Rather than face the inadequacy of your preparation to play the role of the facilitator and grow along with the people, it seems safer and more comfortable to fall back on 'packaged' solutions.*

From the stories shared throughout this book, it is not at all unusual for 'authorities' to try to dictate what should happen throughout a project and let the participatory process fall by the wayside. In such cases, it becomes pseudo-participation at best. If you are not willing to follow the difficult pathway of participation, then don't talk about participation. My advice:

Don't 'talk the talk' unless you 'walk the walk!'

But, take heart and look more closely at the complex dimensions of the development context. Pause a moment to reflect and seek to understand those dimensions. The points I would like to make, and the questions that seem pertinent to our understanding unfold as a finale for this book. Let's take a closer look.

Confronting 'self'

As a facilitator, it is critical to put one's self into the situation in relation to the individuals or agencies with whom we work. In order to do so, you must be aware of yourself and ask yourself some important questions in relation to the facilitator role:

- Am I dedicated and confident about my own career focus?
- Am I enthusiastic about my facilitator role and am I well prepared to assume it?
- Have I reflected on my own 'life story' so that I can understand my own behavior?
- Do I understand my motivations? Is 'what's in it for me' a driving force?
- Am I concerned about the issues of poverty, oppression, lack of resources, and opportunities for people in the developing world?
- Am I observant of the conditions of community that surround the people? Do I really *care* about people?
- Am I comfortable in my interpersonal relationships with the people?
- Can I listen without being judgmental? And do my 'answers' credit for achievements? Return a reflective response that will enable others to look to themselves for ideas and answers?
- Can I get beyond my own ego needs, my quest for status, a goal to make a name for myself, or my desire to receive?

Am I Able to Enable?

I saw this in Zambia

You are an intervention by your very presence in a community. You are in a position to *en*able or *dis*able. When you focus on your interaction with people, probe and listen without being judgmental. This requires getting beyond yourself, forgetting your own vested interests or hidden agendas, *if* you started out with them. Ask people what they want and help them identify their own thoughts and needs.

- Do they know what they will have to do to get what they want and can you help them understand how to go about it?

- Do they think what they want is worth what they have to do to get it?
- Are they willing to modify their life-style to reach out to others?
- Do they have the desire to build trusting relationships?
- Can they make a commitment to the social relationships necessary for collective action?

[handwritten margin note: Both parties need to be accepting]

The successful facilitator goes beyond 'self' when helping people learn how to solve their own problems, to become assertive about their wishes and rights, while simultaneously learning to accept and respect the wishes and rights of others. Accepting others is a requirement for the facilitator as well as for the people with whom they are working. Working toward positive relationships and courses of action implies that one is able to identify tensions among people and guide them toward confrontation and resolution.

To be able to communicate, identify, evaluate, empathize, reflect, and analyze helps us see ourselves and others more clearly as well as our partnerships for learning and action. The 'self' issues must be confronted *prior* to entering into a facilitator role. In fact, self-confrontation is an ongoing process.

Willingness to Take Risks

Even if you have all the *godlike qualities* that seem to be required to be a facilitator (and no one person does), there is no guarantee that you will be effective. So, a philosophy of risk taking is necessary for playing your role. Human relationships are complex and far too often, unpredictable. This means that a facilitator has to be a risk taker. That is implied when we say 'go beyond self' because once that step is taken, risk is at our feet on the development path.

Once you assume a facilitative role in any development effort, you immediately become vulnerable. Mary Jo Dudley, put it pretty straight in a recent seminar she presented to a group of people aspiring to do Participatory Action Research: 'I became a catalyst the minute I began my project with the domestic workers (in Cali, Colombia). From the very beginning, they *used* me. I had to *go with the flow* and feel good about it. This is the reality of doing PAR!' But what is the *risk* in letting people take control of a project and make it theirs? When this happens, we have succeeded, *internally*, with the people. However, the risk for the facilitator is in how 'success' is perceived *externally* by the outsiders—colleagues, sponsoring agencies, power figures. There is a certain amount of fear, legitimately so, of the consequences of people's actions.

There is risk involved in confronting power, in bringing diversity face to face, in exploring unknown territories. Giving people free rein to come up with their own questions, their own goals, their own options, and solve their own problems, makes the facilitator play a purely supportive, consultative role. Playing this role successfully requires careful guidance and response to the people, making it possible for them to control the process throughout the partnering. Fear of failure is also a factor. Not everything will go right; the challenge is to learn from failure as well as the successes. It is important to keep in mind that these definitions are to come from the people, inside, not from the outsiders.

Another risk factor for the facilitator is that of doing the 'politically incorrect.' Worry about political correctness isn't usually a factor for the competent facilitator. This is indeed a trap when the concern for political correctness becomes an overriding force. The concern leads to inconsistent positions on issues, confusing changes in interpersonal behavior, and ultimately the erosion of credibility and trust. *Political awareness*, however, *is* necessary.

The Need to Build a 'Culture of Cooperation'

When I first began working in India, I had been teaching a process learning course in organizational communication. This course took students through a process of relating to each other, acquiring interpersonal process skills and ultimately lead them to a team effort to pursue a final project of their own choosing. I was (still am) a firm believer in team building and participatory decision-making and collaborative work, in regard to organizations.

I was eager to share my enthusiasm for the 'process' approach with my Indian colleagues. Based upon my knowledge and limited experience with Indian culture, I believed that because the family kinship ties were so strong and seemed to foster sharing of resources, it would be a cooperative environment in the workplace as well. So, one of my first objectives was to work with my collaborating partner to set up the project administrative unit using a cooperative, team building model—one which equalized relationships of all people involved in the project. I thought this would be much easier to achieve than in a highly competitive western environment.

My colleague, K. Sadanandan Nair who was the research director, was committed to the team model as well and wanted to give it a try. We soon discovered that this was not a totally realistic expectation, or at least one easily reached. It was difficult for people to function in a participatory fashion, because in every aspect of the organizational structure, a rigid hierarchy-guided organization functions. I would say that he was unusually democratic and did achieve a participatory model within his own unit and in their projects. But, it was nearly impossible to carry the model beyond his unit into the university structure because of hierarchical thinking and acting. He admittedly found it difficult to keep his positional power and authority in perspective at all times.

Based on this and other experiences and observations, I have come to believe that in order for a facilitator who wishes to bring about *authentic participation*, whether in an organization or in a community, conscious effort must be made to create a *culture of cooperation*. Geertz, (1973) perspective on culture, in the broadest sense, can provide a conceptual base for explaining what I mean by this. He looks at culture as an intertwining of symbols and meanings in which people develop and interact socially:

> (One can consider culture as) a historically transmitted pattern of meaning embodied in symbols, a system of inherited conceptions expressed in symbolic form by means of which men communicate, perpetuate and develop their knowledge about and attitudes toward life. (Geertz, 1973: 89)

This perspective on culture centers on the processes of communication as a defining structure. This is useful for framing the concept of a *culture of cooperation* in the development context. While the socially shared activities of a community evolve from traditional conventions it is necessary to confront present day realities. Moving toward a culture of cooperation, these conventions would gradually be transformed into a new pattern of relationships. These patterns would contain cooperative behaviors, recognize diversity, and individual needs but embody the *collective mind* of the community.

What would characterize the *culture of cooperation*? Most important is the recognition that every person's voice is important, and their points of view equally valid. *Equality is a goal*, achieved through mutual *trust, respect* and *tolerance* of *diversity, equal opportunity*, and *access to resources*. Ongoing *dialogue, consensual decision-making*, and *mediated conflict* characterizes the patterns of interaction. Responsibility and accountability for action outcomes is *shared*. People would have the desire to work toward common goals, making their unique contributions to the process. They would put a high value on collaboration, team building, and teamwork, and participatory decision-making on all fronts. They would automatically engage in critical reflection each step of the way.

A *culture of cooperation* is democratic, providing individual freedom but at the same time requires consideration of how individual freedom impacts on others. A sense of social justice prevails among the people. Building such a culture is evolutionary, not revolutionary. The evolution would require a facilitative, supportive, participatory, and transformational leadership within the community and ultimately beyond the boundaries of community. This culture not only derives from the people, but also would be learned by new people entering the community. It would be dynamic, but not without structure, synergistic but not chaotic. Community structure and patterns of relationships would be constantly changing in order to meet new needs and respond to new goals. The culture allows for self-definition that would take into account the collective identity of the community. The boundaries of social behavior will emerge as people become the architects of their own development, and in turn will impact on the institutions within the social structure.

The outcomes of the process of creating the *culture of cooperation* would be a blending of diversity, unity, solidarity, and full understanding as to how to collectively build a community. The networks of collaboration established would continue to provide information, enable sharing of knowledge, and provide resources for learning and competency building. One can look at these outcomes as *building social capital*, to use the current development terminology. Social capital can be thought of as the networks of communication and cooperation that facilitate trust and reciprocal collaboration which

344 The Art of Facilitating Participation

can lead to both an increase in, and access to, resources for sustainable development.

The model of *participatory development communication as cultural renewal*, which came out of our collaborative research in India, is pertinent:

> Cultural renewal takes place through a dynamic, ongoing, interfacing process which undergirds and simultaneously anchors social, economic, and political development....The goal of cultural renewal is to revitalize, preserve, and evolve dimensions of culture which can provide a stable and vital context for development (Nair and White, 1994: 175).

Facilitation, which embraces a goal of human resource development and cultural renewal, most certainly can be an enabling force for creating the *culture of cooperation*.

The Imperative of Appropriate Tools and Techniques

As we noted in Chapter Two, it is apparent that the facilitator as a catalyst communicator needs a wide array of competencies which link beliefs, knowledge, and skills in order to provide services, initiate, and guide processes, and successfully engage action projects of development. The matrix we presented identified specific skills that would be necessary for the facilitator in order to effectively play essential roles in the development process. It is useful to be more specific about the tools of the facilitator and the ability to employ those tools in the 'real' situation.

I pointed out in Chapter One that enabling an environment for ongoing learning and honing communication competencies is necessary to building partnerships for participatory planning and action. Further, technique must serve the *content* of development, and be the *art* which effectively promotes learning and effective communication. Mastery of the art is evident when, through participation, we *feel* the impact of human dialogue and interaction, and find ourselves in the 'flow' of progress toward renewal and change.

Communication skills, based on a sound understanding of communication theory and practice, particularly *participatory communication*, are the foundation upon which the facilitator builds. This translates into the ability to engage in supportive dialogue, active listening, unbiased observation. It also means that the facilitator must have 'hands on' capabilities to use the tools of communication, i.e., oral, written, and visual forms to be encoded for mass media or media for community action.

Group process tools are essential in staging environments for group interaction, orchestrating group interaction, and discussions, conducting focus groups. Knowing how to organize search conferences, how to plan and conduct communication training is highly important. Counseling, mediating, and negotiating conflicting points of view, arriving at consensual agreements, handling prejudice and discriminatory behaviors are all critical process skills.

An important point to be made is that people cannot begin to participate effectively without learning how to do so. This means that *training for participatory development is an essential requirement*. Don Richardson makes important points about this training:

Participatory development communication training requires significant attention to human relation's practices such as group facilitation and group dynamics. Learning contexts need to be flexible and participatory. If our training programs are based on bottom-up, teamwork, participant-driven approaches, learner initiative, and learner determination of content, then the learning context will, in and of itself, provide many of the important learning moments. Top-down instructor-as-expert learning approaches lack the human relation processes that encourage learner understanding of participation. In other words, the training experience must reflect the field (Richardson, 1996: 99).

Putting together training programs for participatory development communication requires that the facilitator be a competent trainer. However, allowing the community to control the training process puts a different light on the planning process. The facilitator must enable people to utilize indigenous knowledge, tools, and techniques to achieve training objectives. As Don rightly points out, we must 'be prepared to ask and answer difficult questions about the nature and expected outcomes of (our) initiatives.'

Thus far we have centered our comments on the tools and techniques for working internally in the community. The requirements are not essentially different for interacting with external parties that we may encounter on the *pathway of development*. The essential difference is that the power structures become more complex and explicit. The critical issues of development are for the most part, power issues. Understanding the nature of power of individuals, both positional power and personal power, is necessary to minimize the vulnerability of our actions. But as I pointed out earlier in this discussion, one cannot be preoccupied with *political correctness* when the community's well being is at stake. It is useful if the facilitator can directly interact with power figures and negotiate with them, but power encounters should not be entered into without some degree of finesse. The facilitator must know when to call for help in handling negotiations with power figures, and when to go it alone.

Where is Our Vision?

It is no longer necessary to confine our vision of the future to that which we can achieve in a single community, or within local limitations. Communication technologies have given us the potential for reaching out and becoming more global in our contacts and in our thinking. The means for networking on a person to person level is available. But, as Don Richardson has so aptly pointed out in Chapter Sixteen, *access* to these technologies, is a critical issue. A vision of one's community is even more important if these linkages are to be useful. We need to put boundaries around our 'searches' and channel what we learn from them back into plans and action for shaping our own lives and living environs. The power of global communication technologies and travel on the information highway is no longer beyond imagination. It will without doubt shape life in the 21st century.

The facilitator finds herself/himself in the difficult position of helping the people of a community move to a point where they can envision their future. In impoverished, resource poor, areas it is pretty difficult to have a vision when survival needs are barely met. Moreover, getting people to realize that they can take control of their future and leading people toward their own vision is a difficult process but also a sophisticated concept. Simultaneously exposing people to the powers of their own internal communication, and the technologies for reaching out more globally is a necessity for creating a vision of their future.

In this heavy duty process, the facilitator is challenged to let the people's agenda dominate the process, keeping in mind that one is after all an outsider and will eventually leave the community. The success of the facilitator can then be evaluated. Criteria include evidence that the capacity of community members is increased, that they can meet their own requirements and sustain the development process. There will be evidence of the community's collective ability to create their own vision and construct their own future. The networks, alliance, and leadership structures, which have evolved during the facilitator's presence, will be sufficient to sustain the development and renewal processes which have been put in place.

Final Thoughts

I asked Jim Lees what he thought accounted for the gaps between 'walk' and 'talk.' He told me: 'I believe that deep thinking and re-thinking is not standard operating procedure for most organizations. I don't know if they actually have the time to do so, or are even trained to challenge and think at deeper levels. If participation as we know it is about self-reflection and challenging ways of thinking, then that is not what is happening across the board.'

He continued: 'On a cursory level, yes, there are participatory things going on. But when I go back to the funding issue, I wonder how willing funders are to support such things. In our Bombay effort, we had to constantly challenge what we thought and what we believed in. I don't think that that is a comfortable activity for most people, particularly when they are overworked, under pressure and have several projects going at the same time.'

His conclusion certainly is consistent with many of the themes throughout this book: 'Perhaps participatory work should be thought about differently, with the stress on *participatory* and not on development. I mean…it needs to be thought of as a creative process which takes time and must be allowed to emerge rather than a process that has to focus on meeting production quotas and the demands of a time table.'

Ndunge Kiiti agrees that there is often a difference in the values and philosophy of funding agencies, the implementing agency, and the local communities/people. Unfortunately many people are committed to development as a business-driven rather than a human-driven matter. 'We quickly forget that development starts with the heart. We are often purely knowledge-driven. But, if your heart is not in it, it's difficult to have the compassion, passion, and commitment to people that we need to make development a success.'

I asked her how her international agency plays out the commitment to *people's participation*. She told me that they begin with their hiring practices; they look for people who hold values that can uphold the organization's commitment. They build strong networks/partnerships with grassroots people and organizations, and continuously share information on projects and practices, creating a culture of dialogue and respect. They seek collaborative linkages and constantly monitor the use of resources. They have an in-built monitor evaluation system, to which they listen, and make project adjustments accordingly.

Few would disagree that poverty, limited access to education and information, and deteriorating environmental conditions which deplete natural resources are critical factors which limit the opportunities for human development. It becomes obvious that while the doors are open for aggressive human resource development, the scarcity of facilitators with exceptional communication capabilities becomes a limiting factor for how quickly people can walk through those doors. In order for people to participate, they must learn how. Building the capacity to be an effective communicator is the core of their learning.

The facilitator is at the center of it all. And participation gives life a new meaning:

> ...to participate means to live and to relate differently. It implies, above all, the recovery of one's inner freedom, that is, to learn to listen and to share, free from any fear or predefined conclusion, belief or judgment. As inner freedom is not necessarily dependent on outer freedom, its recovery is an essentially personal matter, and can be done...under the most repressive conditions. Yet it enables one not only to acquire a tremendous life power for the flowering of one's life, but also to contribute, in a meaningful

way, to everyone else's struggle for a better life (Rahnema, 1992: 127–28).

All this is to say; that the reality of people's participation rests on the beliefs, knowledge, and skill of the facilitator as a communication professional. Although there are other competencies necessary, it is imperative that communication expertise provide a foundation for the facilitation role. In a meaningful relationship with the people, the first step will be an act of persuasive communication—creating awareness and persuading people that they have the capacity to bring about the changes they hope for. At the same time, the facilitator will be capable of designing the necessary learning experiences for grassroots people to acquire the knowledge and skill necessary to communicate. It is communication that enables people to express themselves, to collaborate, to become effective participants, and act on their own behalf.

To be able to *walk the talk* we must honestly try. The contributors to this book have shared their experiences which can give us the assurance that there is substantial effort being made to go beyond lip service to the participation concept.

Fuglesang, in 1973, reminded us that 'The essence of development work is not to try to change people, but to create...new opportunities. Then people will change themselves.' He goes on to say that participation on the individual level becomes a question of attitude towards one's fellow men. 'If the "expert" or the field worker feels that (s)he is not understood by the others in the process, (her)his problem is...to understand them. What language are people speaking and what language is (s)he speaking (her)himself? What are the people's ways of thinking?' (1973: 24) This early insight is painfully relevant.

'*So, what's all the limping about?*' He has answered our question in a simple but profound way: the facilitator's challenge is to listen, to speak the people's language, to understand, to walk the path of opportunity with them so they can reach that '*higher ground.*'

References and Select Bibliography

Fuglesang, Andreas (1973). *Applied Communication in Developing Countries—Ideas and Observations.* Uppsala, Sweden: The Dag Hammarskjold Foundation.

Geertz, Clifford (1973). *The Interpretation of Cultures.* New York: Basic Books.

Nair, K. Sadanandan and **White, Shirley A.** (1994). Participatory Communication as Cultural Renewal. In Shirley A. White, K. Sadanandan Nair and Joseph Ascroft (Eds.), *Participatory Communication: Working for Change and Development*, pp. 138–193. New Delhi: Sage Publications.

Rahnema, Majid (1992). Participation. In Wolfgang Sachs (Ed.), *Development Dictionary.* London: Zed Books Ltd.

Richardson, Don (1996). Training Needs in Participatory Development Communication. In Guy Bessette and C.V. Rajasunderam (Eds.), *Participatory Development Communication: A West African Agenda.* Ottawa: International Development Research Centre Southbound.

About the Editor
and Contributors

About the Editor

Shirley A. White is Professor Emeritus at the Department of Communication, Cornell University, where she conducts research and outreach programs in development communication and in video, organizational, and interpersonal communication. Prior to this, she was Chairman, Department of Extension Home Economics, Kansas State University; Associate Director, New York State Cooperative Extension of Cornell University; and Director, Communication Arts Video Communication Laboratory, Cornell University. She has previously co-edited *Perspectives on Development Communication* and *Participatory Communication: Working for Change and Development*, and *Communications for Social Change*.

Shirley A. White
485 Van Ostrand Road
Groton
New York 13073
USA
E-mail: saw4@cornell.edu

About the Contributors

Chike Anyaegbunam is the United Nations Food and Agriculture Organization Regional Communication Training Advisor to the

SADC Centre of Communication for Development based in Harare, Zimbabwe. He is the creator of Participatory Rural Communication Appraisal (PRCA), an innovative communication research methodology for human and rural development purposes, and designer of an experiential communication training program for extension officers and other rural development workers in the Southern Africa region and beyond. He has worked as a communication trainer and advisor with a variety of international development agencies, including UNICEF and USAID. Between 1988 and 1993, he edited two University of Iowa publications, *Journal of Communication Inquiry (1993)* and *International Studies Newsletter of the Center for International and Comparative Studies*. His doctoral degree is in Communication from the University of Iowa with specialization in instructional design, participatory communication, and Third World development.

Joseph Ascroft is Professor Emeritus, co-founder and former head of the Development Support Communication Masters Degree program, Department of International Programs, University of Iowa. The program is dedicated to training professional communicators to facilitate effective involvement of Third World development beneficiaries for participation in decision-making concerning their own capacity building and development. Graduates of that program have assumed leadership in communication for development worldwide. Joe was the major architect and consultant to the current FAO project with the Southern Africa Development Community's Centre of Communication for Development, SADC-CCD.

Renuka Bery is Dissemination and Advocacy Manager, Support for Analysis and Research in Africa (SARA) Project, Academy for Educational Development. As a project director and development video trainer with *Communication for Change*, she facilitated participatory training processes to use video as a tool for communication. In that capacity she worked with grassroots women and men in Bangladesh and India and adolescent school children in Nigeria. The training transferred skills that enabled participants to gain the confidence needed to make informed decisions and voice their opinions. She writes and consults on health and communication issues. While pursuing a masters degree in public health, she worked on family planning and health issues with Columbia University in

New York and the Association for Reproductive and Family Health in Ibadan, Nigeria. She was consultant to the PBS series, '*Where in the World is Carmen Sandiego?*' and served as an advisor to Apple Computer's Multimedia Laboratory. She has lived, traveled, and worked extensively in Asia, Africa, Europe, and North America.

Kathleen E. Colverson is currently the Southeastern USA Project Manager for Heifer Project International, a non-profit organization dedicated to empowering people through training and provision of quality livestock. In this role she collaborates with local organizations and universities to improve rural communities. Prior to this position, she was an Associate Professor of Animal Science at the State University of New York, completing her Ph.D. from Cornell University in 1996. Her research interests include gender roles in agriculture, and leadership training for young adults.

Meredith Fowlie received her bachelors degree from Cornell University in 1997. She completed an Honors Thesis on Science, Development, and Participation, which examined the concept of participatory development as understood by international graduate students—development professionals of the future. As part of her study, she interned with agricultural scientists in Nepal. She has since conducted a comprehensive study of a community oriented micro-hydropower development initiative in Northern Pakistan, working closely with engineers, administrators, social organizers, and community members. The project, under the auspices of AKSP (Aga Khan Rural Support Program), sought to better understand and interpret design considerations, existing management institutions and maintenance regimens, economic and financial cost-benefit analysis.

Josh Galper is an independent research analyst. For the last three years he has worked for UNICEF, the Harvard Institute for International Development, and as an independent consultant. He has assisted state, local and non-profit agencies in the US and Brazil on the use of statistics for planning, with an emphasis on participatory processes. He holds a Master's Degree in City and Regional Planning from Cornell University which focused on statistics and planning.

Ricardo Gómez is a Development Communication Research Specialist with the International Development Research Centre in

Ottawa, Canada. A native of Colombia, S.A., he has worked with communication technologies in participatory processes for community organization in Latin America. Having learned to value the role of the facilitator in stimulating the participatory processes learning from grassroots practitioners and researchers alike, he is now active in promoting participatory development communication programs in different regions of the world. He completed his doctoral program in communication at Cornell University in 1997.

John L. Hochheimer completed his Ph.D. in Communication from Stanford University in 1986. He is Associate Professor and founding coordinator of the journalism program at Ithaca College at Ithaca, New York. Experienced in all facets of community radio and other mass media in the United States, he has assisted with the development of journalism education in the newly democratizing countries of eastern and central Europe. His research interests include the uses of community media and educational programs in the development of locally based journalism in the developing world. Assuming the role of a facilitator, John employs the Freirean notion of dialogue both in terms of working with students and colleagues and with local media developers, enabling people to initiate and sustain dialogue for meaningful growth. He believes media can be used to promote dialogue in communities and that students can become involved and facilitate those dialogues within their own communities.

Marilyn W. Hoskins is an independent consultant. From 1984 to 1996 she was Senior Community Forestry Officer, Policy and Planning Division, Forestry Department, Food and Agriculture Organization of the United Nations. She directed FAO's community forestry development and management including the *Forests, Trees and People Program*. Marilyn was the first social scientist to work within the FAO Forestry Department, bringing to it an anthropology and communication background along with a personal commitment to local control and governance and participation methodologies. The challenge was to make forestry knowledge and resources support community development in a manner which would address poverty and inequity issues and create understanding of the dynamics of the tree and forest interface with local people.

Ilias Hristodoulakis received his doctoral degree from the University of Iowa in development communication in 1998. He has gathered data on some eighty-eight Child-to-Child projects selected from a list of 170 sponsored by the London based Child-to-Child Trust. The data, gathered in some twenty Third World Countries, was analyzed as a part of his dissertation research. Currently he is serving in the Greek Army, but returns to the United States in 1999 to launch a career in development communication.

Anne Marie Johnston is a Senior Lecturer for International Programs, Faculty of Medicine, at the University of Melbourne. Anne had a MacArthur Leadership Fellowship at Harvard University's Center for Population and Development Studies (1993–1994) and completed a doctoral program at Cornell University in 1998. She has served as Director of Women in Development and Advisor for Women, Health, and Population in the South Pacific for the Australian Aid Agency, representing Australia on the OECD Development Assistance Committees for Gender and Development as well as Population. As an international consultant, she has facilitated training programs and research projects in the areas of gender relations, program planning, and project design, group dynamics, community participatory development, and conflict resolution with respect to environmental conflict.

Ndunge Kiiti is pursuing her Ph.D. in Communication at Cornell University. Prior to coming to Cornell, Ndunge served as the Director/Assistant Director for a global health organization working in community development—Medical Assistance Program (MAP) International's communication department for Eastern and Southern Africa. Ndunge has done extensive work in HIV/AIDS prevention and education. She managed a WHO sponsored study of community barriers and resources for home care in Kenya and played a key role in the design and implementation of MAP's AIDSCAP PVO Grant (funded by USAID) for AIDS education and prevention in Kenya. Ndunge has served on various networks and boards in international health: International Scientific Committee for Track D (Social Science: Research, Policy & Action) for the XIth International Conference on AIDS in Vancouver; UNDP Kenya Country Research Team for the Interregional Partnership Program to Enhance National Capacity to Analyze and Respond to the Psychological, Social, and Economic Determinants and Consequences of the HIV Epidemic; Editorial Board Member of the Health

Education Network in Kenya; Board member of the Kenya AIDS NGO Consortium (KANCo)

Peggy Koniz-Booher is a reproductive health communication consultant who has played the role of an outside facilitator dozens of times in a wide variety of nutrition, family planning, and health-related projects throughout Latin America, Asia, and the United States. Her commitment to participatory communication and team building spans more than two decades. Beginning with her master's work at Cornell University, she emphasized the potential power of grassroots organizations in interagency communication, coordination, and collaboration. Her research documented the design of a national-level communication strategy for the promotion of breast-feeding in Guatemala. Since 1980, she has worked extensively and simultaneously with multilateral donors, bilateral agencies, international and local NGOs, policy-makers, academic institutions, health care professionals, community health workers, peer-support groups, clients, and local media with the aim of building creative partnerships to improve program coordination, encourage community leadership, and strengthen local capabilities. She was IEC Resident Advisor for a USAID-supported Family Planning and Health Project in the Dominican Republic, 1994–1996.

Jim Lees is a cultural anthropologist who has worked closely with out-of-home youth for the past decade. In San Francisco, he developed and managed a direct-service program for street children with HIV and AIDS. Jim recently co-directed a two-year project with street children in India, developing an educational package on risk behavior related to HIV/AIDS and drug use. The project placed children in the central role as creators of the concepts, methodology, and content of a curriculum which brings children and adults who work with them together in a participatory process of inquiry into the emotions, lives, and needs of street children. Along with his co-author, Sonali Ojha, Jim has recently formed a non-profit, non-governmental organization, mapintee, Inc., to continue participatory work with children throughout the world. Their goal is to help children better understand their own lives and options, and to assist adults in defining their role in relation to the children that they are striving to support.

Paolo Mefalopulos is the FAO Regional Communication Trainer in the SADC Centre of Communication for Development and collaborated in the development of the Participatory Rural Communication Assessment (PRCA) research methodology. After obtaining his Master of Arts in Telecommunications at Michigan State University, he worked in the FIAT training company in Turino, Italy, where he participated in the development and production of a number of interactive multimedia training programs. He then joined UNESCO as a media specialist working in the Middle East and in Guatemala where he came directly and dramatically in contact with the realities of development work with rural people. This experience further motivated him to investigate and apply the principles of communication to empower rural people to play a more active role in making decisions that impact their lives. He has participated in a number of audiovisual productions including a short film '*Spari Dispari*' for which he was the assistant director. This film has been presented at various festivals in Europe.

Titus Moetsabi is a lawyer by training, a development professional by practice, and a writer, actor, theater director by inclination. Currently he is a Regional Communication Training Advisor with the SADC Center of Communication for Development. He is a visiting lecturer in participatory rural appraisal and intercultural communication for the masters degree program in Tsetse Control of the University of Zimbabwe. He is presently conducting field research on *communicating legal issues using theatre* as part of his M.Phil degree program at the University of Zimbabwe. For eleven years he has worked with several rural communities of Southern Africa in participatory project conceptualization, planning, implementation, monitoring, and evaluation. He is a trainer in participatory planning, participatory communication research, and program planning. His publications include *A Trainer's Guide for Empowerment*, and *Fruits and Other Poems*.

K. Sadanandan Nair is Professor of anthropology at the University of Poona, Pune, India. He teaches and directs research of advanced graduate students in anthropology, development, and communication studies. From 1985–1990 he was research director and principle investigator for the University of Poona's Development Communication Research Project which was funded by the US Department of

Agriculture. He has taught summer courses in Participatory Research and Development Communication at Cornell University for the past seven years. He currently serves as research advisor for the National Addiction Research Centre in Bombay, India. His consultancies with the FAO, have focused on participatory communication issues.

Erik Nielsen completed his Master of Science Degree from the Department of Communication at Cornell University in 1998 with a focus on international development communication. His research was a participatory analysis of collaborative multi-stakeholder relationships among local institutions in Central America and their cooperative management of natural resource conflicts. Cornell's International Institute of Food, Agriculture and Development, the International Development Research Centre in Ottawa, and the Cornell Graduate School jointly funded this project. He was awarded an internship with the UN Food and Agriculture Organization's (FAO) Community Forestry Unit in 1997 and returned there (September 1998) for an assignment in their Policy and Institutions Division. He is a graduate of the University of Guelph, Canada, majoring in Natural Resource Management and International Development.

Sonali Ojha, after completing post-graduate work at the Paul. H. Nitze School of International Studies in Bologna, Italy, has maintained a strong commitment to participatory processes in all aspects of development. Her latest work was co-directing a two-year project with street children in India, developing an educational package on risk behavior related to HIV/AIDS and drug use. The project placed children in the central role as creators of the concepts, methodology, and content of a curriculum which brings children, and adults who work with them, together in a participatory process of inquiry into the emotions, lives, and needs of street children. Along with her co-author, Jim Lees, Sonali has formed a non-profit, nongovernmental organization, mapintee, Inc. They will continue participatory work with children throughout the world, hoping to help children better understand their own lives and options. They will also develop programs to assist those adults working with children in these contexts.

Ricardo Ramírez is currently pursuing a Ph.D. in the program Rural Studies for Sustainable Communities, University of Guelph, Canada. Trained in Crop Science (Guelph) and Adult Education (MSc., St. F.X. University, Nova Scotia), he is experienced in design and management of agricultural knowledge and information systems, participatory learning, research and evaluation, communication for development, and pluralism and stakeholder analysis. He is a member of the International Support Group: Linking local experience in agroecosystem management *http://ids.as.uk/eldis/isg/isg.html*. Ricardo returned to Guelph after two years as coordinator of the Information and Communication Unit of the Centre for Research and Information Exchange in Ecologically Sound Agriculture (ILEIA), The Netherlands. He was posted in Rome for over five years in the Development Support Communications unit of FAO, where he backstopped projects mostly in Latin America, the Caribbean, and Asia. Between 1985 and 1989 he worked as a freelance consultant with short-term contracts for Latin American and Canadian NGOs. He spent two years in Colombia working with campesinos in search of improved production systems in subsistence agriculture.

Don Richardson is an Associate Professor of Development Communication and Rural Communication Studies at the University of Guelph. He is director of the Don Snowden Program for Development which promotes, through training, research, and advisory activities, communication for community development and the mobilization of human resources in the developing regions of the world. Their web site is: *http://tdg.uoguelph.ca/~drichard/snowden*. He has done extensive training, consulting, and writing on the issues of Internet access in developing countries and on participatory communication for development.

Simone St. Anne was born in Goa, India where beaches and coconut trees abound, and grew up in Mumbai amidst the crowds and excitement of India's busiest city. Creativity has been long linked to her family, infecting her with a passion for creativity from early childhood. Painting, music, graphic design, and dance have combined to give her a varied background in the arts. She is a graduate of St. Xavier's College in Mumbai with degrees in History, English Literature, French Literature, and Ancient Indian Culture. Research for her masters degree in Communication from Cornell University, was a case study of 'Impact India: an initiative against avoidable disablement.' This facilitative project brought India the world's first hospital train, the 'Lifeline Express'—a model that is now being adopted in many countries from China to Zimbabwe. She is currently studying the management of creativity.

Shirley A. White is Professor Emeritus, Department of Communication, Cornell University. The first decade of her career was spent at the University of Nebraska where, as an extension communication specialist, she produced television and radio programs for agriculture and home economics for statewide University Television. She has pioneered the field of participatory communication through her teaching, graduate student guidance, and research. Over the past twenty-five years, her work has focused on organizational renewal and change, video communication, and development communication. After completing a Ph.D. in Communication at Michigan State University in 1967, she spent ten years in university administration at Kansas State University and Cornell University, providing leadership to Cooperative Extension programs. She has collaborated on development communication projects in India since 1982. The major thrust of her collaborative work there has been as the US Department of Agriculture's Chief Cooperating Scientist for the Development Communication Research Project at the University of Poona.

Index

362   Index